The Loss of Lacey

A Mother's Story of Facing Her Greatest Fear and Coping with Devastating Grief

The Loss of Lacey

A Mother's Story of Facing Her
Greatest Fear and Coping with
Devastating Grief

Nancy Jarrell O'Donnell

Editors: William Harryman, Alanna Nash, and Barbara McNichol
Proofreader: Peggy Henrikson, Heart and Soul Editing
Cover and interior design: Peggy Henrikson, Heart and Soul Editing
Cover photo of Lacey Jane Jarrell by April Simmons
Cover photo of "Starry Sky over Mountains" by Cliford Mervel, Pexels

ISBN: 9798674765370

Printed in the United States of America
First Edition

Dedication

To my mother: Had you not instilled in me the spiritual beliefs,
the trust in pursuing self-exploration, and had you not modeled
the grace and acceptance of faith under adverse conditions,
I would not be.

Acknowledgments

I have so many, many people to thank for being there for me in the most trying of times. I am afraid of attempting to name all of them as I would not want to inadvertently leave someone out.

Thank you to all the staff employed at Sierra Tucson from July 2006 through April 2011: You were my lifeline.

The teachers and students from St. Gregory College Preparatory School (now The Gregory School): I am grateful to you all.

The Vail School District including teachers, students, and the Vail community: Thank you for loving us.

The Lacey Jarrell Foundation Board of Directors: You all modeled kindness and compassion and taught me through your actions what true benevolence is.

I thank my family, living and deceased: You all contributed in varying ways to my resilience.

To my friends: You carried me, held me, and kept being there for me. There are not adequate words to convey my gratitude for each of you.

To the strangers whose names I never learned: Your anonymous gestures and gifts of support gave me continuing faith in the human condition.

To those who entered my life and I now call friends: You chose to stay in my life when you easily could have run. You are all heroes to me.

To the children who are Lacey's and Will's friends, now adults: The consistent and genuine love you supplied Will and me is not forgotten.

Contents

The very essence of instinct is that it is followed independently of reason.

~ Charles Darwin

Preface

Completing this manuscript about my daughter's death has taken more than thirteen years. What started as journal writing for managing tragedy morphed into something more. I did not work on this manuscript regularly over the years. There were many years I couldn't bear to return to it. Yet my initially selfish goal—to help myself—transformed into the hope of helping even just one person from my experience. I maintain my hope and faith that those who may benefit will come across my humble writing.

All the individuals in this book are real people whose real names are used. The contents contain my personal perception of events based on my experience in real time and from my memory. The story is mine as it happened for me based on my truth. In no way is there an intention to hurt anyone. I am aware I may be hurting myself by sharing my story and thus placing myself in a vulnerable position as I allow people into my highly personal thoughts and behaviors following tragedy. I am willing to take the risk.

This book holds my clinical thoughts and learning process, as the psychotherapist part of me does not turn off outside the therapy rooms. It is interspersed with neuroscientific research I found along my journey and provides evidence for those coping skills that helped me to keep going day after day despite often doubting I could continue to live.

Whether you are a clinical professional, therapist, medical provider, counselor, religious teacher, parent, child, sibling, friend, or family member, may my writing either help you personally or allow you to assist someone who is suffering.

Nancy Jarrell O'Donnell, MA, LPC, CSAT, CCTP, Tucson, 2020
integrativetherapyservice.com
njotherapy@protonmail.com
https://laceyjarrellfoundation.info/

PART ONE: THE IMMEDIACY OF GRIEF

Lacey and Me, 2005

Chapter One: The First Day

Love the rising of the moon
Broken glass
Bright day
The mask of truth awaits.
Fire burns
Rain hammers the ground
Afraid of life
Afraid of death
No.
Yes.
The walk of shame
The day of the dead
The day of life
Eat and smell sweetness.
Breathe in the good
And out with the bad.
Life flows like a river
Death stops still like a rock.
Hear the ocean
Be like a river
Not like a rock
Be swift like the wind.
Touch, feel, smell, see, observe.

"My Poem"
~ Lacey Jarrell, age 12

It was 10:50 a.m. I had just noted the time when someone tapped me from behind. I was in an obscure part of Sierra Tucson, the hospital in which I worked, and in an area one would not usually find me. I was working with two women whom I generally did not supervise, but that morning found me taking on extra duties due to a crisis. This level-one licensed acute care psychiatric hospital with level-two residential treatment units provided daily crises that needed my attention.

The tap on my shoulder startled me, though, and as the woman said my name aloud, I turned. *Who was she and why had she sought me out?* I quickly recognized her as one of our new nurses, but I did not know her personally. I turned and met her eyes with a sudden thought. *She is coming to tell me something terrible has happened to my daughter Lacey.*

Instead, she came to inform me that her department could not cover some patient monitoring for me. I immediately smiled with relief and thanked her. I even let out an audible sigh and noticed her surprise with my lack of concern about the problem. Her staring grey eyes brought me back into reality. *Nancy, what is wrong with you? Why do you have these terrible kinds of thoughts?*

One hour later, my daughter was dead.

Lacey was killed in a rollover car accident in front of our gated community in Tucson. She was allegedly the driver who lost control of her car on a curve on a downhill grade. The vehicle rolled over down the hill three to five times. Lacey was not wearing a seat belt, it was said. She was ejected from the vehicle and landed face down, and the car landed upright on top of her. I do not know how long she was under the car before first responders were able to extricate her.

Although Lacey had a pulse for an indeterminable amount of time, she was never responsive. By the time they lifted the car off her, she was dead. She died of lacerations to her brain and skull—blunt force trauma to the head.

It was July 6, 2006. Lacey was sixteen years old.

Work was so busy that July 6th that I had to call a lunchtime meeting. I generally called Lacey at 11:30 a.m.—she was out of school for the summer—but that day I decided to call her after the meeting. At 12:30 p.m., my cell phone rang. Thinking it could be my daughter, I excused myself from the meeting and took the call.

It was my housekeeper, Kelleeyn, calling to say the road to my subdivision was blocked, and she could not get to my home. I disregarded her concern. July is monsoon season in Tucson, and we live near the Rillito River. A monsoon is a large area weather pattern that is generated by a seasonal shift in the wind bringing a concomitant increase in precipitation and humidity. A cloudless blue sky and burning heat are present most of the day during Tucson's monsoon season until suddenly robust cloud formations appear over the Santa Catalina and Rincon mountains. As the clouds move over the Tucson basin, intense thunderstorms develop. Rain begins like a sudden explosion and pours down on the city hard and fast. As a result, the long dry riverbeds—washes, as we call them—swell with a wall of water rushing down from the mountains. Sudden surges of run-off flood the once-dry riverbeds and streets. Flash flooding occurs as the rushing rivers cross the streets, making them dangerous to enter, at times impassable. Over the years, I have had to find a variety of routes home during monsoon season.

I told Kelleeyn the Rillito was running, and she needed to go a different route that would bypass the wash. She seemed hesitant at first, but she agreed to take an alternate route and would call me back if she ran into a problem. I returned to my meeting.

Before long, Kelleeyn—now highly agitated—called a second time. She reported the road was closed to eastbound traffic due to a car accident that involved a fatality. She now knew from the police the car involved was black. My daughter drove a black Subaru Impreza WRX, a four-door sedan.

Although it was not spoken, by this point we both knew the victim was my daughter, Lacey. I explained to those in the meeting I was concerned about Lacey and needed to call her. I repeatedly made calls to her cell phone and our home telephone numbers. I never got an answer. I began to panic and called her employer to see if she was there, and then called Kelleeyn to ask if she knew anything more.

This all occurred between 12:30 and 1:45 that afternoon. I kept telling myself I was catastrophizing. *The drive from my work to home would take me forty-five minutes.* Thinking about that, I dialed her number again, praying to reach her this time. I asked two staff members I had been meeting with if they thought I was overreacting. One of them said I likely was, so I went with that thought— not because she had said it but because I could not bear to think otherwise.

Still, I continued to call Lacey and any of her friends I had numbers for. No one had heard from her that morning.

I felt myself entering a state of panic coupled with "the freeze." As a therapist who works with traumatic stress clients, I know that people faced with traumatic events fight or flee. If these options are not successful or available to them, then they freeze. It is called *tonic immobility.*

I felt frozen in my office. *What do I do next?* At about 1:50 p.m., I heard a knock on my door. An administrator, Connie Gavel, said I needed to come to her office. "No," I told her. "I can't leave the phone; I am waiting to hear from my daughter." She softly told me that I *must* come; people had come to see me. At that point, I knew. My worst nightmare was about to become a reality.

I entered Connie's office. A sheriff and a victim advocate introduced themselves and greeted me. I began to cry and scream: "What happened to my daughter? Is she dead?" The sheriff softly asked me if Lacey had any tattoos on her ankle. *Why wasn't he just telling me?* I shouted at him. "She's sixteen!" She did not have any tattoos, I told him, but she did draw stars on her ankle with a black or green marker. Stars were her symbol. Green was her favorite color.

That was the confirmation he needed. He told me Lacey was dead.

The world turned black as I spiraled back in time to an unknown place. Everything around me became surreal in an instant. Figures appeared, some in slow motion, while others seemed to move like lightning. I screamed (or thought I did) as I held my belly and rocked back and forth. I could not stop or control the hysteria. The victim advocate knelt by me and began talking to me in a gentle voice. I could see his mouth moving, but his ceaseless sounds made no sense. I could not make out a word he said. I could not hear anything but my whimpers, which must have sounded like a distress call from a wounded animal. My scream came from some part of my inner body with which I was not familiar. At times, it was barely audible, and at other times, it was as deafening as a jackhammer. I felt detonated. I looked for my body parts on the floor before me. A nonphysical pain engulfed me. Severe.

"Nooo, noooo, not my baby girl! She is just a little girl! Oh please, oh please, not my little girl!" I shouted.

Nearby staff members who already knew why the sheriff had come, entered the room and held me. People came out of their offices, and as someone guided me to a more discreet place, I registered familiar faces looking at me with tears and disbelief in their eyes. *Why were they looking at me like this? This was not real. They must stop acting as though this is real!*

Word spread like wildfire throughout the hospital, and staff members lined up to hug and see me. Some fell to their knees around me. I still could not make sense of what was going on. I could not speak. I could not walk without assistance. Traumatized, I went into shock. I collapsed in the medical director's office, and one of our physicians ultimately gave me a sedative. I begged for confirmation that Lacey was *not* dead. I begged them to take away my pain.

Once the sedative took effect, my questions came. "Where is she? Shall we go now and identify the body? We need to call people."

Staff moved around me frantically, getting numbers from my cell phone to call people who needed to know, including my brother and my ex-husband's family. (Buddy, Lacey's father, was in Thailand, and I had no way to reach him.) I knew I had to call my son personally; Will was a student at the University of Colorado majoring in business law. But before I made that unbearable call, I continued to ask about identifying the body. The sheriff told me I was not needed for that because they had positive ID. There had been a passenger in the car.

"What? Who was in the car with her?" I asked.

He could not tell me who it was, but I knew at once. It was Ernesto Chavez, Lacey's ex-boyfriend, who was trying desperately to get back with her four months after their breakup.

I then became extremely focused on when I could see the body and what Ernie was doing in the car with her. I asked these questions over and over. I gave the sheriff a report about how the boy had been stalking Lacey by calling her excessively and leaving black roses at our doorstep. I told him we were planning to change her cell phone number.

Before long, I was practically carried to another office farther from the patient area so our patients could not hear my continuing screams of despair. At some point I remember saying to the sheriff, "I am so sorry for you having this as part of your job. How horrible it must be to tell a mother that her child is dead." His sullen face registered an odd look of disbelief.

Many people gathered around me, and someone asked me for the number of my boyfriend, Jack O'Donnell. He and I had an on-and-off relationship, and things were rocky at the time. I responded, "Oh, please, don't bother him. He lives way on the other side of town." Fortunately, no one abided by my irrational request. Someone called Jack, and he came at once to be by my side.

Seated in a stiff, oversized chair, I felt raw and fragile and small in it. My breathing became irregular, and my emotional wound left me chilled and cold to the touch. I turned to the sheriff. "Where is my Lacey Jane? I need to see my Lacey Jane! She is my baby! Who is watching her?" The sheriff attempted to explain she was with the coroner now, but this made no sense. I was the one who made decisions about where my daughter would go or not go. *Who was making decisions about my child without me?*

A group of staff members lined up outside the office door waiting to console me, and they came in a few at a time. I was still seated in the chair, and each one dropped down and hugged my legs. I sat stiff and frozen, continuing to wonder why they behaved as if this were real. This could not be true, and *I had not seen Lacey's body yet.* "I want to see her!" I cried.

Another group planned the next move: organizing a caravan to follow me home, driving my car for me, picking up food, and deciding who would stay the night with me. They were all amazing. Clinical Director Johanna O'Flaherty, who was new at Sierra Tucson, immediately took charge and planned the next steps. She and I had grown close quickly. Johanna was one of two women, along with Carol Ross, a therapist and friend, who planned to spend the night with me after Jack drove me home. Other staff I considered friends began calling people from contacts in my cell phone and arranging to meet them at the airport if they had to fly in. I was unaware of this activity until weeks later and could not figure out how all the people connected.

Meanwhile, I continued to feel as if I were missing body parts. I grew silent and scanned the area, almost looking for them. I was desperate for a clue to explain this new, raw, agonizing, and ferocious emotional pain. I felt as though all the cells in my body were violently shaking and moving about to find their new homes. The image of a Christmas snow globe from childhood came to mind. I would shake the globe and watch the snow particles inside relocate to the bottom of the globe. *That was happening to me now.*

Again, I stiffened, held my belly, and let out a wail. I knew my wail was unique to a mother who has lost a child. That realization folded me over. Like a rag doll, I fell sideways in the chair over the armrest. Someone gathered me up while I whimpered. A waterfall of tears landed in my collar.

I remember little about the drive home with Jack and have only in-and-out memories of the rest of that day and evening. When people began to appear at my house, I was still unclear why. *Who are all these people? Why are they coming to my house in tears?* From that point on, my memory seemed fractured, challenged. I felt disoriented all the time. I was stupefied and bewildered, living in a world of surrealism.

Lacey's accident was reported on all the local TV stations. I felt compelled to watch, but for some reason, I never did see any of those reports. The newspapers called, but I could not speak, so Jack talked to them for me. He and others took the nonstop phone calls. People arrived with food, and others took over for me. I just sat and cried.

When I called Will in Boulder, he knew immediately by my voice something was terribly wrong. There was no way to ease into telling him his little sister was dead. He hung up the phone quickly, and I later learned he jumped on his bicycle and rode frantically to his best friend's place of employment. Will and Lee McLoughlin had grown up together in Tucson, and Lee immediately left his job that day. Within hours, they drove to Denver's airport to get on the next Tucson flight. They seemed to walk in the door only minutes after my phone call. Time had become distorted for me—an obvious symptom of *traumatic grief*, a severe form of bereavement.

☆☆☆

Shock can have a potent effect on the body, especially after the cataclysm of losing a child. Shock protects us from feeling the seemingly unbearable. Numbness sets in. I could not shake the feeling that I had lost a vital internal organ, and that I could not exist without this organ. *How could I still walk around?* I developed stomach problems I had never experienced before. I sometimes found it hard to catch my breath.

I would later learn that some of the screams I perceived I had emitted couldn't be heard by anyone else. A specific part of our brain, called Broca's area, is responsible for our ability to emit sound and produce speech. When humans experience severe distress, shock, or terror, this part of the brain may go offline, rendering us speechless. Hence the phrase "I was speechless," which is used to describe surprise or shock. This response is often factual, not just a metaphor.

The physical symptoms I felt were a minor distraction from the indescribable pain of traumatic grief. I remember feeling increased distress when someone played music that first day at my house. *Why are they listening to music? Don't they know Lacey is dead?* I wanted the world to stop. It all seemed fallible—a mistake. *This could not be true!*

I wanted to be dead, too, although that did not equate to feeling suicidal. I wanted to be with her.

Amid all this, it hit me that my son, four years older than Lacey, was still alive and needed me. *I could not die.* I struggled to know how to help him, as I could barely help myself.

In the weeks and months afterward, Will was devastated. His appetite decreased, and he went into a deep depression. My family was shattered, fragmented. My entire world as I knew it was torn away from me as suddenly as Lacey was ejected from her car and killed.

Chapter Two: What Comes Next?

Not the prophetic call
A visit, unwanted by all.
The sheriff's face
Screaming silence
Wreckage, no violence.
A routine visit;
What is it?
No routines ever more.

"The Visit"
~ Nancy Jarrell

People began to arrive from all over the country. I found out later that Sierra Tucson covered the cost of several of these flights, including my son's. I was never asked to reimburse the company, and all along my most dreaded journey, the staff and Jack took charge of all the things I could not.

However, no one else but me could make the essential decisions in the wake of death and traumatic loss. I am not sure how I did what I did over the next few days. The sedatives, which had to be monitored, were given to whoever was taking care of me at the time. I asked for more every ten minutes, expecting to feel relief and not receiving it.

Lacey's father, Buddy, did not get home from Thailand until I was well into planning the services. I wrote my daughter's obituary and designed the schedule and format for her funeral, the church service, the speakers. Jack arranged for a reception at a local resort.

From early on, my primary focus was seeing Lacey's body. Jack escorted me everywhere to ease the hideous formalities and arrangements. I remember going to the funeral home and feeling incredibly angry that the room was so cold. I thought the woman assigned to us, Belinda Motzkin Brauer, was lying to me when she said she turned off the air conditioning. I still felt so cold and could not stop shivering. I did not like the atmosphere, either. *Of course* I did not like the atmosphere—it was a funeral home. I found the place worn and substandard and wanted my daughter to have something better. I was consumed with planning for a surreal event, and I wanted it to be perfect. *But how does a mother create a perfect funeral for her daughter? And what is a perfect funeral?* Everything now was far removed from perfection.

During one of our first meetings, Belinda asked me where I wanted to have the funeral. This question gave me pause. I was aware of my silence and my sudden emotional paralysis. My oneiric state was interrupted by Belinda's second question asking if we attended a specific church. The question brought me back to the moment. I shared that I was raised Catholic and that both the children had been baptized and received their first communion in the Catholic church, but that we were not compliant Catholics. With that, she handed me a list of local churches and phone numbers and the receiver of a landline phone. She said she would enter the phone number once I found my church on the list.

I gave her the number of the Catholic church we had attended closest to our home. When a woman answered, I explained I was inquiring about having a funeral and the circumstances. After placing me on hold, she returned and stated, "I checked your record and you are not a regular financial donor so Father will facilitate the service, but everything will be selected by him and no other speakers or special requests or readings will be allowed."

I do not remember my exact response but knew it was brief, clear, and direct. I was shaking. *I had no desire to have a funeral at that church.* In recent years, I had exposed the children to several other religions, and we had attended a variety of services. We particularly gravitated to a certain Episcopal church, and so I called and received a kind, warm, and empathetic response to my request. I was appalled at the way in which the Catholic church responded and made a grand statement that I would never attend a service at that Catholic church again.

Buddy and Jack had never met until the day we were planning next steps at the funeral home. Coming straight from the airport, Buddy walked into a conference room where Jack, Will, Belinda, and I were gathered. Buddy and I had divorced four years prior. I could not even think about Buddy's and Jack's first meeting being awkward. I introduced them, they shook hands, and everyone moved on.

As the hours passed, I began to realize that Belinda was there to help. The mother of a sixteen-year-old daughter as well, she was visibly shaken by my grief. And so she understood my outrage that two days had passed, and I still had not been allowed to see the body. *I want to see my baby!* The funeral home convinced the coroner to let us have a private viewing.

This depended, however, on the funeral home being able to make the body presentable. I did not grasp this at the time, but over the next weeks, as I learned the details of the accident, I came to understand why they initially did not allow me to see my daughter in death. Fortunately, Jack and I, along with Buddy, Will, and Buddy's two brothers Brad Jarrell and Todd Jarrell, were eventually allowed to see her. This was vital for me and more deeply emotional than I can convey—even after all the years I have had to reflect and process this event.

While at home waiting for information about the viewing, our phone rang. One of my cousins answered it. I eyed her as she moved toward two more of my female cousins. I watched them as they whispered in a huddle, heads bowed. In seemingly slow motion, they moved in a line toward me. One of them sweetly took my hand as the others encircled me on the couch. "Sweetheart," my cousin said, "that was Bring's Funeral Home calling. They need us to provide some clothing for Lacey."

"Why?" I asked. "Her little blue jeans and green tee shirt are exactly what she so loved to wear. I brought these to them yesterday."

"I know, sweetie," my cousin said. "But we need something different now. They want us to bring a skirt with an elastic waist and a loose blouse with long sleeves. You see, her body has become bloated since death."

I do not remember my response to this horrible realization except that I could not find any skirt. And no matter what I brought out of Lacey's closet, my cousins said it was "still too small." I gave in to their offer to go buy her a larger skirt with an elastic waistband and then deliver it and a blouse I found to the funeral home. I did not like the blouse I selected; it was long-sleeved, loose, and large. I did not recall Lacey wearing it. It would have looked silly on her tiny body.

Later that day, we learned her body was ready for us to view. *How I longed to see her, to touch her again.* Jack, Will, and I arrived at the funeral home and were seated in a conference room at a long table. Buddy arrived, and Will and Lacey's two uncles walked in soon after. Buddy's face was long, drawn, and vacant. We said a quick, "Hi," but there was no dramatic hug, burst of tears, or conversation. We all seemed frozen.

The funeral home staff gathered us all and instructed us to be incredibly careful touching her body and avoid moving her at all. She was fragile from the preparation work they had done to make her body "presentable."

The six of us walked in. I approached her face as her father and uncles drifted toward her feet. Jack glanced at her and then stepped away in a gesture of respect for the rest of us. For Will, the sight of his sister immediately overwhelmed him. She did not look like our Lacey. The frumpy, flowery clothing was not her style. And the bloating made her look heavy, not like the petite, slender, long-legged, button of energy she was.

I did not care, however. I could still see my Lacey, and it was critical that I kiss her cheek, touch her hair and skin, and look at every detail of her precious body. *Her newly polished fingernails still looked the same as they had a few days ago.*

I noticed the makeup could not hide the bruising on her right cheek. I flashed on her in the driver's seat of her car and calculated that her right cheek would have faced the passenger side. She looked as if she had been punched in the cheek. *Was that what happened?* Thoughts of those possible moments in her car raced through my mind.

Then I turned my attention to her feet. Her feet! We had joked about her feet. The family sometimes called her "sweet feet" and told her she had "perfect feet." This was fun and funny. After her death, we developed the photos in her camera and noted one from our recent trip to Hawaii—a photo of just her feet.

As I slowly moved down the side of her casket, I was shocked and angered to see Buddy's two brothers draped over half of Lacey's body, crying and hanging onto her. I feared their heavy weight would damage her, and that they were hurting her. I could not make sense of why they were slobbering over her body and seemingly trapping her. Knowing she would not like this, I instantly became as protective as if she were alive. That's when I yelled to Buddy, "Get everyone off of her!"

At that moment, I could not integrate her uncles' innocent behavior into a cognitive process. I could not wrap my mind around the fact that Lacey was really deceased, that her loving uncles and father were just shedding their tears of grief, and that hovering over her was not harming her. The three men backed away just as I stood at her feet and softly touched them, kissed them.

It is the last thing I remember of that day. I have no idea how long we were in that room. Fractured memories, time distortions, and flashes of the car accident I never saw became my new life without my Lacey Jane.

I will be forever grateful I was permitted to see her body privately with the family that day. I needed to see her so desperately. My only regret is not preparing Will for viewing his sister's body. I wish I had thought to explain to him what it could be like, or that I had offered him a choice. I was so swept up in *my* need that I did not think about what *he* might need. There was simply a silent understanding that we must all go and see her.

☆☆☆

The visitation and viewing at the funeral home as well as the service at St. Philip's in the Hills Episcopal Church a few days later were exhausting and overwhelming. Lacey's body lay in an open casket the night of the visitation, and many people seemed shocked with how she looked. Hundreds of people showed up, and I was shaken to see people from my past going back thirty years: co-workers, neighbors from communities we had lived in, teachers, students, and families from The Vail School District where we had lived for twelve years, Will and Lacey's friends and their families, and St. Gregory College Preparatory School families, students, and teachers. I had never experienced such an outpouring of love and support.

I was surprised to see how many friends had flown in from various parts of the country. At the funeral home, the reception line snaked out to the parking lot. I stood with as much grace as I could muster and greeted each person one by one. We hugged and cried, and I thanked each one for coming, saying I loved them.

At some point, I became aware that many who came were in even more emotional pain and agony than I, if that were even possible. That moved me. And so, I took on the role of caretaker and stepped outside of my pain to embrace theirs as best as I could. That included children I had cradled in my arms who towered over me now. They bent down to hold me and tell me they loved me. A family I knew when we lived in the Rincon Valley stepped forward, and the three children, so grown up, hugged me and reminded me of when I gave each of them horseback riding lessons. Jamin had been Lacey's first boyfriend when they were both four.

Kind teachers from both kids' schools whispered reminders of how special both Lacey and Will are. People told me I was beautiful, a role model, an example of grace and dignity. I felt the love at a depth only accessible in the wake of such a tragedy.

The funeral took place five days after her death. I walked through the motions of making these arrangements feeling like a ghost floating through the air but separate from my physical body that somehow kept moving across the land yet still influencing all the preparations.

The chief paramedic who responded to my daughter's accident came to the funeral. I was standing in the back of the church when Alan DeKalb introduced himself and asked permission to attend, along with the other firefighters from his station. I was taken aback and touched that they wanted to do so. "Absolutely," I said. "I'm so glad you are here." I sat down with Alan, wanting to know every detail of what happened to Lacey. Suddenly, Jack interrupted and said, "Nancy, we have to go to the procession." I immediately invited Alan to the reception at La Paloma so we could talk. I later became friends with him and the other paramedic on the call, Paul Smith.

I don't know how I spoke at Lacey's funeral, but it was extremely important for me to do so. Uncannily, only a few days before she died, I stood in my closet and imagined being at one of my children's funerals and speaking there. I did not know which child it was, though I was in tears at such a morbid and frightening vision. *A premonition?* I often shamed myself for these painful thoughts and visions. *Did my thinking bring on the tragedy?* I had experienced premonitions before, and they confused me. I never received enough detail to act on them and prevent tragedy. Rather, I dismissed them. They presented to me as visual scenes in my head, and I sought to purge the thoughts rather than embrace them when they occurred.

About a month before Lacey's death, her school college advisor, Melanie Drake, had asked me to write a few paragraphs about my daughter for her to reference when writing letters of recommendations to colleges. So I typed a three-page summary of how I saw my daughter, describing her talents and attributes, and saying (among other things):

> Lacey is intelligent and bright in a worldly way. Her natural common sense and "know" has and will serve her well. She is a great conversationalist. Her social skills are wonderful. Lacey is a direct communicator and engages in honest and open sharing of her feelings. She is genuine. All these traits seem to naturally draw others to her. Her charisma is constant. Her attractiveness is increased by her humility and her lack of pretentiousness or grandiosity. Her depth and self-reflection seem well beyond her years.

After the counselor read this, she wrote me to thank me and said my description conveyed so much love for Lacey that she wept when she read it. Little did I know I had written Lacey's eulogy.

She had died on Thursday, and now on Tuesday I was dressed in black. Everything around me still felt surreal. *How did this happen? How can I be alive and attending my child's funeral?*

I was the first to speak at the funeral. As I arose, I beckoned my son to escort me to the podium. The church was full beyond capacity.

Suddenly I felt wobbly, and unsure. How could I stand up and speak about Lacey to these hundreds of people? As I turned around to face the congregation, weeping faces stared up at me, many looking bewildered and shocked. And then, as though from the heavens, these unplanned words came out of my mouth: "I am the most fortunate person in this church right now, because I have had the privilege of being the mother of Lacey Jane Daly Jarrell for almost seventeen years." If anyone took a breath, nobody heard it.

After my reading, Will got up and spoke of his sister, then read her poem titled "The Star," which we found in her room. I was so proud of him. He did not waver. He spoke with strength and fortitude. After that, Janey and Eddie, my sister and brother, spoke. Eddie talked of the way Lacey lit up a room, her humor, her flirty smile, and her ever-present kindness. He then read the lyrics to the song "Yesterday" by Paul McCartney. Janey read a beautiful, heartfelt piece she wrote about what Lacey brought to her life—the joy, the love, the laughter. Their writings were beautifully sophisticated and well thought out.

Next spoke my former stepdaughter, Anne Marie, eighteen years older than Lacey. I remember feeling surprised when she said,

Lacey and her father, Buddy Jarrell, 2005

"Lacey is my sister." Annie, as we called her, had been living in Colorado, and we did not see her much. Lacey and Will's Aunt Travis (Buddy's sister) also spoke and verbalized her deep love for Lacey and offered words of peace, love, kindness, and comfort.

Then Buddy spoke. I had not expected him to do so. Someone had placed his name on the agenda, but I knew he was never comfortable speaking publicly and he kept his deep pain private. As he stood up, I held my breath. "I am sad," he began. "I am just so sad. That is all I can say." His voice was flat, and his face pained. His bowed head told me how much guilt and shame he carried. He loved the children deeply, but he had not been a very present father. I separated from him when the kids were ten and fourteen, and two years later, I filed for divorce.

All the speakers both moved and quieted the room. I was mesmerized. Following the service, I was unable to greet all the people at the church. All I had already done was now taking its toll on me. I was falling apart physically and emotionally, so the priest, Meighan, announced that anyone wanting to greet us could come to the reception at La Paloma Resort's ballroom. This gave me some time to compose myself. Quickly recognizing I was weak and depleted, Jack snuck me out of the church through a side door. I saw two people gesturing to me to talk and almost chasing us to Jack's car and calling my name. I could not stop. I jumped in the passenger side and locked the door. An odd response to people I cared about yet this behavior of fleeing when overwhelmed was a post-traumatic stress response I had employed before.

Just days before she died, Lacey told me she had a new boyfriend. His name was Joey. She shared with me how much she liked him and asked if he could come over to the house on Tuesday to meet me. I was thrilled, and enthusiastically responded "yes." I did meet Joey on Tuesday. I met him at the reception following her funeral.

One of Lacey's close friends, Christina McAlpin, took me by the arm and walked me a few steps toward a boy who stood with his head bowed, seemingly shy. "Nancy," she said, "I want you to meet Joey, Lacey's boyfriend." Joey and I locked eyes, but neither of us said a word. I was tearing up, and then I watched as tears streamed down his boyish face. I approached him and we held each other. I felt him shaking, and it registered with me that Lacey had asked that I meet him on Tuesday. *Her wish came true.* But meeting Joey in this context threw me back into the freeze, a place of slow-motion escape wherein I became silent and locked down, only going through the motions of things I had to do. As I let go of Joey, we locked eyes again before I turned away, never to see him again.

Buddy and I had Lacey cremated after the funeral. We had never discussed what she would want, burial versus cremation. We certainly never considered we might be making such a decision about one of our children. I come from a long line of Irish Catholics, and traditionally we always had a wake and buried our dead. The decision to cremate intuitively felt right, as did my selection of the beautiful urns for her ashes. She had not left a will, of course. But weeks later, I found a story she had written about her life. At the end, she stated she wanted to be cremated and placed in a blue, green, and silver urn. I hadn't known her wishes at the time, but this was exactly the description of the urn I chose.

The day of her cremation, I received a call from Belinda, who had helped us at the funeral home, to say Lacey's ashes were ready to be picked up. I detected a lifting air of excitement in each nuance of her voice. It seemed incongruent, considering the subject, but I dismissed it and promptly drove to the funeral home.

As soon as I saw Belinda, I knew that something happened out of the ordinary. "Nancy," she exclaimed, "a miracle has happened! I have never seen anything like this!" Puzzled, I approached her slowly. She pointed me to a sofa table adorned with three urns. The large one held most of Lacey's ashes, and two smaller ones held ashes for Buddy and me. We had both selected smaller, individual urns so that we might keep some of her cremains.

I had chosen a green and gold urn. Belinda directed me to it and dramatically lifted the top. There, sticking straight up out of the ashes, was the silver cross from my grandmother's rosary beads. I gasped. At the visitation at the funeral home, during the open casket viewing, I had placed Grandma Daly's rosary beads on Lacey's chest and strung them through a finger and palm of her hand. Growing up, I saw my grandmother saying the rosary on these treasured beads daily, but I never expected to see any part of that rosary again, especially not in such a jarring way.

Still animated, Belinda went on to say, "This is a miracle!" I began to cognitively process all the reasons it could not be a miracle. *This can't be real; it must be a type of metal that does not incinerate.*

Over time, I came to recognize that Belinda was a gift to me. Her quiet patience and genuine compassion and empathy shone through all the horror I was facing. She never judged my mood changes from profound pain and sorrow and immobilization to anger and energy and impulsivity. For some reason, though, I dismissed Belinda's clarity on "the miracle" until eight years later. I had established a roadside memorial to Lacey by then, and I was tending it one day when Belinda happened to drive by. She saw me, stopped, crossed the road, and hugged me. She updated me on her change of employment since I last saw her, saying she now worked in hospice care. "I will never forget you," she said, "and I have told your story over and over—the miracle of the cross in the ashes."

Belinda had been involved in so many cremations, and her belief and memory about the cross was so strong that I had to rethink it all. I had researched what happens to metal mingled with or in a body during the process. There was no consistent, concrete answer to this question. I read that dental gold melted and that salvaging any metals depended on their type and size. But my reading had focused on metals implanted *in* the body during surgery. After hearing Belinda's beliefs so many years later, I accepted how profound the survival of this cross had been.

☆☆☆

Although traumatic grief often involves complications of memory, recent interactions with Lacey were as crisp as early morning when the sun inches over the Rincon Mountains. I remembered her approaching me in the kitchen just three days before her death. I was standing at the stove cooking, and she came up and threw her arms around me tight and told me she loved me. "Mama," she said, "you are the best mama in the whole world!" I started to come up with reasons why I was not, discounting what she said. But as always, she interrupted me and refused to let me do that. She insisted it was all true, and that I should not deny these good things about me. Then she told me in list form all the things that *made* me the best mom in the world. I felt so blessed at the time, not knowing how precious a gift she gave me that day. Through the weeks, I began to wonder if I had been a good enough mother to her.

As the days passed, I became obsessed with figuring out how my daughter died. On the days I felt strong, I talked to the investigating sheriff, combed the police reports, reread the autopsy report, and drove up and down River Road at varying speeds, trying to figure out what had happened when Lacey lost control. I could not let it rest. I was told a toxicology report had been completed and the results were negative. It had never occurred to me that drugs or alcohol had been a cause of the accident. The autopsy report stated her death was "due to blunt impact to the head with skull fracture and laceration of brain."

Questions continued to plague me about whether Ernie had caused the accident. After their breakup, I worried that his pain would lead him to persistence and an inability to let Lacey go. That, of course, was true, evidenced by his calling her all the time. After he dropped the black roses at our doorstep, Lacey defended him saying he liked black. "Well, *you* don't," I told her, "and if the roses are for you, why wouldn't he bring what you like?"

Ernie continued to be a worrisome conflict in my life for months after Lacey's death. I had already dealt with the ups and downs of their relationship for three years. Now I veered between love and anger toward the boy. Most days, I felt both together.

One day I received a call from Alan, the first responder to Lacey's accident. He told me one of the other paramedics on the scene had been struggling since the accident. Alan wondered if I would come to the fire station and speak with this man. I was a bit confused by this request but agreed to do so. *Maybe it would be helpful to get to know these men better.*

When I arrived at the fire station a few miles from my home, I was greeted by Alan, who introduced me to Paul Smith. The three of us went into a private office. Both men had been in their jobs for decades and had seen many horrible things. They explained to me, however, that Paul was thinking about quitting his job due to "having seen too many kids die." Lacey's accident affected him at a time when he felt unable to hold any more tragedy. He was clearly suffering from post-traumatic stress disorder and had not been to work since Lacey's death. Alan had invited me to speak with him in hopes that Paul would not quit, and that he would see the difference he made in others' lives. I spoke to them about my pain and knowledge that I had to keep going. I was not trying to intervene with this man in any way. I was just talking through my thoughts at the time. Spending time with these men connected us deeply, and our connection became a gift.

A few days after our meeting, Alan called again and stated, "After you left the fire station, Paul said 'if this poor woman who lost her daughter can continue on, then I certainly can.'" Alan shared that Paul had agreed not to leave his job. I was grateful to learn our conversation had helped Paul. I was also intrigued that they had been so impacted by Lacey's accident that they made a point of reaching out to me twice. As time passed, I learned a great deal more about what happened that tragic day from these two special men. For now, however, I felt enough of a comfortable connection with them that I courageously picked up the phone a few days later and asked Alan to tell me more detail about how Lacey died. I needed to hear the truth about whether she had died instantly. I was fixated on an image of her lying under the car, still alive, desperately fighting to be extricated. Alan explained what had happened, insisting she had died instantly. I chose to believe him rather than thinking he told me this to spare me from more agony. *Choosing your thoughts* is a critical part of being able to survive each day following the sudden loss of a child. Had I chosen *not* to believe the paramedics and believed instead that they told me she died instantly so as not to upset me, then walking through my days would have been harder. By choosing to believe Alan, I experienced some relief.

Lacey was to enter her senior year of high school at St. Gregory College Preparatory School. My son had also graduated from this school, and Lacey had been a student there since the sixth grade. She was looking forward to being captain of the soccer team after being a dedicated player for the past three years. She adored her coach and reveled in the camaraderie with the other girls. She fully engaged with everybody and in anything she did. Her coach described her as "the fiery spark plug that ignited the team." Just days after her death, Coach Jeff Clashman came to our home with the graduating captain and presented a precious scrapbook to me that

Lacey playing soccer

the girls had put together. Filled with photos of Lacey and letters of loss, the words "I love you" showed on every page. The three of us sat on my living room floor going through it.

Although I felt wholly grateful for this time with these two special people, I was also struck by the fact that one day I was a soccer mom and the next I sat tugged toward the heavens, looking for my daughter in a place I never knew. *I am a bereaved parent, lost in the woods of my extraordinary despair.*

These visits on my living room floor became familiar, as so many of her friends came over with other scrapbooks, videos of Lacey, poems to her, and photographs taken when she modeled for her photography class. I did not even know she had modeled or that videos were posted of her on YouTube. Slowly, I learned of the impact she had made on so many. This outreach stopped my heart with conflicting emotions of astounding gratitude and deep, searing pain.

☆☆☆

Ironically, Lacey's birthday, August 29th, fell on the first day back to school. The kids did not want to return that day. Instead, someone arranged a meeting for her classmates and me, and someone else brought a birthday cake. (I imagine the head of the high school, Susan, whom I knew well, had arranged the meeting and brought the cake per the headmaster's instruction.) Susan's daughter, Emily, had been one of Lacey's closest friends through the years. They'd recently had a fracture in their relationship, but I knew both Susan and Emily loved Lacey completely.

Though well intended, the whole event felt incredibly awkward. I cried throughout, and the kids were tearful and speechless. The new headmaster spoke, a man who had arrived that summer and had never met Lacey. He had his hands full with this tragedy. Later, the kids went to Susan and demanded something more be done; this was not nearly enough to honor Lacey and their feelings. Some weeks later, the school held an assembly program where they showed a classmates-created video of her. Despite the funny scenes of Lacey laughing, dancing, and playing, the room was as silent as death. Middle school and high school students and teachers all attended, with her teachers from over the years all providing incredible support. They included Jeff Clashman, Kate Oubre, and Linda Mount, just a few of the significant teachers in our lives. Lacey's classmates remained after the program, allowing me to speak to them through tears. I presented each of them with a double-faced card I had made with two of Lacey's poems on each side and a photo of her above each poem.

We then walked outside and placed colored marbles in a large cement star they had made in her memory. A parent I did not know stood in the background and sobbed. Some of the boys stood with their arms around each other's shoulders, tears streaming, and at times rocking side to side in anguish. Teachers held me and cried. Then Cheryl Pickrell, a middle-school teacher who taught seventh-grade English to both Will and Lacey, came over. I knew she had lost her son, Chris, some years before. She allowed me to collapse on her, her slight figure holding me up with the strength of God.

This scene is forever etched in the memory bank of my soul.

Each day, I became more and more obsessed with finding out everything I could about the accident. This need to know was part of my grieving. It was also a small way in which I could medicate the torture I felt all day, especially every morning when I awakened to the reality of Lacey's death. *Why was Ernie with her in the car? How did he escape injury? How did he convince her to drive to the corner that morning to pick him up? And was that what really happened? Had he done something to make her lose control of the wheel?*

Lacey was named as the driver based only on Ernie's report, though the positioning of the seats indicated that a shorter person was driving, as the seat was closer to the steering wheel than the passenger side, and Ernie was taller than Lacey. *But if she had been driving, why did he give me her keys three days after the accident and tell me he did not know where he got them?*

Kelleeyn shared with Jack that, when she arrived at the house, it did not appear that Lacey had been awakened suddenly, as Ernie had reported. The television was still on and all her art supplies were out, suggesting she had begun work on a new project. But even if Lacey had not been awakened suddenly, it appeared she had *departed* suddenly. She also left behind her purse and was still dressed in her sleeping clothes. One of the doors was unlocked, and she had left barefoot—two things she never did. *What caused this instant departure?*

I stayed close to Ernie, wanting to hear anything he could remember from the accident. He was the last one to see my daughter alive. He called and texted her constantly. *Why was he in the car? What were they doing together?*

I was also concerned about Ernie, since he had suffered an enormous trauma himself. He, too, was in shock and pain. He finally admitted that my daughter had refused to pick him up that morning. But he said that after he made several calls to her, promising they could eat doughnuts (in fact, a box of Krispy Kremes was later found in the vehicle) and that he had something else to give her, Lacey eventually agreed to come get him at St. Francis in the Foothills Church, less than a mile away. She was angry at him, he said, and as a result drove her Subaru too fast on the curvy, hilly River Road close to our house. Ernie asked her to slow down, he said, but Lacey said only, "Why?" Right after that, she lost control of the vehicle and uttered a mild epithet. He remembered bracing himself with his hands pressed to the roof as the car rolled and tumbled counterclockwise down the hill.

Still, I had questions. *Exactly what had happened when the car began to roll?* The police report noted marks on the roadway but no obvious or distinct yaw or skid marks. But that could have been due to the downgrade and the possibility of Lacey's car not displacing all its weight on the roadway. The velocity of the vehicle could also have been a factor. Some surmised Lacey was knocked unconscious before she was ejected from the vehicle. Others thought that, with her hands on the wheel, she would have had no way to brace herself as Ernie did. She was also a petite little girl, weighing a slight one hundred ten pounds at barely five-foot-three. I pressured officials to get those police reports, and I spoke with the investigating sheriff daily. All were exceedingly kind to me.

I acquired the phone bills for both Lacey's cell phone and our home phone. Then I studied them and listened over and over to Lacey's voicemail. The only documented call from Ernie came in *after* the time of her death. Things were not adding up. As a result of experiences both as a child and an adult, my suspicious nature finds it difficult for me to trust. In the past, people I least expected to do so had violated my trust. This made me question the simplicity of Ernie's report. *How could something as simple as a one-minute car ride end with loss of life? And how could the explanation not be complex, dark, and mysterious?* I could not accept what I had been told, and I experienced a major meltdown and incapacitation as I realized *I would never have Lacey's side of the story.*

✩✩✩

Meltdowns and incapacitation soon became a way of life for me. When alone, I often found myself on the floor in the fetal position, crying like an infant whose mother had abandoned her. My fixation on what caused the accident resulted in increased back-and-forth travels on that specific quarter mile of River Road. The day after the accident, I had gone there to pick up glass from the windshield and anything else I could find, looking for answers and understanding. I saved everything I could find. I drove the same stretch at different speeds, trying to determine how Lacey flipped her car and at what speed. It was all I could think about.

I heard that the car had landed on Lacey, and only her feet protruding from under the vehicle could be seen. This became a haunting vision in the form of flashbacks about something I had never seen. Prior to Lacey's death, I had been meeting with a therapist on an as-needed basis. When she heard about my loss, she came to the house and I shared this intrusive vision. She generously worked with me on it, sitting on the floor in Lacey's room. To help reduce this symptom, she facilitated a neural-somatic psychotherapy treatment called EMDR, or Eye Movement Desensitization and Reprocessing.

EMDR is a therapeutic modality initially designed to reduce trauma symptoms. The theory behind it is that trauma gets compartmentalized in the right hemisphere of the brain, which explains how some of us get stuck in the symptoms. EMDR activates both the right- and left-brain hemispheres, allowing the traumatic event to be processed across the whole brain and consequently freed as a result of the bi-lateral stimulation. The process involves using light, or an object, or even sound or vibration, which a therapist controls. One method employs an object that the therapist moves in a consistent left-right, left-right motion and the client's eyes follow. One theory is that the eye movements mimic the rapid-eye-movement sleep phase in which dreams appear. That phase is directly involved in memory formation. EMDR therapy can be transformative in normalizing once terrifying memories into ones that are no longer emotionally charged. The process supports clients in recognizing they are safe now, that the memories are in the past and that what happened is over. This process is not for everyone and must be facilitated by a trained clinician for safety and efficacy.

The EMDR in which I participated involved the use of wristbands that gave off a vibration and sound. As I closed my eyes, the sensation pulsed back and forth from my left wrist to my right wrist. During the process, I experienced being outside of my body, in the sky, watching over Lacey's accident. It almost felt as though I *were* Lacey after leaving her body. Looking down on her accident gave me brief comfort, as I felt no pain and understood that she felt no pain. Rather, she felt wonder and disbelief. I did not imagine her shocked by it all, for at some level, I believed both she and I subconsciously knew she would die at age sixteen.

Several years later, I learned that this kind of obsessive behavior—the engraved vision in my mind and my need to know—was typical for someone suffering from traumatic grief. At the time this was all happening, I just felt crazy.

☆☆☆

I continued to look back at the days before Lacey's death, trying to retrieve every word of our conversations. I remembered recent occasions when I had come down the stairs at a trot and had stopped cold when I saw her big green eyes and long brown hair cupping her tiny face. Her beauty often stunned me, but on these occasions, her expression stopped me. She appeared so worried and disturbed, and said, "Mama, I have a bad feeling in my stomach." When I asked her about it, she said, "I feel that something bad is going to happen."

I never dismissed her statements but questioned her thinking and tried to calm her. I listened deeply and did not let on how much it frightened me when she said these things. Just days before the accident, she told me she wished she could remain sixteen years old forever. Currently content and happy, the thought of going off to college was one she didn't want to entertain. She also spoke to me about knowing she was an "old soul," and that she had a mission on earth to "make people happy."

Only two days before her death, she shared with increased anxiety that Ernie's persistence with his calls and texts was escalating. She spoke vaguely about him bothering her, saying I did not know "how bad it is." I begged her to please tell me what she meant. I asked if I should go to his home and speak with him and his mother. Adamant that I not do that, she said, "That will just make everything worse." I remember exactly where I was standing when I said, "I'm afraid he will harm you and even kill you with his jealousy." We made eye contact and held it for a full breath.

My own words shocked me. I could not believe I spoke these words aloud. *Did I really think this?* Such a thought did not fit in with what I regarded as our normal, blessed, safe lives. I shuddered. Yet, she told me there was nothing she could not handle. That's when I asked if she wanted to go on Saturday and have her cell phone number changed. When she said yes, my fear escalated. I *knew* what a big deal it was for a sixteen-year-old girl to change her number and risk being out of touch with friends until she got the word out. Once we agreed to do this, I felt better that we had a plan of action, although Lacey did not live until Saturday. The conversation ended, but for me it is still going on, haunting me.

We kept in closer touch over the next day until that final day, when for two hours I could not reach her. I realize now that she was already dead when I first started trying.

I could not stand to think for any amount of time that anything I did, did not do, or could have done would have changed her fate. Some of my thoughts about her "premonitions" are still too unbearable to think or write about.

☆☆☆

Sometime later, I learned that a woman named Michelle St. Rose witnessed the accident. She was standing on her second-floor porch talking to her sister on her phone when she heard screeching tires and saw the car come around the first bend, westbound. She thought the car was traveling at an excessive rate of speed. Michelle counted three rollovers before the car hit the berm on the south side of the road and called 911 before the car came to a standstill.

Two separate female drivers also came upon the accident and stopped. I later became close to Michelle, who ended up with Post Traumatic Stress Disorder (PTSD) due to witnessing this tragedy.

She could see both Lacey and Ernie moving around in the car as it rolled over again and again, but she could not tell who was driving. Michelle later reported that Ernie was walking around the car asking, "Where is the girl? Where is the girl?" She and the two women could see Lacey's foot, sole face up, protruding from under the car—the foot with the three green stars she had drawn on her ankle. Before the emergency team arrived, one of the women, a physician, found a pulse in the *dorsalis pedis* artery in Lacey's ankle, but she was unresponsive to their voices.

The three women, two of whom were mothers, knelt in a circle, held Lacey's ankle, and prayed as my little girl transitioned to a higher place. I will forever be grateful to these three loving women that they were there for my daughter when she passed. Later that day, Michelle and her seven-year-old daughter, Robby, went back to the road, and Robby placed one of her personal teddy bears on the side of the road. Thus, began what would become Lacey's memorial site.

☆☆☆

Months later, I was told that Ernie and his mother, Mel McBeath, came to my home in the early evening on the night of the accident. Approaching them both with tears and open arms, I was told I said, "I'm so glad that two of you did not have to die today." I do not remember this. It was months after that I learned that one primary symptom of traumatic grief is impaired memory. Other symptoms are preoccupation with what happened, scanning the environment for cues and/or the presence of the loved one, and talking incessantly about the deceased.

As a clinician, I knew the term "grief" was not used as a diagnosis in the *Diagnostic and Statistical Manual of Mental Disorders* (DSM), but the manual did include the term "bereavement." Bereavement is the response one has to the death of a significant other. I was aware that my response was profound in that the pain was all encompassing and constant, and it filled every space in my life.

I had worked with trauma patients for years at Sierra Tucson. In my lectures to their family members, I defined trauma as "an overwhelming emotional experience when one has a real or perceived threat to their life and/or safety or the life and/or safety of someone else." Further, I said that "trauma is not an event but rather how one experiences or perceives an event." I also shared a well-known quote from Anaïs Nin, a French American writer, who said: "We don't see things as they are, we see things as we are."

People feel traumatized when they are unable to control the outcome of an extreme life stressor. I also knew from my experience in the field that people could experience grief without trauma, but rarely did anyone experience trauma without grief. So, there I landed, *self-diagnosed with traumatic grief.* Now I at least had an explanation for my behaviors, other than just feeling insane.

I buried myself in research on the topic. Traumatic grief is defined as the result of loss of a loved one in which the death is sudden and/or unexpected and violent in nature. The nature of the death and its circumstances play a significant role in experiencing traumatic grief. Without any psychological preparation for such a loss, the unexpected and untimely aspects of suddenly losing a child exacerbate the struggle of how to cope. It was not until the late 1990s that grief and trauma were addressed jointly. A clinician-generated movement advocated for traumatic grief to be recognized as a true diagnosis in the next edition of the *Diagnostic and Statistical Manual of Mental Disorders* (DSM), scheduled to be released in 2013. I found the book *Traumatic Grief* by Selby Jacobs,[1] which included proposed criteria for the diagnosis. I could identify with all the criteria! One proposed general criterion centered on "symptoms involving intrusive, distressing preoccupation with the deceased, manifested in yearning and engagement in searching the environment for cues of the loved one." I knew about that in spades. It seemed that every day, as a small black vehicle shot by me in traffic, I saw Lacey's long auburn hair against white skin. Other times it was a young female jogger with her hair pulled back, wearing a baggy sweatshirt. Such sightings provided me with a flash of false validation that Lacey really hadn't passed.

☆☆☆

In the years following Lacey's death, I became an expert on traumatic grief and began to train other clinicians in how to recognize and treat the condition. This was not what I wanted to be known for, but I realized I was doing a service. I eventually traveled to London, where I presented at a conference on traumatic grief. There, I explained how the symptoms were similar to—and different from—those of PTSD.

Traumatic grief as a diagnosis was not approved for the DSM-5 published in 2013, but I still use the term while working with bereaved parents. The DSM-5, which in 2019 is still the most current version, does have a chapter titled "Conditions for Further Study" and includes *Persistent Complex Bereavement Disorder,* which lists proposed criteria similar to Jacobs' traumatic grief definition.

Early on, I began to recognize I suffered from *separation anxiety*— a diagnosis reserved for children under eighteen who experience severe distress or anxiety when separated from a loved one. It is also defined as *excessive preoccupation* with the feeling that one might lose a loved one to an uncontrollable event. There are many more symptoms and criteria defined for this disturbance, but these two were enough to convince me I was suffering from an adult form of it. I was often enveloped in fear that Lacey might not be in a good place. I missed her all the time, everywhere I went. The gnaw was constant.

In the worst of it, I had to fight hard to keep functioning and remember to focus on gratitude, positive thinking, and the knowledge that I have the power to choose my thoughts. I knew I had a long road ahead of me, and that I would need to adopt compensatory behaviors and thoughts to find my way through this unfamiliar maze of tragedy.

I also had to engage my rational and logical thinking very consciously time and time again to alleviate the sense of guilt I felt. *As a parent, my job was to keep my children safe, and I had failed.* When I was plagued with all the "I should have's," and thought about what I could have or should have done to prevent her death I learned to stop this thinking. It would not bring Lacey back and it only resulted in my feeling worse than I already did. (I did not think that possible, but it was.)

Knowing that my guilt only produced more agony and I needed tools to help me walk through this field of pain, it just made no sense to mire myself in guilt. Parental guilt comes with the territory of just being a parent. Not allowing guilt or shame to seep into my drastically changed life became work in progress for me day by day.

Terror and shock, the twin monsters, grew and lived inside of me. "Please give me something for this," I remember begging my doctor. I did not want to feel the pain anymore, and yet I knew I was not feeling fully—I was somewhat numb. *There was no medication for this pain!*

A few years later, I learned more about how endorphins, the chemicals produced by our bodies to relieve pain or stress and increase our level of happiness, numb us when we experience trauma. These natural painkillers are released in the brain within moments of a traumatic event to help mask emotional and physical pain and allow our protective survival responses to kick in. The overall job of the brain is to help us survive.

When considering trauma, an area called the limbic system is a collective term for multiple brain parts responsible for our emotions, survival instincts, regulation of impulsivity, aspects of memory formation, and automatic motor activity. Within the limbic system, an area known as the amygdala acts as the brain's fire alarm alerting us to danger and identifies if there is an actual threat to our very survival. The amygdala generates fear activation and responses to sensory information—specifically, any external potential danger. Its job is to prepare the body to respond to a real or perceived threat. In turn, the amygdala alerts the hypothalamus, another brain structure within the limbic system that regulates blood pressure, heart rate, sexual arousal, hunger, and thirst. The thalamus—the communicator—relays motor and sensory information to another part of the brain known as the cerebral cortex. A two-fold process begins as the adrenal glands release the hormones epinephrine and norepinephrine, resulting in increased heart rate, blood pressure, and rate of breathing to provide more oxygen and enable quick movement. Epinephrine, also known as adrenaline, activates our fight or flight response.

Simultaneously, a process involving the release of the stress hormones cortisol and corticotrophin activate our systems to supply us with the best opportunity for survival by turning fatty acids into energy for our muscles to use, if needed. Once the danger is over, these same hormones work to stop the production and release of epinephrine and norepinephrine, allowing the body to return to homeostasis. This hormone release initiates survival actions of fight and flight. Mammals automatically fight or flee (depending on which is most available to them) or, lastly, they freeze when escape from the terror seems impossible.

In 1995, Dr. Steven Porges[2] identified an evolved portion of our nervous system that he called the social nervous system. This system engages when we feel safe, comfortable, and connected to others. He surmised that when faced with threat, we look to this system first, seeking close others for safety. When this approach is not available, we engage our sympathetic nervous system (fight or flight response) and lastly default to our parasympathetic nervous system (freeze state or immobilization or dissociation). This can happen in a matter of seconds.

In psychology, *dissociation* refers to mild-to-severe detachment from our surroundings as a defense mechanism for seeking safety. In laymen's terms, dissociation is when we essentially check out. We are not fully present. A mild example is highway hypnosis after driving for hours and falling into a mental lull without being fully focused on the task.

Dissociation is also defined by *distraction,* such as driving home and then later realizing we have driven past the exit to our neighborhood. These symptoms can be severe when an individual detaches from reality and suffers significant memory loss and even loss of identity.

Metaphorically at least, I did all three of these over time. For most of the first year, however, I was simply frozen.

☆☆☆

Grief is a process. It has no defined stages, and the many myths—such as "time heals"—are just that, myths. As John W. James and Russell Friedman wrote in *The Grief Recovery Handbook,* "Time does not heal; it passes."[3]

Grief and loss had become familiar to me. The year before I lost Lacey, my parents passed away a week apart. And I had lost my brother, Thomas Farley, sixteen days before Lacey's birth. He died after being in a bicycle accident in a beautiful park in Greenwich, Connecticut. He was discovered unconscious by a passerby, who performed CPR on him and called 911. Tom lived in a coma for three days and was then taken off the ventilator. He died soon after.

Just the year before, Buddy, Will, and I had gone to visit him and his wife, Brooke, and visited the very same park. I was torn, conflicted, and devastated, as I was due to deliver Lacey any day and ultimately could not fly back to Connecticut to see my brother or attend his funeral. My father called me and begged me not to come, saying he could not bear the thought of worrying about me delivering on the plane or experiencing travel difficulties. Thus, the decision was made for me; I would not cause my parents more anxiety.

As it turned out, Tom and Lacey died of the exact same injuries. The autopsies both stated: "Cause of death: laceration to the brain and skull."

Before losing Lacey, I thought I had avoided grieving my parents' deaths through busyness, although I did express my feelings through the writing of poetry. Although I knew how important it was to talk about my feelings, I feared burdening others with my pain. A close friend asked me if the accumulation of all these deaths plus my divorce and other losses compounded my pain over the loss of Lacey. I quickly answered her with a "no." So many past experiences seemed to have flown by like pages in a book, one I had flipped backwards with my thumb. Yet none of those other losses felt big anymore. *This* was the tragedy of my lifetime. Nothing else compares.

✩✩✩

In 2008, I began reading about liminal space, or liminality. So much of what I had experienced regarding change and transition seemed to fit into what was described as the "state of liminality." I decided to research this concept.

Arnold van Gennep authored *Rites of Passage* in 1909, in which he coined the word "liminality."[4] He described liminal space as the realm between two worlds of status; for example, a boy leaves childhood, enters the liminal space of ritual and transformation, and then emerges as a man.[5] In 1967, Victor Turner discovered van Gennep's work and wrote *The Forest of Symbols,* expanding on the concept of liminality.[6] He described a process wherein one's sense of identity dissolves into a state of disorientation as a result of a major life-changing event. But he postulated that if one could transition out of the disorientation successfully, the possibility of gaining new perspectives existed. He noted how a sudden event affecting one's life left that person "between and betwixt," and yet opportunity for growth existed if one successfully resolved the conflicted state.

Neurological psychology uses the term "liminal state" and describes it as "subjective" and "of or between two different existential planes."

I thought about myself, of course, but also of other bereaved parents I knew. We all had described our lives in similar terms: *between two worlds; I don't know who I am anymore; I have lost my identity since my child's suicide; am I a mother still?* And *I will never be the same.* As bereaved parents, we had been thrown into liminal space and existed as "transitional beings."

The final phase of development in Turner's process of liminality was the "re-entry" of the individual back into the culture as a "new person."

I became a new person. No question. Jack tells me I have "become quiet." He describes my whole way of being in the world as having changed to a quietness and physical slowness. I carefully measure my words. I have adopted a second internal world that only I seem to understand. I realized that a life spark was blown out. But from that, I truly know gratitude now. I am wiser. I am more comfortable with most of what I do and say.

In that first year, I gave myself permission to just be, do, and say whatever I needed to if it pushed me through the pain. I worked hard trying not to hurt others. When that became challenging, I tried to look inside of them and see their pain. Early on, I asked these questions: "How could this have happened to her, to us, to me?" And then arrived at "why not me?" For I am just another person on this earth striving to extricate myself from a mire of grief, yearning for the possibility of relief.

Chapter Three: Time Passes . . . Slowly

Grief is a tidal wave that overtakes you
Smashes down upon you with unimaginable force
Sweeps you up into its darkness, where you tumble and crash
Against unidentifiable surfaces, only to be thrown out
On an unknown beach, bruised, reshaped
And unwittingly better for the wear.

~ Stephanie Ericsson

Almost immediately following Lacey's death, Jack became my major support. During the first months, he devoted a great deal of time helping me through the grief process. He took care of me, fed me, looked out for my overall well-being, and protected me from any perceived sources of overwhelm. He vigilantly ensured I not hear or see too much information about the accident. He worried it could re-traumatize me or even spiral me back into a dependency on alcohol, which I had worked so hard to overcome.

I had been in recovery for seventeen years when Lacey passed. I felt grateful every day that my children had not experienced me when I was actively drinking. After family members who flew in for Lacey's services arrived, I learned that many of them were concerned I would relapse and begin medicating with alcohol. This shocked me, not because I could not be vulnerable to relapse but because the thought of turning to alcohol never entered my mind. I wanted relief from my emotional pain but never thought of alcohol as a solution. By this time in my sobriety, I had to consciously recall the number of years I had been sober. Not feeling attached to that number, I preferred to just be grateful for another day of sobriety. The large Irish Catholic family I was raised in drank when someone married or when someone had a birthday, an anniversary, a death, a funeral, or just because it was a new day, or in some cases because they were alcoholics. My parents did not understand that I could be an alcoholic and decide not to drink. However, they did respect my decision and asked early on if it would bother me for them to drink in my presence. My siblings, though, were well aware of how alcohol affected me.

A few weeks after losing Lacey, I attended a meeting of Alcoholics Anonymous. There, I recognized that now the only time I thought about alcohol was in these meetings. I tearfully shared my loss and listened as others shared their stories or offered me condolences. Most importantly, they reminded me that it would make no sense to begin to drink again now. Lacey had not experienced me that way and so why would I dishonor her memory by drinking now? I agreed. And I also had my son to consider. Drinking was not an option nor was it a desire.

My once-best friend of fifteen years, Kim, suddenly reappeared in my life. She and I had gradually grown apart when I became sober. My sister, whom I had not spoken to in a year, came back into my life, too. In these early months, I no longer had fractured relationships. Everything was about love and pain—two intertwined emotions.

Additionally, some new people entered my life who later turned out to be significant, especially in their support of my development of a nonprofit organization in my daughter's name. Others helped me find answers to my questions regarding the accident. I believed that Lacey provided her brother, her father, and me with all these people to help us cope. In fact, many encounters seemed to be miracles from my precious child. As people carried us through the harrowing days, I felt she was still very close to me.

Most people do not know what to say to bereaved parents unless they have experienced such a tragedy themselves. Many are so uncomfortable with the mere thought of such a loss that they will smile to hide their pain, unaware of the incongruency. I worked consciously not to become angry with these people. I realized they did not know how to help me, though they wanted to desperately. In fact, I felt stunned when someone smiled, suggested I play music, or told me it would get a little better every day. It does not get better every day.

The profound level of trauma in my loss sometimes triggered people into projecting their own unresolved grief onto me. Many would want to tell me stories of how they managed a loss. Others wanted to share with me their deepest grief and pain, unconsciously using me as a mirror with which they could reflect their own sorrow.

But I could not carry their pain, too. I had to distance myself from anyone who used my pain to help them process their own unresolved grief, even if it was unintentional. I became irritated if people told me they understood what I was going through. I remember shouting my planned response to an empty room: *Unless you have gone to work one day and by lunchtime had your sixteen-year-old daughter, whom you were closer to than any other human being, lose control and wreck her car and roll three times down the road, be ejected from the car, and then have the car land on her, lacerating her brain and skull, then you do not have a clue!*

☆☆☆

As a therapist, I was accustomed to hearing horribly traumatic, life-changing stories, and I supported people in their healing through validation, empathy, and listening. But these experiences of projection often left me worn and unnerved by people's insensitivity while instilling in me a fervent desire to flee. One woman demonstrated how she repeatedly hit herself in the head with her fist as hard as she could when her twin brother died from an infection after what was considered a routine surgery. Another insisted I listen to tragic-sounding music that her mother played "to never forget the impact her husband and my father had on our lives." It seemed her mother intentionally worked at keeping the pain close and was attached to the suffering. This disturbed me. Another man told me he did not know how I felt as he had never been a parent "unless we count when I was a parent to a cat in a previous life." My response was a vacuous stare. People told me these kinds of stories day after day. Completely full of my own grief, I had no room to carry their pain and think about their tragedies.

Despite this, I was told I presented myself with dignity and grace, which became especially important for me. I did not want to become bitter and morose. While every sinew in my body felt ripped apart and bleeding, people referred to me as courageous, a role model, and compassionate—words I would use to describe my daughter.

I dealt with my grief by forcing myself to remain active but also accepting it was okay if I did nothing but stay home and cry. The loneliness and quiet in my house were my best friends and my worst enemies. Some days I could not push myself out of bed, and even if I did, I returned to it so I could escape through slumber. Basic human needs such as safety, food, and water disappeared as my priorities. I could only think of the pit of anguish in my stomach and the all-embracing misery. I knew no adjectives to describe how I felt. Words imprisoned me.

☆☆☆

I often wondered if Ernie ever came to Lacey's roadside memorial. Within days, it had transformed into a thriving site with an amazing number of flowers, cards, stuffed animals, photos, jewelry, and wind chimes hanging from the trees. Then I heard that Ernie went there late at night. *What did he do there? How long did he stay? What did he think? How did he feel?* I monitored myself when these questions arose, as at times, my assumptions took me to a dark and useless place. So I consistently worked to turn my thoughts around.

The memorial became sacred space to me. I felt fiercely protective of this blessed plot of land. Because Lacey had been cremated, Buddy, Will, and I did not want a gravestone, but we knew we needed something to anchor the memorial and define its purpose. At a granite store, we discovered a large boulder-like piece of rock with a flat surface that we agreed was exceptionally beautiful. We happened to notice it lying in the large outdoor yard of the store. When we asked about it, the owner told us about an old cowboy rancher who had donated the rock two years earlier. The rancher had said, "Perhaps the right person who could use it will come along."

That rock was meant for us! Miraculously, the storeowner did not even charge us when he learned what we planned to do with it. It was perfect for the site, and we requested the store add a marble cross to the face as well as engrave Lacey's name, birth and death dates, plus an indentation of a star. Later, Buddy had our friend, Randy Mendoza, make a copper star to place in the rock, knowing the copper would turn green in memory of Lacey's love of stars and her favorite color.

Lacey's roadside memorial

When the engravings were completed, Will, Buddy, and Lacey's uncle Brad Jarrell dug a deep hole at the site, poured cement, and somehow carried the heavy boulder from Buddy's truck and set it into the ground. Still July, the sun was merciless as all three of these men—strong, shirtless, and in tears with physical and emotional agony—carried what would be a permanent marker commemorating the place of Lacey's death. I watched as they did this, knowing that this terribly painful scene would also become a permanent memory in my mind.

As the weeks passed, people added more and more objects to the memorial site—crosses, Buddhas, Virgin Mary statues, angels, and all kinds of personal things, including clothing, books, and china. When some of the religious relics were stolen, I felt shattered and fragmented, but I told myself they were small setbacks. I went to a church supply store and bought ten more relics. When I told the women in the store what had happened, they prayed over the objects to guard them against theft. My upkeep of Lacey's memorial became a source of desperation but also penance for my inability to keep her safe. My life still revolved around Lacey in every way.

☆☆☆

That summer, my continual drives up and down River Road became excruciating. I was obsessed with trying to understand how the accident happened in order to make sense out of what seemed to me to be implausible. I knew the primary job of the human brain is to ensure our species survives, and the brain's reward system plays a significant part in this. To secure our chances for survival, the brain seeks novelty. The chemicals in our brains that reward our behaviors are activated during seeking; as this provides opportunities for learning that, in turn, motivate us. From our brain's perspective and from an evolutionary viewpoint, "seeking" behavior is considered positive and necessary for survival. The seeking circuit urges us to be curious, interested, and motivated to fulfill our needs.

At the time, I was not aware of anything that might be occurring in my brain, but some years later came to recognize this early seeking of answers gave me a push to keep going, to have purpose, to be motivated, to live. Albeit small, I was receiving some benefit from the behavior. As my sometimes-risk-taking drives on River Road increased, Jack and a few friends decided I had to stop torturing myself and get away from everything that reminded me of the accident.

Prior to Lacey's death and unknown to me, Jack had rented a house in Aspen, Colorado for the month of August 2006. As the end of July approached, a group of caring individuals thought it best I drive to Colorado with Jack and stay in Aspen for a bit. Doing something I would not normally do, I gratefully allowed others to make decisions for me. *I had no idea how to help myself.*

Will agreed I should go as well. We decided he would first stay in Tucson and then come join us in Aspen in a week with his girlfriend, Carly. Jack's daughter, Laura O'Donnell, would also join us. At that point, Will was unsure if he would return for his last semester at the University of Colorado. He was finding it increasingly difficult to stay at our home where he and Lacey had shared the whole bottom floor. They each had a bedroom and shared a living room and a game room, which included a ping-pong table and Lacey's electric piano. The guest room housed her drum set.

It felt eerie downstairs in our home now, her absence palpable in every corner, and I understood why Will might not want to be there. So he stayed at the home of his close friend, Ben Schwartz, during my absence. The Schwartz family was extremely good and kind to him. When I left for Aspen, I felt as though I were abandoning him and had to fight off the potential for more misery. I had no more space in my body to carry my failures.

Our drive to Aspen was both beautiful and painful. Leaving Tucson felt as though I was leaving both Will *and* Lacey. Jack was also grieving, so he patiently understood without discussion that I needed to take Lacey's ashes with me to Colorado. He had come to know Lacey, winning her approval after he gave her a few driving lessons and allowed her to drive his Volkswagen. On the trip, whenever we packed or unpacked the car to stop overnight, rest, or walk Jack's dog (a pit bull mix named Wally), we attended to Lacey's ashes first. Jack handled the urn as if it were the most precious item in the world. To us, it was.

We arrived the first of August at a beautiful home in the middle of Aspen with spectacular views and luxuries most of us only dream of. Stunning! Yet, not long after our arrival, I had a complete meltdown. The pain of living and breathing seemed more than I could bear. I got into bed and cried myself to sleep. Jack had to take care of me, literally waking me up to make sure I ate and drank. At times I was inconsolable or despondent. He was unbelievably good to me. Try as I might, I could no longer deny the reality of my greatest loss and fear.

☆☆☆

I got out of bed as often as I could and committed to doing so for the long term, knowing I could not medicate my pain by hiding under the covers all day. I also knew that lying around would increase my depression. Many times, though, I could not get through the entire day without going back to bed for hours. If not in bed, I spent many afternoons and evenings on the couch sobbing, feeling sick to my stomach, or sitting frozen in shock.

When I felt able to go into town, I scoured bookstores and libraries for books to help me learn what was ahead of me. I found an abundance of literature on how to raise a child but absolutely none on how to deal with losing one.

Despite my being inconsolable, Jack somehow helped me step through the doorway many a morning, along with his dog, to go on long hikes into the grand, healing mountains of Colorado. Every evening, he carefully made hiking plans for us, so the next morning we had a fresh new destination.

Still, I often walked with my head down, my senses dulled while engrossed in deep thoughts of Lacey. At times, I seemed to forget to feed my lungs with the fresh mountain air. At other times when I would look up, it was as though I were viewing the environment through a strong camera lens, and I could see the scenery in all its perfect detail. I felt insignificant on the planet during these moments, yet also embraced and cared for by its majesty. A green-feathered hummingbird caught my attention. A single pine needle dangled ahead of me like a unique and stunning ornament. My senses were both muted and heightened—a strange dichotomy I became used to.

I did not know then that this trip to Colorado and Jack's care likely saved my life. We walked for hours; sometimes we spoke and sometimes there were lengthy periods of silence. Sometimes I walked way behind him, lost in my thoughts of Lacey. It was not until 2015 when I read an article in *Proceedings of the National Academy of Sciences Journal*[7] that I learned the results of a research study demonstrating that a ninety-minute walk in a natural setting decreased rumination—repetitive thoughts focused on negative aspects of the self. Subjects in this study who walked in nature also showed a reduction in activity in an area of the brain linked to risk of mental illness. Other subjects walked for ninety minutes in urban areas and did not have the positive results that those who walked in a natural environment did.

In 2018, I read an article in *NeuroscienceNews.com*[8] summarizing a study researching the effect of exercise on recovering drug addicts. The research showed that recovering addicts who exercised regularly were not as triggered to use as those recovering addicts who did not exercise when re-exposed to drug-related cues. Triggers or cues include seeing drug paraphernalia, being with people one used with, or being in the neighborhood one frequented when seeking the drug. The research concluded that exercise changed levels of peptides in the brains of those who exercised by altering previous learning that associated drug use and the resulting feeling or sensation. Previous research has shown that regular exercise could reduce cravings and consequently relapse in addicts.

During those weeks of walking in the Rockies, I intuitively knew the activity had to be helping me in some way. Due to my feeling consumed with unfamiliar grief and angst, I could not compare it to any other time in my life as proof these hikes were helping me. At the time, nothing felt healing.

In fact, I feared nothing except the pain I felt and not knowing how I could live with it. And then I no longer even feared the pain, as I did not care to live at all! I just kept hiking and crying and thinking and talking about Lacey. I tried to be the best company I could be to Jack, but this was futile. I could not even think about what this was like for him.

Jack's daughter, Laura, came for a few days with her little dog, Jesse, a Chihuahua mix. Our two dogs, particularly Wally, gave me comfort, and it became apparent this sweet, special dog intuitively knew my condition and looked out for me.

One day, Jack asked his daughter and me if we wanted to go parasailing. We had seen people doing this from the mountains above the town, and both Laura and I said yes. Feeling little excitement about it, I was just going along with the plan. Jack scheduled the adventure for the next morning. None of us had parasailed before, and I had virtually no fear about it, which would have been unlikely before Lacey's death.

We met our instructors in town, climbed into a van, and drove higher and higher above Aspen well into the magnificent Rocky Mountains. We arrived at our take-off location and were given what seemed like two minutes of instruction. We stood on a flat, square pattern of soft sea green and jade-colored grass. Noticing the colors more than anything else, I thought about how Lacey would love these blends of green, and how thrilled she would be to do this.

Anytime I'd find a green rock in the dirt or a green piece of paper, or anything green I believed it was her saying, "Hi."

I was still thinking about all of this when I was told to run off to the edge of the mountain with my instructor behind me. I remember stopping short at the edge for barely a second. My brain was operating enough to discern that "jumping off" was counterintuitive to staying safe.

Like so much going on in my life, jumping off made no sense.

Then the instructor pushed me off. The next thing I knew, he and I were sailing above the town and the lower mountains. *I was in awe of all I saw.* There I was, carrying all my pain while soaring over one of the most beautiful locations on earth, one that offered mixtures of Lacey's favorite color. Hues of emerald, beryl, sage, sea, and malachite rose up from the magenta and amethyst-like mountains. The scent of pine and the sight of flat rocks like hearthstones evoked memories of happier times. For moments, I was able to feel gratitude, as I knew I was privileged to be doing this—hiking, soaring, and just being in the town of Aspen. Had I been home alone in Tucson, I do not know that I would have lived.

As a clinician, I knew that exercise was equally as effective as antidepressants in the treatment of depression. I also knew that the blue light emitted by the sun provides us with natural melatonin, allowing us to fall asleep with ease and maintain a healthy sleep/wake cycle. When we are exposed to direct sunlight, we also produce more of the mood-lifting neurotransmitter called serotonin. By comparison, low levels of serotonin are associated with depression. (Note: 2020 research is questioning this now.)

Soaring over Aspen under the golden watch of the sun allowed me to feel fully present in those thirty minutes or so. The walking and hiking must have helped me too, but at the time, I noticed no true improvement. Just pain, pain, pain like no other.

☆☆☆

Not long after settling in Colorado, I replaced my obsession with driving by Lacey's accident site with writing a thank-you note to every person who had sent flowers, written a card, or attended the funeral and wake. The list totaled well over seven hundred people, and it became an obsession I engaged in for months and months to follow. It was an almost impossible task, as I lacked so many addresses, but I committed to writing at least ten a day while in Colorado. I read every card and note as I responded and doing so helped.

It was also at this time that I began to write in a journal. The following is what I wrote.

☆☆☆

August 2, 2006. There was life *before* my precious Lacey Jane Daly Jarrell died, and now there is life *after.* Today, I am twenty-seven days without her on earth. "Shock," "grief," "sorrow," and "devastation" are just small words that merely teeter on the edge of describing what I feel. A part of my heart, soul, and being left with Lacey that brutal and tragic July Sixth. Some days it is hard to breathe. It feels as if someone grabbed my internal organs and snatched them from my insides, leaving me minimally functional. I've no words to convey how much I love her.

She gave me a gift in early morning sleep today. She appeared to me in not one dream, but three—the first time I have seen her in a dream. In dream one, she had the accident, but in addition, terrorists appeared and cut off her limbs and took out her eyes. I awoke with a start, and then I realized that these things did not happen. As odd as it sounds, the dream was a good one. I have obsessed over how much she suffered in the accident, but the message I received was that she had not suffered greatly as I had imagined. I had likely catastrophized how much she physically felt.

In dream two, she was ten years old. She came downstairs and said to me, "Where have you been? I've been looking for you." And I said, "Where have *you* been? I've been looking for *you!*" We found each other in the dream.

In the last dream, she was at home wearing her soccer clothes and playing with one of her friends. She was sixteen, and it all seemed happy and normal. The message I took from this dream was that she is okay and in a loving, comfortable place. I felt better because of these dreams. Yet I ache for her every minute. *I will love you forever, Lacey.*

August 13, 2006. Yesterday was very bad. I so desperately wanted to hear Lacey's voice on the phone. I was trying so hard to feel some greater connection to her. I did not get it. I think my grief was too great. I have decided today to accept that she will come to me when she is ready, and the time is right. I feel her everywhere and miss her everywhere, every day. I melted in the afternoon and had to cancel dinner with Jack and Laura. I wanted to be alone and went back to bed. I have been sleeping more than ever. My body is shaky, and I am often on the verge of tears. Jack is spending his vacation watching what must be one of the saddest things—a mother who lost her daughter in a tragic accident. My guts ooze constant pain.

I want to know that Lacey is at peace. This plagues me. I know I am severely depressed. I must look for the positive, but it is so hard to do right now. I have no fear of death now. I hope to find a way to honor Lacey by helping others—kids, parents, whoever. *Lacey, please direct me to what you would like me to do that would please you. I love you forever, darling daughter.*

August 18, 2006. My son, Will, and his girlfriend, Carly, are here with us now in Aspen. It has been nice. I feel great relief having him close. Will and I had some alone time his first day here, and we were able to grieve Lacey together. He had cut his head in a recent fall in Boulder, but his stitches are out now. Still, I am so worried about him. He struggles to eat and frequently feels sick. His pain became clear to me when he shared how alone he feels in having lost his only sibling. He described Lacey as "my back up." I understood the uniqueness of his situation, as he has no one of his generation left in our family. His cousins are all many years younger and live across the country.

Yesterday, I felt hopeful after talking on the phone to another bereaved parent from Tucson. He said we could memorialize Lacey in the incredible park he developed in memory of his daughter. Today, though, I feel sick, sad, and scared about going home in ten days. Home to our house with no Lacey. Will is going back up to Boulder to try to finish his last college semester. I support that choice and am so proud of him.

I continue to cry every day, throughout the day. I continue to feel as if I am living without internal organs. I struggle to believe that my precious daughter, my cherished child, is gone from this earth. If life is Hell, Lacey must be in Heaven. God, bless her and keep her safe.

August 26, 2006. I have received many signs and communications from Lacey since her death. I do not know what it means that the last three nights I dreamed of being in near tragedies—a car accident (that was peaceful, not scary), a plane with mechanical problems, and then a boat with mechanical issues. There were accidents in each of these, and I lived through them.

The other day, I found a silver heart pendant on the floor of St. Mary's, the Catholic church here, near the candles Jack and I light every day for Lacey. The statues and figurines in the church felt alive at times, especially one six-foot replica of Jesus hanging on the cross. It was sculpted in such intricate detail that with his bowed head, piercing eyes, and blood, Jesus seemed almost real, and I felt uncomfortable kneeling down and praying in front of it. Next to Jesus was another detailed figurine of the Mother Mary. This figure soothed me, however, and I chose to kneel and pray before it when we visited the church.

Heart pendant
found at
St. Mary's, Aspen

I asked for the wisdom and open heart to receive any messages from Lacey. I made the sign of the cross, and as I turned to my left to rise from the kneeling position, I noticed a silver object on the floor close to me. My first thought was, "I wonder why I didn't see that when I walked over and knelt down?" I was positive it had not been there when I first walked in to kneel and pray.

I walked a step and picked up what was an old silver pendant. The pendant was round with a small heart in the middle. An arrow pierced its center. There were two thin bars of silver attached to the heart. I always preferred the look of silver to gold. I picked it up and instantly fell back on my knees as I interpreted and believed this pendant was a message of love and acknowledgment from my daughter.

Did it mean Lacey shared my broken heart? Did she even know about my broken heart? I decided not to make any painful interpretations about it, other than to think it meant that Lacey was still connected to me.

I often hear her voice in my head. I have been finding dimes that I believe are her saying "hello" to me, since many are dated the year of her birth. The ringtone on my cell phone changed by itself one day, playing the tune "Angel Bells." While I was visiting Will's apartment in Boulder the other day, the television and music players went on by themselves. Will and I just looked at each other and said nothing. He turned everything off, and in about five minutes it happened again. This continued for something like two minutes. Will and I were on the couch, nowhere near any controls.

August 27, 2006. Today, Jack and I went again to St. Mary's to light candles for Lacey. Much to our surprise, there were no candles in the church to light. We went down to the rectory and found a young man dressed in jeans. He was truly kind. He apologized to us and said he would look for candles. I told him my daughter, Lacey, had died and began to cry. He could not find any candles, and so we told him we would come back later that evening to see if they had any then.

When we returned that night, the young man was kneeling in prayer. As we entered the church, we saw two chairs sitting by a special large candle with a note attached: "To the parents of Lacey Jarrell." I had never told the man her last name. Jack and I were stunned. He and the parish priest had written some lovely words of comfort, reminding me of how Mary had lost her son, Jesus. I had not thought of that before. I found great comfort in their words and the trouble they went to in finding the candles for us.

Last night, I dreamed that I had to go through another woman before I could see Lacey. I do not know what that means, but her name was Grace.

☆☆☆

Grace was born May 5, 2007. Gracie, as she was called, would have been Lacey and Will's first niece. Perhaps a month or so after Lacey's funeral, Will and Lacey's half-sister, Annie (Buddy's daughter from his first marriage), announced to the family that she was pregnant. The joy that Annie hoped to find from the family was muted, as most were fearful for her. Annie was fourteen years older than Will and eighteen years older than Lacey but was not married and had little employment or relationship stability. I had heard she became pregnant by the man she brought to Lacey's funeral. At some point during those first tragic days, this man and Annie had an argument and he flew back home.

When I first heard that my stepdaughter was pregnant, I was also told she planned to name the baby "Lacey" if she had a girl. She was determined to have this child, and when the sonogram confirmed that she was, indeed, carrying a girl, others and I feared she would actually name the baby after my daughter. The family dynamics involving Annie and Lacey were hard on Annie. She loved Lacey but often felt she did not receive the attention from her father that Lacey did. All I knew was that I did not want any attempt made to "recreate" my Lacey. At the time, this seemed rational, and I fretted about it. However, Buddy took control by telling Annie, "There will never be another Lacey." With that, the child was named Grace.

Was that what my dream was telling me? Not to worry about Lacey being at peace? Or was this yet another premonition? I never considered myself a religious person. I had become a disillusioned Catholic many years ago. I do believe in a Higher Power, whom I refer to as God. And I do think of myself as spiritual. Upon Lacey's death, I had clearly sought out certain rituals from Catholicism without a second thought. I was kneeling and praying in a Catholic church almost daily in Aspen and would years later recognize how my faith in God and turning to Catholicism to heal was an instinctive behavior I engaged in. My religious upbringing began to be braided into my coping methods in a more prevalent and profound way than I was aware of at the time.

The lyrics of "Amazing Grace" came to mind—perhaps a message to me that Lacey was happy and safe.

> *Yea, when this flesh and heart shall fail,*
> *And mortal life shall cease,*
> *I shall possess within the veil,*
> *A life of joy and peace.*

Many definitions exist for the word "grace": as a verb, to bestow mercy; as a noun, a reprieve; divine love and protection; and divine assistance given to man when in spiritual rebirth. I knew intuitively I was going through a "spiritual rebirth." My life was changing in ways I could not yet fathom. *Was this, too, the message in the dream—that I would be helped through the pain? Wasn't every-thing that happened in my dreams or around me a message from Lacey?* Believing that was my way of keeping her alive.

When studying traumatic grief years later, I recognized how of-ten I looked for clues that Lacey was there in those first twelve months. This is a classic hallmark of traumatic grief. My hypervigi-lance and attention to dreams provided me the bit of connection I so desperately craved. The sudden separation—our relationship in-terrupted—seemed to require my full attention if I were to live. Still, thinking my dream involving the word "grace" meant I would receive divine love gave me a sense of protection and safety—like being embraced by a veil of love.

✩✩✩

I continued to write in my journal until September 23, 2006. I also kept searching for books, spending hours in bookstores scanning shelves to find books on bereavement and the afterlife. Although I purchased ten different volumes, I found little relief from their con-tent. *I wanted a book written by a mother who struggled with the loss of her child. I could not find one.*

I journaled about the excruciating pain of returning home to Tucson to my empty house. I suddenly felt alone. For three years after Will left for college, Lacey and I had lived alone together. Now I was returning to a vacant home with symptoms well be-yond empty nest syndrome. It was a house of sorrow once filled with laughter, fun, learning, and hurts—and above all, uncondi-tional love.

I also wrote about going back to work two months after Lacey's death. Journaling is a coping mechanism I had used even as a little girl. If I could not verbalize what I was feeling or experiencing, at least I found my voice through writing. And journaling helped me find clarity in the past, which is why I recommend it to patients.

That same September, I decided to author my own book—the book I could never find. I typed my thoughts and feelings into my computer as many mornings as possible until the one-year anniversary of her death. I'd wake up at five a.m. each day and write whatever came to mind. I paid little attention to grammar or language; I just let it all flow.

The chapters in Part Two: Grieving a Deceased Child include the edited version of what I wrote for ten months following my daughter's death. The story relates how I coped that first year while providing a synopsis of what I've learned looking back. I hope the details resonate with you—and that a sense of grace will come through as you read on.

Lacey looking lovely for prom

PART TWO: GRIEVING A DECEASED CHILD

Chapter Four: First Steps Back
into the World

And still driving to work each day
Half a woman
Looking for her in the sky.

"Then and Now"
~ Nancy Jarrell

I came to learn that if I accepted whatever I did to cope as permissible, this helped. There was no benefit in judging my behaviors and actions. I no longer placed a great deal of importance on what others thought about my behavior (or me, for that matter) as I struggled to find my way through this living darkness. I had to accept that others did not understand my experience—nor did I want them to. Instructions on how to raise a child abound, but I could find absolutely none on how to take care of yourself once you have lost a child.

One book I had found while still in Aspen shared stories about parents who had lost children and described how the deceased child communicated with them. One involved the child taking over her mother's writings while she was on the computer and sending her messages this way. This author explained that the deceased often try to communicate with the living through the same type of medium they used to communicate in life. For example, if the deceased child watched TV, used a cell phone, a landline, or the computer, the grieving family might hear from their lost child through those devices. It reminded me how much my daughter and I were both active cell phone users and texters. Another story described a mother's experience of text messaging her deceased son and how he responded and continued to communicate with her through the cell phone. I would have believed anything at that time as I searched for a way to connect with Lacey.

One night while in bed in Aspen, I began to text message Lacey. When Jack asked me what I was doing, I burst into tears as I told him, and then I felt embarrassed. He never judged me. The next day, when I did not receive any return message from Lacey, I felt devastated. I cried all day and needed to stay in bed. I was ashamed that I felt devastated over such ludicrous stories. I was childlike. *Why would all the people in the book receive such clear communications and I could not? How had my thinking become so fatuous?*

I quickly learned not to read these books anymore. My daughter *did* come to me in other ways, but it required being vigilant about everything around me. I needed to look, listen, and smell.

☆☆☆

As the days progressed, I recognized that my deepest times of grief came when I was in the house. I looked for signs of her, even her scent, everywhere. I kept everything quiet. Noise bothered me for a long time; only after five months could I listen to music occasionally, mostly at the gym. That I was able to get there at all was an enormous accomplishment. I went when I could but not regularly. On weekends, it often took me hours to get out the door to drive the one mile to the gym. I mostly went to alleviate my depression, not to get into shape. Once I got there, I put on my earphones and refused to engage with anyone. I'd board the elliptical machine, listen to my music, and let the tears roll, not caring if people noticed.

I learned I was not the kind of mother who needed to preserve her child's room exactly as it was. Perhaps it was my need to keep my body moving that allowed me to go through Lacey's things and save or donate some of her clothing. I created precious containers to keep her most cherished items with sentimental value: her soccer clothes; her favorite jeans, shirts, and shoes; her makeup; her jewelry; the poetry she had written; all the photographs she had taken. I felt blessed to have so many photographs of my daughter.

During the first days following her death, Will and I went into her bedroom to look through her things. Her room was a typical teenage disarray of clutter. Tee shirts, jeans, music CDs, eyeshadows from MAC cosmetics, papers, markers, and books were strewn across the barely visible oatmeal colored carpet. Splotches of nail polish with the names Raz-berry and Dazzle Me streaked across the closet floor in front of the full-length mirror where she sat and applied her makeup. The state of her room was no longer a concern for me. The almost daily demands I'd made to "clean up your room" I recalled like echoes shouted into a cave. They bounced back to me—meaningless, empty, and unheard.

Will and I sat on the floor going through what turned out to be piles of pain. We found little pieces of paper that stated what she liked or wanted, many of them written in case she passed on. One said: "If I die, I want to be placed into ashes." She had even left instructions: "If I die, give my phone to . . ." and so on. We also found a poem she had written for a school project that was a metaphor for her death. We were stunned.

My Wings
were clipped again
Torn apart
then they left me
My fire was burning out
without a frown
I had died that day
Feeling the pain in every way
And I was gone
Now I see the cries
Deep inside innocent eyes
Forest Green
I see you sitting there
As my cage disappears
And I'm free
Shed no tears for me
You can't even see
But I still fly

~ Lacey Jarrell

Lacey's bedroom became a place of angst for me. Many of her friends would come over and ask to sit there. Some wanted something special of hers as a memento. Unfortunately, items were stolen. I understood this need to have a possession to remember her by, but I wanted to oversee who received what. When I caught some of the kids stealing her jewelry, I told them how and why this was unacceptable. I did so with compassion, and we always ended up in tears and hugs. In effect, I protected her room like I was protecting her life.

I started thinking I should move to a smaller home—one not filled with all the memories. As this transition into my new life began, odd things happened—a broken toilet, for starters. Then all my outside lights quit functioning; the timers stopped working on the inside lights; the blinds fell off their tracks; the irrigation system malfunctioned; the security alarm went off in the middle of the night for no reason. On top of it, lights also went on and off by themselves throughout the evening. An electrical party was going on all around me, but I wasn't in charge of it.

I interpreted these occurrences as signs from Lacey, pushing me to get out. The added repairs overwhelmed me. Mold was detected in the guest room, resulting in a major renovation that forced me to live on the upper level of the house. Lights continued to go on and off at random, especially when I was alone at night. I finally asked Lacey to stop; I could not take it anymore. "I'm trying to move," I told her, "but all the repairs are slowing down the sale of the house." I noticed after I asked Lacey for help, the house quieted down.

☆☆☆

I was also starting to become afraid. Fear reappeared for me, despite months of no connection to it at all.

For the first few years after Lacey's death, I never slept in my bed. For some reason, I needed to lie on the couch where I could see most of the house and not feel closed off—a result of post-traumatic stress disorder (PTSD) from years before. Years later, when reflecting on these early days after her death, I recognized I'd slept on that couch the last night of Lacey's life. I continued to gain insight into how I'd remained frozen in time. Even after years passed.

I had been diagnosed with PTSD earlier in my life after experiencing multiple traumatic events, and I was aware that my symptoms returned following Lacey's death. As a result of the shock, my memory was impaired at times, and time was distorted. Other symptoms of PTSD often include hypervigilance, difficulty sleeping, exaggerated startle response, nightmares, mood swings, and flashbacks.

When an individual tends to be hypervigilant about her surroundings or is hypersensitive to stimuli in the environment, these behaviors are known as hyperarousal symptoms. The term defines an extremely elevated state of reaction to benign situations that the PTSD patient may experience as a threat, consequently increasing anxiety.

With hyperarousal, the body prepares itself for flight or fight as though danger were present. By contrast, a dissociative sub-type of PTSD has characteristics with hypo-arousal symptoms. Responses such as depersonalization, lack of focus, and derealization are passive or reduced responses to perceived threat. I primarily suffered from dissociative symptoms, often feeling separate from others and as though the world was surreal. I sensed my whole nervous system had been compromised. I had not ceased reacting to loud and sudden sounds with an exaggerated startle response, but this was contrary to my reduced attention to my environment resulting from preoccupation with Lacey's death.

In general, the treatment for PTSD is to reduce the emotional and behavioral disturbance resulting from a devastating traumatic event that affects an individual's ability to function normally. As a therapist, I was familiar with the process and symptoms of PTSD. I also knew I suffered from traumatic grief. When one has PTSD symptoms, it is not unusual to have memory problems, to dissociate at times, and to not hear everything people say. For example, I frequently had to ask Jack if I had talked to someone or if a certain person had been at Lacey's services. I learned that organizing things, writing down what I needed to do, and checking things off a list reduced my anxiety about what I could not track.

☆☆☆

When I returned to work after two months' leave, I worried if I could actually *do* my work. I did not want to be there. To me, it did not make sense to get up in the morning and drive the same route to work five days a week. *Lacey was dead. How could I do these ordinary things when Lacey was gone?*

I truly lived by the one-day-at-a-time concept, saying, "Today I will go to work, but I have no plan for tomorrow." Without that approach, I would have felt I had resumed life just as it was before Lacey died. In reality, it did not matter what I was doing. *Nothing remains the same after a parent loses a child. Nothing.*

I quickly learned I was still able to perform at work. I was even promoted after one month back. With my overwhelming workload, I was worried that I would so immerse myself in my job that I would abandon the grieving process. Yet nothing I did could stop the grieving process. I was filled with enormous sadness 24/7. When I was not distracted by my job duties, I swam in a deep, endless ocean of pain and could only think and talk about Lacey. But I had to curb this while at work, even though she and the sorrow I felt filled me all day.

Slowly, I could see that work was a positive distraction for me. The amount of emotion I contained each day needed some outlet or distraction or I might die from it. I mean this literally, knowing an intense amount of emotional pain often results in physical symptoms. And I had so much distraction that I feared I would not keep myself safe—or that I'd suffer an emotional breakdown and end up institutionalized.

Exploring every way to find peace and learn more about the accident, I spoke with a psychic. She related a Jewish belief that, after a person's death, a loved one will experience three accidents; therefore, it was important to be alert. I am not Jewish, but this made sense to me, as I know any dissociation could easily make me vulnerable to harm. Then I thought, *What do I care if I have an accident?* I defied other vehicles and almost dared oncoming traffic to hit me, especially when I crossed the road on foot at the curve of my daughter's accident site. Visiting her place of transition, I dared death to take me.

My consultation with the psychic, Maggie Garbarini, occurred just two weeks after Lacey passed. She often did readings for people at Miraval Resort, once the sister company to Sierra Tucson. Kind and nurturing, Maggie had lost her husband, David, and possessed a great deal of knowledge about the grieving process.

We conducted my reading by phone when I was still in severe shock and disbelief. So much of what she shared I could not fully absorb. I was not even close to accepting Lacey's death as reality yet. Years later when I listened to the reading on a cassette tape, I realized that many of the things she said were accurate. The impaired areas of my brain had prevented me from making sense of them at the time.

For example, she kept coming up with the initials "J" and "O." These are Jack's initials, but when I stated that to Maggie, she replied, "No, the J and O are not about Jack. It is something else." In addition, she and a few other psychics I talked to that first year mentioned the name "Steven" or "Steve" multiple times.

None of us, not our family or friends, could come up with the significance of the name "Steven." Again, I could not see this name connected to anything until eleven years later. But while driving on River Road one day, his identity became as clear as the Arizona sky. The name of the dealership where Lacey and I purchased her car was "Steven Jory"—the "J" and "O" Maggie referred to I recognized as the first two letters of the auto dealership "Jory." Maggie had been adamant the name "Steven" was also connected to the two initials "J" and "O." Because we purchased the vehicle in another town, only Lacey, Ernie, and I would know this.

I had never visited with psychics before Lacey's death, but I was willing to try any possible route to connect with her.

☆☆☆

Lacey and I were frequently surrounded by drama, a normal part of raising a teenage girl, and other unusual events including an attempted break-in one night. Months before she died, a woman rang our doorbell around midnight and proceeded to pound on the door when we did not answer. She was speaking loudly claiming she was in trouble, afraid, and needed to use our phone to call for help. Lacey immediately wanted to assist the voice behind the closed door, but I did not trust the woman's pleas for help. *It might be a ploy to convince me to open the door, followed by this woman and others who might be hiding entering our house with mal intent.* The woman kept pushing on the double doors to the point of the wood cracking down from the knob to the floor.

My intuition was accurate. The sheriffs arrived and arrested her along with another male. A third male had run away. The woman had a cell phone and did not need to use our phone for help. I used this scare as a teaching moment for Lacey on how to react when in an uncertain situation that warrants a response. We reviewed a verbal checklist of what alarmed me in the scenario, resulting in not opening the door. The incident left us both unnerved, and neither of us felt completely comfortable in the house after that.

Other disturbing incidents continued after her death, well beyond the malfunctioning of lights and an errant security system. Some were so painful and others so bizarre that I let only a few people know what happened. I especially kept any incidents secret from my son; I wanted to protect him from any further pain.

☆☆☆

One incident involved Ernie. He asked if he could see Lacey's car one more time before the insurance company took it over. He couched his need in wanting resolution to the traumatic event. Understanding this element of trauma, I agreed, although I did hesitate. Even the investigating sheriff had told me to stay away from him, because he did not believe Ernie had been honest with him about the details of the accident.

At any rate, one day I did take Ernie to where the car was stored. On the drive over, he asked if he could take some parts off Lacey's car. Instantly stunned and angry, I told him, "No." But he continued to badger me, saying, "Why should I have to buy new parts when there are perfectly good parts on Lacey's car?" And "They will just junk all the parts, anyway." I did not acquiesce.

When we entered the building and met the insurance woman, he asked *her* if he could have some parts. I again said, "No! It's still my car, and my decision is *no*." I also told him the insurance company probably didn't want parts removed from a car for which they were reimbursing me.

When the agent took us to see the vehicle, the first thing Ernie did was kick a few parts underneath it. "Oh, well," he said. "I don't want this one anyway, because it's busted." I began to go through the car to find any last mementos of my daughter. I had come to the salvage yard twice already and searched the car, which was harrowing each time. I even sat in her driver's seat to experience and connect to the last place she had been sitting. *It was all so surreal.* Then I looked in the trunk and found some poems she had written. *How had I missed them before?*

Suddenly, I wondered where Ernie had gone. I lifted my head to see the car's hood open and raised. As I approached him, I saw he had an Allen wrench and was attempting to remove a part. I screamed and asked him what he was doing. He again became verbally pushy with me, saying it was just a universal car part, so why should he have to go buy one when there was a perfectly functioning one on Lacey's car? That's when I confronted him about whether or not he came for trauma resolution or to get free auto parts. He said, "Both," but I could see where his energy was.

As he continued to try and remove the part, I told him he had thirty seconds to do it. If he could do so, then I'd believe Lacey wanted him to have it. I counted. *He removed it in fifteen seconds.* "We are done," I said in a fury. "Go back to my car."

In that moment, I felt as though a dozen daggers had entered and exited my body, and they'd be coming back for Round Two. Although I was furious with Ernie, I also felt enormous sadness. *Now* I understood how much he'd pressured and pushed my daughter into doing what she did not want to do. Here I was, an adult woman who had no problem saying "no" to him, and yet he kept attempting to coerce me and disrespect my wishes, if not my orders. That's when I realized how tough it had been for Lacey who would say, "Mom, you don't know how bad it is! He won't leave me alone!"

Our ride back to his drop-off place was tense and difficult. Ernie and I conversed about what had just transpired. I expressed exactly how I felt. He ended up crying and disclosing that he felt he had caused the accident. I told him I did not blame him for her death. That was hard to say. However, I believed Lacey would not have left the house that morning if Ernie had not allegedly called her repeatedly, begging her to pick him up after she'd refused several times. In fact, Ernie had reported he knew Lacey did not want to come get him.

I suggested he not blame himself, as I believed this happened by fate, and that God needed Lacey that day. I shared my belief that feeling guilt contributed to nothing except more pain and depression. He thanked me and hugged me. After he exited the car, I told my daughter I had gone above and beyond for this boy. *Now I was done.*

That statement didn't prove to be true.

Another incident I later learned about also involved Ernie. He had tricked Lacey's best friend into giving him my daughter's e-mail password and then deleted her Myspace page. He led her friend to believe he was seeking the password at my request. Myspace, for the uninitiated, is an online social networking site that allows people to create a personalized profile page. On its pages, users spotlight their interests, likes and dislikes, and share photographs, music, and more with friends and family. (Facebook, Instagram, and Twitter had not yet dominated social media in 2006.) Before Lacey died, she and her friends were active on each other's Myspace pages, communicating either through the Comment section or via private messages. Lacey's page featuring many personal photos, was incredibly detailed, and of course, it depicted her as the sixteen-year-old girl she was. It had many graphics and a list of more than three hundred friends as well as music she'd selected as her favorite. Looking at her site in the early months after her death was a crucial lifeline for me. It kept her alive for me, and I looked at it several times a day.

When her page first disappeared, I must have had thirty phone calls from people of all ages who went on her site just to see the beautiful pictures of her. The fact that Ernie believed he had the right to delete her site frayed me—I felt out of control. And it was days before he admitted to doing it. "I didn't want people gawking at her," he told me. I spoke with his mother and told her he was obsessed with Lacey in life and that needed to end *now* in her death.

After that, I worked for a month trying to access her former site and learn how to re-create her Myspace page. Although I could not bring back her former page, I was able to rebuild a new one, adding graphics and music. I had never done anything like this before involving technology. I felt I was fighting for my daughter's life all over again. *I still needed to protect her, even in her death.*

I often found myself vacillating between feeling terribly angry with Ernie and extremely sad and concerned about the trauma he'd experienced. I also grieved for his mother and family, as I imagined how the tragedy held many layers and conflicted feelings. But, honestly, I could not focus on that too much. Sometimes, I could barely get myself through the next five minutes.

Ten years later, I visited an auto dealership in Tucson to look at new car inventory and possibly trade in my vehicle for a new model. While having my car assessed for its trade-in value, I circled my vehicle with one of the managers and answered his questions about the car's history. At one point, he kicked one of the front tires and stated, "I have to beat you up on price because of these bum tires." Suddenly, I experienced a desire to flee, to quickly get away from this man and this dealership. I asked for my keys back and went inside to tell the puzzled young salesman I was leaving. Then I left abruptly.

My sudden reaction disturbed me for the next twenty-four hours; it made no sense. And then the connection emerged. The manager's action of kicking my tire and making a negative statement brought me back to the day with Ernie when we went to see Lacey's vehicle one last time. Ernie had kicked the tire under the car, stating, "It is busted anyway." *I was experiencing the result of a trauma memory.*

After one suffers trauma, the human survival system that triggers action for self-preservation can become stuck in a permanent state of alert as if the danger and threat could return any moment. Those who carry the emotional damage of trauma often *overreact* when others aren't reacting at all, and they *underreact* when others are having intense reactions. Once I identified the connection between my behavior and its cause, I was able to relax. Identifying cause of behavior can have profoundly healing results.

As I continued learning about trauma, post-traumatic stress, and traumatic grief, I concluded again I was suffering from an adult form of separation anxiety, and that my experience was different from those who had experienced other forms of trauma. Not everyone who is exposed to a potentially life-threatening event will develop PTSD. Those who do may present with avoidance symptoms. Examples of symptoms involve excessive efforts to avoid people, places, thoughts, objects, or anything that represents a reminder of the experience.

Trauma survivors attempt to avoid anything that reminds them of the traumatic experience. *So where did I fit?* I sought information about the accident and was preoccupied with anything relevant to Lacey. I concluded I approached and even summoned memories and reminders of the accident. My persistent intent was to gather and then confine all I learned about Lacey's death. I wanted my discoveries immured in a neatly compartmentalized area of my brain where I could retrieve them on demand. I was serving a self-imposed sentence, believing release couldn't occur until I solved this perceived mystery. Then perhaps, just maybe, I could rest, I could live, I could transcend the harsh reality that Lacey was not coming back.

Lacey and Me, 2006

Chapter Five: Dreams and Signs

She captured the universe with her jump rope.
A littler girl then, skipping and jumping higher than the rest.
Her ponytail almost touched the sun.

"Then and Now"
~ Nancy Jarrell

In October 2006, St. Gregory School published two articles "Remembering Lacey Jarrell" in its school newspaper *The Gregorian Chant*. One article was written by one of her teachers, Kate Oubre, and the other by her coach and Latin teacher, Jeff Clashman. Both articles fervently and compassionately demonstrated how much Lacey had impacted their lives. Photos of Lacey covered two full pages. I was moved and so grateful.

When October turned to November, I looked at someone and asked, "How did it get to be November already?" *What had I been doing since July 6th?* In reality, I had done a lot. When I was not at work, I was visiting Lacey's accident site, trying to promote a safety program at her school in her memory, meeting with people who were reaching out to me, and authoring this book. I was not interested at all in socializing.

At four months post Lacey, I still felt extremely raw and fragile. I knew it was ludicrous to expect any state other than this. My tears, an everyday part of life, were not subsiding. At work, I could perform my administrative duties with a surprising amount of ease using sound judgment and decision making. Outside of work, though, I struggled.

My grief was so prodigious that the slightest discomfort filled me to the brim. One morning, for example, the handle on the coffee cup broke, and coffee spilled all over me. This certainly was unpleasant, but it literally sent me to bed with unstoppable tears, my head hidden under the covers. *It was not about the coffee spilling; it was about having no more room in my psyche. I just could not take anything else.*

My life script became that of a bereaved parent—a woman with multiple losses and then the ultimate loss, a child's death in a violent accident. I did not like this new role, but I worked on accepting it. I had no choice.

☆☆☆

The previous year when my parents passed a week apart from each other, my mother had been expected to die but not my father. Yet my father passed first, literally starving himself to death, refusing all food, water, and medication. I will never forget the fist he gave me when I tried to convince him to take water through a straw.

After years of fighting Parkinson's disease, my mother died peacefully under hospice care. I spoke at both of their funerals and wrote their obituaries. A year after that, their estate had not yet closed. Shortly after Lacey's death, the attorney for the estate contacted me saying he had three books to distribute to my two siblings and me. He planned to pull names from a hat, and then each of us were to choose the book we wanted in the order our names were drawn. The choices were a book autographed by Richard Nixon, an autographed book about Dwight Eisenhower, and an old book of poetry by Alice and Phoebe Cary. The Cary book, written in 1908, bore an inscription to my grandmother for her volunteer work at the Holy Rosary Academy in New York. The first two books had assigned values. The poetry book did not.

My sister won the lottery and chose the Nixon book.

Being more attracted to family heirlooms than anything with financial value, I knew without seeing it that I wanted the poetry book. Besides, I love to read and write poetry, and I loved that it had been given to my grandma for her altruistic work. Fortunately, my name was drawn second in the lottery, so I chose that book. The attorney said he would send it to me from his office in New Jersey.

Some weeks passed before I received the book, and I remember a conversation with Jack in which I said I now believed that Hell existed on earth—one of many emerging beliefs and theories I'd developed since Lacey died. *Hell is on earth.* I certainly believed I was in Hell right then.

My nature is such that I tend not to focus on the negative incidents I experienced in childhood. I sought positive twists on personally experienced disturbing memories. I called this practice finding a "workaround." Thus, deciding *Hell is on earth* was a divergence from my typical practice. While in Tucson for Lacey's funeral, both my brother and sister said to me, "I can't believe this happened to you. You have had so much hardship in your life." I hadn't seen my life that way, but as they recounted traumatic events in my childhood—abuse, difficult relationships with my parents, a distressing marriage and difficult divorce, single parenting, multiple deaths— these things coupled with my pervasive sadness and gut-wrenching sorrow influenced my thoughts. I understood why my siblings said this.

Jack and I were discussing my *Hell is on earth* belief while in his car. When we arrived at my house, I checked the mail and found a small package wrapped in brown paper—the book of poetry from my parents' estate. I opened it to find a bright green piece of paper marking a page. *How odd that the attorney would write me a note!* But the green paper was blank. A chill ran through me as I registered the color of the paper—Lacey's favorite color. When I opened the book to the page where the paper was placed, I was shocked to read the poem's title: *Heaven on Earth* and the poem itself. Its message encourages us, even after great loss, to look for the beauty and goodness in life and recognize *Heaven is here on earth.*

Those words challenged my new theory about *Hell on earth* and showed I had reverted to polarized thinking. In later years, I became aware that, following my loss, I perceived many things in the extremes—all or nothing with nothing in between, or black-or-white thinking. I was also engaging in filtering—that is, looking at only one part of a situation to the exclusion of everything else.

I noticed a second poem on the same page titled *Far Away,* which was equally powerful. Its last lines offered me comfort.

> *Though dark are the billows between us that roll*
> *We'll meet in that home far away.*

Many things happened that I chose to justify as communication from my daughter. I could have made other interpretations, but it helped immensely to view any mystifying occurrences as her way of talking with me. I often felt her around if I kept my heart, mind, eyes, and ears open to possibilities. As a result, I had never noticed the desert, the sky, the moon, and the stars as much as I did following her death. *So how could such splendor exist in Hell?*

At that point, I buried the contradiction to preserve the analysis for another time.

Sometimes the experience of magnificence in nature transformed me into an awareness of having glimpses into existence on a higher spiritual plane—another level of connectedness and wisdom I felt privileged to have. Yet simultaneously, I mourned that the experience kept me feeling separate from others—one of many dichotomies that presented themselves.

I did not experience life the way I once had, and due to my lack of familiarity with the new emerging me, I felt as though my sense of perception about the world differed significantly from people I knew. Yes, I had noticed tiny objects or aspects of them before, but by now, I had developed a heightened appreciation and awareness of the *esoteric* detail around me. A flower petal, a pebble, the sound of a calling cricket—all seemed amplified. At the same time, I could also completely miss that I was speeding at the wheel of my car or had driven past the turn leading to home.

Despite this, I felt inexplicably connected to something All-Powerful. As I had in Aspen, I continued to notice every bird and song, sunrise and sunset in detail. As I scanned my environment, often everything seemed magnified a hundred times. Lights were brighter, colors more vibrant. I could see not only a caterpillar on the ground but all the intricate features that made up its beauty.

Yet other times, I checked out and drifted off when someone was speaking—another among the many paradoxes and symptoms of traumatic grief.

One day after work, I was particularly depressed about returning home to an empty house. When I went to retrieve the mail, to my surprise, I found hanging on my lamppost a beautiful crystal bracelet with a half-moon and a star in the middle. It was blue, my favorite color. I have no idea how it got there or who put it there, but it felt comforting to me. *Perhaps Lacey had used another person to send me that message of love.*

These incidents were treasures to me.

Then something shifted in my thinking—I started to feel sorry for myself. I knew my ongoing grief and crying was becoming more difficult for Jack to watch. He was my rock. So I tried to hide my pain from him, but when I could not contain it, my anguish came out in indirect ways.

For example, one night Jack drove me to Walgreen's to pick up my prescription for an antidepressant I was taking. Although I had received an e-mail stating the medication was ready, the pharmacist at the drive-through window told me it was not ready. With that, I decompensated. I was persistent and angry, and I started to cry. "You *do* have my medication, and I want it now." I did not believe the pharmacist. I ended up with a partial prescription to get me through a few days. Later, I was ashamed of my behavior, and I knew it had upset Jack. I felt flawed and weak. My mood would swing from zero to sixty at times. *What was happening to my thinking—not believing what a salesclerk or pharmacist or business operator told me?*

During these moments, my distrust was impenetrable and, even to me, abstruse. I began thinking I was not fit to be in a relationship with *anyone*. I isolated more at home, not wanting to bother others. In my isolation, I ruminated on all my losses, my trauma history, and my lack of family in Tucson. Why *was I going to work, coming home to an empty house, and just waiting for darkness to put another day behind me?*

Jack and I still did things together, but I did not spend as much time with him as I had, and this contributed to my thought process. I felt as desolate as ever. I didn't tell anyone when I was having a horrible night and did not want to be alone. I felt like a hazard to myself and anyone around me. I did not want the cart of pain I pulled to ruin anybody's pleasant day.

One night, the pain was particularly excruciating. I called out to Lacey, asking her why this had to happen and telling her I was sorry she had been taken in such a gruesome way. Not sure how to get through the night, I wandered around the house in tears.

I went to the kitchen to prepare my coffee for the morning, and as I looked down at the floor, I saw a beautiful white feather. *How did it get there?* It was not there earlier. As I picked it up, I found great comfort as I believed it was a message from Lacey telling me she was okay . . . that I would be okay. I went to bed peacefully after that, and my mood picked up considerably in the following days. From that time forward, I scanned the environment for white feathers, and whenever I found one, I interpreted it as a sign from her. Choosing these types of interpretations allowed me to feel that Lacey was still with me, since her well-being continued to be of paramount importance to me. *If I knew unquestionably she was not feeling the pain that tormented me—that she was safe and at peace— then I could begin to heal.*

The following morning after finding the feather, I decided to engage a medium, someone a friend told me about. I called the woman and scheduled an appointment, though it would take four months to talk with her. Over the next few months, another series of what I believed to be communications from Lacey arrived. I was saddened by how rarely I dreamed of her now. I desperately wanted her to visit me in dreams and talk with me. The dreams I had soon after she passed were what I considered to be "message dreams," and they often soothed me. I longed for more.

One such dream occurred when I was still obsessed with what happened in the accident. In this dream, I saw two unbelievably beautiful women with white hair standing on a scenic curving road bordered with lush green trees that provided an umbrella of shade over the roadway. Their flawless features added to their ageless appearance. Each of the women stood by the side of Lacey's car, one by the driver door and the other by the passenger door. They were touching the car and looking directly at me. The odd thing was that Lacey's car was no longer black but all white and clean, with no scratches, dents, or broken glass. The women looked kind and gentle. They had gorgeous white hair piled high in buns, and they wore long, lacy, wispy, white gowns. I woke up believing that Lacey was at peace and being taken care of by loving souls.

On November 11th, I received a call from a distraught Emily Heintz, one of my daughter's friends. Emily had experienced several dreams of Lacey, but she needed to share this particular one with me. She described walking with Lacey as they held pinkies, which they often did. They were at a birthday party with friends from Lacey's school. In the dream, Lacey was focused on getting the box underneath the cake rather than the cake. Emily described her as not speaking yet having a calming and peaceful presence. I often heard people who dreamed of Lacey repeat this same description.

When Lacey finally freed the box, Emily said, Lacey found a pen and wrote on the box: *Please tell my Mom that I will be coming back to her, and that only she will recognize me.* When Emily spoke those words, I doubled over onto my kitchen counter and cried uncontrollable tears. I asked her to repeat my daughter's words so I could write them down.

We had a long talk, but after our conversation ended, I became afraid. While at home alone, I had been shouting to the ceiling that all I wanted was my daughter back. Of course, I knew I could never have her again in this physical world, and that I could never again live in this house with her or watch her grow into a young woman.

I initially interpreted Lacey's message via Emily's dream to mean she planned to be reincarnated and return to earth in another family. *I did not want this.* So I talked to her and begged her to *please* not make any decision that would compromise her soul. I did not want her to jeopardize herself to satisfy my needs as she would do in life for those she loved. *I truly did not, and do not, care more about my own well-being than hers or my son's.*

I then settled down and chose another thought.

I cannot emphasize enough the value of changing our thoughts after becoming aware that a chosen thought can place us in a state of greater depression and anxiety. We experience enough of that with the source of the depression itself. *What logic exists in exacerbating our distress with distorted and paralyzing thoughts?*

Somewhere along this journey of suffering, I learned that I had choices. Whenever I thought of something that debilitated me, I would then identify a variety of viable options and choose the least painful one from a buffet of thoughts. This shift helped me immensely.

So my new thought was that Lacey was letting me know I would recognize her in the future when she came to me in unusual ways—through people, places, or incidents. I told her I wanted her to be there to greet me when I passed, that I did not want her coming back to earth to another family. I also told her I believed we would meet again in *"that home far away."*

Four years following Lacey's death, I finally had the emotional strength to revisit drafting this book and work with an editor. He pointed out how profound the presence of dreams was in my story and suggested I research after-death communication. From the immense amount of material I found on this topic, I realized how common it is to have "message dreams" after a loved one dies.

At a personal level, I know that these types of dreams—those in which Lacey came to tell me something clear and direct—are vastly different from other dreams I have involving people I know. Message dreams are noticeably clear, visual, vivid, and in color. Lacey's words in these dreams were brief, direct, to the point, and delivered with aspects of her personality standing out.

My research led me to early tribal people and how their dreams contribute to a belief that a part of the deceased managed to survive the dissolution of the body. Some of the ancient cultures believe that one's body held two or more souls that split off from it upon death. Many Native American tribes believe the deceased travels to a wonderful, peaceful, and glorious land, but to ensure this, family members of the departed must perform specific rituals and rites. I also found extensive writings on multiple cultures that believe the deceased requires many of his or her possessions to survive in the new world. That is why bodies were buried with valuable objects, food, and water.

This tradition lives on. When my brother, Tom, was buried, my other brother, Eddie, placed a Phillies' baseball cap in his coffin. When Lacey was in her coffin at the funeral home, many of the visitors placed notes, small angels, holy relics, and jewelry in the coffin or on her body.

While reading about dreams of the deceased, I discovered a 1992 study by Dr. Deirdre Barrett, who is well known for her research on dreams and dream imagery. Dr. Barrett is an author and psychologist who teaches at Harvard Medical School. She is also past president of both the International Association for the Study of Dreams and the American Psychological Association.

Dr. Barrett discovered that loved ones of the deceased describe four distinct types of dreams. In "back to life" dreams, the deceased person is alive again. In "advice" dreams (much like my "message" dreams), the deceased sends words of comfort. Barrett calls the third category "resolution" dreams, in which the deceased explains the circumstances of his or her death. Last are the "philosophic" dreams in which the dreamer and the deceased discuss the mysteries of death.

I have experienced two of the four kinds of dreams—"back to life" and "advice" dreams—but not the "resolution" or "philosophic" dreams. Perhaps they will still come to me.

☆☆☆

November 11th was highly significant because it was the eleventh day of the eleventh month and eleven was Lacey's favorite number. Considered a highly spiritual number, eleven was also her life number in numerology. She was born on the twenty-ninth of August. If you add the "two" plus the "nine," it equals "eleven." She frequently told me she was an eleven.

On that special day in 2007, I felt a lot of energy, both physically and in the environment around me. Tucson was buzzing, and I sensed Lacey everywhere. I even had moments of feeling content—a first since her death.

Her school, St. Gregory College Preparatory School—a small private institution and a tight-knit community—had been compelled to manage an extremely difficult situation since her death, given it was the school's first experience of a current student's death. The students' emotional state remained labile. By November, the school had facilitated several commemorative efforts

St. Gregory's Star Memorial for Lacey

for Lacey per students' requests. The star her classmates had made from cement and marbles was placed in a new garden for her. Some-one had taken over the school "rock" in the middle of the campus, painting it gold with stars all over it and adding her name and her soccer team jersey number.

I continued to be amazed by the attention my daughter's death received from her schoolmates, teachers, and parents. I was still getting letters from a multitude of adults and young people who shared how Lacey had touched their lives. This fed me and often gave me a desperately needed push to keep on.

At this time, I recognized I had not heard Lacey's voice in four months—not even when the kids put together a slide show and video of her after her passing and played it at a ceremony for her early on. Her friends warned me that her voice was on the video, but when they saw the look on my face, they removed the audio. I felt very anxious about hearing her voice at that time.

On that day in November, though, for some out-of-the-blue reason, I thought I was ready to hear her voice. *Which one of her friends should I call to acquire the original video?*

That night, I went to Jack's house for dinner. When I arrived, I noticed he was a bit hyper and his speech unusually rapid. He immediately told me he had gone on YouTube to look up Lacey's name. The day before, I had told him about the ceremony at the school when the video was played, and that I had a YouTube account so I could see any videos people had posted in her memory. He told me he was not prepared to hear her voice. I asked him what he was talking about. None of the videos I had viewed included her voice. Then he told me about a tribute video on YouTube in which she was interviewed and talking directly to the camera. I was stunned. What timing! As Jack played it for me, I felt lifted.

For all these months, I thought I had seen every posted video of her, yet I had completely missed this one. Things came to me only when I was ready to hear them. I felt taken care of.

Chapter Six: Finding Meaning
in Suffering

The woods are lovely, dark and deep
But I have promises to keep.
And miles to go before I sleep
And miles to go before I sleep.

"Stopping by Woods on a Snowy Evening"
~ Robert Frost

I remember the first time I laughed after Lacey's death. The sound of my own laughter was unfamiliar to me. I felt joy, but also betrayal, as if it were wrong to be laughing when my daughter was gone. *How could a good mother laugh?*

I did not remain steeped in guilt, however, as I knew this was not productive. Shedding tears was the primary emotional expression that occurred for me each day. Even the smallest thing could bring them on. Sometimes it would involve shopping in the grocery store and seeing Lacey's favorite beverage. Because of that, I could not be around certain drinks or foods or visit many stores where she and I had been together. I never went to the restaurant where she'd worked as a hostess—too unbearable for me. I continued to battle between acceptance and denial of my new life script. But I slowly began to recognize the many lessons to be learned from my grief. I had always believed that when the universe pelleted us with pain, we had a lesson to learn.

I also became aware I was formulating new and distinct spiritual beliefs, and that these beliefs supported me in validating I was of sound mind, although I did not feel sane a great deal of the time. When I was home alone, I screamed and cried loudly to God, frequently finding myself on the floor in the fetal position, sobbing and whimpering like an abandoned pup—an all-too-familiar behavior.

I felt I was on a perilous journey through life. *My absolute worst fear of losing a child had come true.* But even with my greatest fear having transpired, I could still function. Despite feeling devastated most of my waking hours, somehow I went on. I was surviving.

Once the loneliness decreased, I *wanted* to be alone more. As I accepted this desire, I felt a heightened closeness to Lacey that allowed me to stay in the moment and not project into the future. I lived either hours at a time or one day at a time. I had few plans for the future—other than to sell my house. Mostly, I let life take me along. *Someone or something was carrying me through what often seemed unendurable.*

☆☆☆

I had never felt anything as devastating as Lacey's death, and my conviction to keep living continued to ebb and flow. At five months, I still had not passed a single day without several bouts of tears while wandering around the house looking for her, talking to her, and then feeling as though I were losing my mind.

Still, I was keenly aware I was medicating my feelings through my work. I worked exceptionally hard, purposefully using it as a distraction from my agony. When not at work, I felt intense heaviness. I knew that if I did not have work or some busy focus in my life, I would struggle to make it through a day. And despite being led to the poem *Heaven on Earth,* my situation continued to support my stance that *Hell was on earth,* too.

☆☆☆

From that first day when I learned of Lacey's death, I felt I existed in two worlds. In one, I was walking the earth doing some of the same things I had done before, such as going to work, coming home, and making my way to the gym. But nothing felt the same as I went about these activities. *I really belonged in another realm.* It seemed I was going through the motions of living, but my heart and soul had departed with my daughter.

- 80 -

I knew the only way to tolerate my continuing life was to uncover meaning in Lacey's tragedy—and in mine. At times, I felt my very survival depended on finding this meaning. *What could be the gift from the suffering?* This need to seek understanding motivated me and pulled me through, day by day.

During those months, I perceived that whatever happened to keep me moving forward was designed by a power greater than I. The arrival of certain strangers into my life could not be coincidental. Through unexpected connections, for example, people supported me in developing a Lacey Jarrell Foundation to heighten awareness of artistic youth in Tucson and to promote education, creative experiences, and counseling opportunities for young people. Ideas came to me out of the blue.

During this time, I also developed a safety program. I designed green wristbands with Lacey ☆ Buckle For Me on them. The wristbands were to be worn on the right wrist as a signal to drivers to put on their seat belts when they first put the key in the ignition. I passed out hundreds of these bracelets.

Somewhere along this journey, I came to believe that both Lacey and I were old souls. We had actually conversed about this just days before her death. We agreed I was an old soul like her, but not as old as she—and then we laughed about it. It struck me that with Lacey being sixteen years old, this kind of conversation was rather sophisticated, yet typical of what we often spoke about. She did not need to ask what I meant by "old soul." She intuitively understood.

Perhaps her death and my loss *had* to happen for the advancement of both our souls. In some small way, this belief allowed me to find a level of acceptance and meaning. Perhaps we also shared previous lives and deaths, and that at some point, we had made a contract that she would die, and I would live. Thus, her death would result in the growth of both our souls.

I came to accept my life at this time as one of suffering, and I did not do that to be a victim or a martyr. It just was reality. I have always been a positive person and consciously took on an attitude of *amor fati* ("love of fate"). Somehow, I was able to turn my suffering into something tolerable by believing it was intended and necessary for something greater. I hung desperately to the belief that she and I would meet again. This connecting thread defined my existence, giving me a wavering light of hope.

In graduate school, I read *When Nietzsche Wept*[9] by Irvin Yalom. A main character in this novel is Friedrich Nietzsche, a nineteenth-century German philosopher who had presented the idea of "eternal recurrence." Finding this book on the shelf one morning led me to researching Nietzsche and his philosophies. In proposing the idea of "eternal recurrence," he wondered how one would react if told that humanity repeated living the same life with all its pains and pleasures exactly as lived before, over and over for eternity. He asked this rhetorical question: "Would you not throw yourself down and gnash your teeth and curse the demon who spoke thus?" His intent, however, was to promote enjoyment of life to the fullest and the embrace of all life experiences.

Nietzsche's philosophy did not conform to my Catholic upbringing in which the idea of a paradise was presented *if we were deserving*. Life on earth was considered inferior to this place called Heaven. I relished the moments I could engage in deeper thoughts like these.

In terms of life after death, I became more open to all sorts of possibilities. I looked at the entire world and how it worked as proof that our lives had been predestined. As I continued to experience myself apart from others, I felt a stillness around me, even in the midst of chaos and noise. The stillness led me to believe that my daughter's death—for all its pain and debilitation—allowed me to see the world in a greater light, with more significant meaning. Although life might feel like a melee at times, I believed there was an exact order of things, and that connection with others was the available remedy for all challenges. Furthermore, I came to believe that there lies only a metaphorical veil between the living and the dead.

The agony I felt, and my daily bouts of tears no longer surprised me. A growing belief that I would receive reward and benefit from my suffering at a later date was another coping method I adopted to keep pushing me through the oppressive despair.

In this way, my spirituality grew and carried me through the days and nights. My life seemed other directed and so did the lives of those around me. I was impelled to learn the lessons so I could meet my daughter again in that faraway place. As a result, my priorities completely changed. Although I would never want to minimize the problems of others, I realized how many things that would have caused me great anxiety before Lacey's death were not significant at all.

In my grief, I also lost many of my concerns about the future. Getting married again, having high career aspirations, not living alone as I grew old—all these mattered little. It was more important to live each day as an opportunity to give gifts of kindness, treat others well, and strive to be a forgiving, nonjudgmental person. My daughter possessed these traits, and I knew that living them *myself* was the best way to honor her memory. Absolutely no other female had impacted my life in the way Lacey had. She became, without question, an angel and a heroine to me.

☆☆☆

I became acutely aware that my precious son, Will, was grieving as well, and I was powerless to soothe him. So absorbed in my own grief, I felt as if I were neglecting him. That, too, brought me great sorrow. As a mother, I could never compare how much I loved my children, who were each vastly different. I loved them both equally.

During Will's college years in Colorado, Lacey and I lived by ourselves. We missed Will a great deal and had gone through many mother-daughter challenges. Some included her wanting to spend time at Ernie's house on school nights, staying on the phone past what I considered a reasonable bedtime, and wanting her nose pierced. This all seemed trivial now. I would have given her permission to pierce her nose a hundred times if I could have her back. We had finally transcended many of these growing pains, though, and joked about how we had become like roommates. Of course, at the time, I had no idea how precious those three years of our living on our own would prove to be.

It was time for Will. Like many young men, Will moves inward and keeps his pain and feelings to himself. Maybe that is why I was so surprised when he said one day, "Mom, I just wish I never existed. Then maybe you could have kept Lacey and the two of you could be together." My heart shattered. Hearing his words, I began to cry. *This amazing young man loves deeply and possesses the same compassion that Lacey did.*

"Oh, no, my darling," I told him. "I don't ever want to imagine you *not* in my life! It would have been equally devastating had it been you and not Lacey. I love you so much, and I never loved one of you more than the other."

Chapter Seven: Thanksgiving?

Let us rise up and be thankful, for if we didn't learn a lot today, at least we learned a little, and if we didn't learn a little, at least we didn't get sick, and if we got sick, at least we didn't die; so, let us all be thankful.[10]

~ Leo Buscaglia quotes his Buddhist teacher in Thailand

One day, I looked at my 2006 calendar and noticed Thanksgiving was approaching. I dreaded it, as most people dread holidays after the death of a loved one. I felt as though I had been walking in a never-lifting fog for nearly five months, but looking back, I realized so much had happened.

I was aware that, from early on, my natural response in terms of "how to live" was to take action. So in that five months, I had re-modeled parts of my home to put it up for sale, and I had looked at more than one hundred houses to buy. At work, I had been pro-moted and was excelling in a challenging position. And, as I mentioned, I had started the safety program in my daughter's name and was formulating ideas to start a nonprofit Lacey Jarrell Foundation promoting the artwork of young artists. I was also drafting this book.

Yet none of these activities stopped my grieving process. *That task proved to be impossible.* As I searched for meaning, I felt a strong intuition that I was to help others as a result of my loss. Moving toward whatever that was became my mission.

I also became clear that having expectations did not serve me in any way. Given that we never know what can happen at any mo-ment, it made no sense to have any anxiety about the future. That translated to expending energy worrying about something that had not even happened yet and may not ever happen. *Holding this idea of no expectations was so freeing.*

I resolved again to live in the moment, and I did that by listening, watching, and trying to connect with the universe around me.

Grieving is a highly personal process. How I coped may not be how someone else would. The goal after losing a child, however, is the same for all of us—*to find a way to live without our child if we have chosen to keep living.* To do that, we must start putting together days that take us further from the date that forever changed our world.

☆☆☆

My son was now a young man, and I was grateful we'd always had a close, connected relationship. I believed he still needed his mother until I realized that belief was more about *me*; I undoubtedly needed *him*. As I became absorbed in my own grief, at times I just

Lacey and Will, 2006

couldn't help my son with his sorrow—not that he expected me to. Still, I desperately wanted to remove his pain. Then suddenly I would get jarred into my new reality—that I had no power or control over my children's suffering or their futures. As any parent, my focus had always been on keeping them safe and providing the best life possible for them. *Yet, I could not prevent my daughter's death. I could not keep her safe.*

Not staying in this thought was a tool I mastered early in my new journey. I knew facing myself and seeing a mother who did *not* protect her child would be fatal, so I again resolved to choose my thoughts cautiously. To some degree, I watched my son go through pangs of guilt and self-blame whenever he remembered an incident in which he felt he had been unkind to his sister. I also watched as he made the adult decision to return to college to complete his final year, dragging all his pain and loneliness in tow. And I saw him go through a process of transformation resulting from the tragedy. I tried to be a role model for him, but at the same time, I just kept being who I was—a bereaved parent who tried to seem okay while struggling in a river of turmoil. I was so proud of him.

Will found his strength in his own way, negotiating his own terms for how he coped.

Living through Thanksgiving week was harder than I had anticipated. I felt the kind of depression others have described as if being sucked into a black hole and unable to get out, no matter what. I was in one of my worst mental states, and at times thought I should check myself into a treatment program. Yet somehow, I was able to go back to my toolbox of coping mechanisms and select *focusing on everything for which I was grateful.* Doing that helped tremendously. The irony of deciding on *this* coping mechanism at Thanksgiving did not escape me.

Will's visit that Thanksgiving helped me immensely. Despite his own grief, he worked extremely hard to comfort me. I thanked God for having him, just as I continued to thank God for giving me Lacey for almost seventeen years. *I felt blessed to have been given two wonderful children.*

On Thanksgiving Day, however, I regressed. I felt like a failure when I found myself unable to cook the holiday dinner. I had expectations of others to take care of me and found myself disappointed when no one extended Will and me an invitation for dinner until the last minute. Feeling exceptionally low, I was especially upset with Jack for going to a dinner without inviting Will and me.

Then through the course of the day, I realized I had given people extremely mixed messages. On one level, I was telling them I wanted to be alone, and on another, I really wanted *not* to be alone. Struggling to communicate, at times I was completely incongruent. Because I did not know what I wanted from one minute to the next, I had a challenging time hanging onto those feelings of gratitude. I had to consistently remind myself to be less self-critical. Remembering that "forgiveness" includes "forgiveness of self" challenged me. Through this life-altering experience, I was feeling emotions I could not name.

I knew the normal signs of grief included an inability to concentrate, sleeplessness, feeling out of control, and being tired, distracted, preoccupied, withdrawn, and forgetful. I was particularly forgetful and felt out of the moment. I also felt pain weave throughout my body with no opening to let it out. There was no escape. Grief filled every space in my body; it lived in me, and I both hated it and loved it. *It meant my condition validated Lacey's individuality and the enormity of my love for her.*

During the darkest times, I called out to God and Lacey for help. Often after these episodes, the telephone would suddenly ring, or I would get an e-mail from someone offering me comfort. Love from others was one of the things I held on to as a reminder that I could find goodness in the world, even after my tragic loss. I also learned to protect myself from anyone who said I should "just move on and get over it" by consciously blocking their face and words. Suggesting I "get over it" felt unrealistic and unkind.

☆☆☆

One night, Will and I went to a University of Arizona basketball game. I had been going to these games for many years and decided to renew my season tickets despite Lacey's death. She rarely went to any games with me anyway. She was not that keen on college basketball, but Will was a huge fan. After he entered college in Colorado, he wasn't home enough to attend many games, so going to one together was a welcome escape.

While we were talking at the game that evening, Will mentioned he had called Lacey once when a home basketball game was coming up. He told her she needed to go with me, especially if I would otherwise end up going alone. I said that, although it might sound strange to him, I was glad she had not come with me. The U of A stadium was one place I could go and *not* have profound memories of her.

A moment after I said this, a woman tapped me on the shoulder from behind. She grasped my hand and said, "Forgive me, but didn't you recently lose a child in a car accident?" I was stunned but answered yes. As she grasped my hand tighter, I burst into tears when she told me she had heard about me and my loss. She shared that she had lost her nine-year-old daughter in an automobile accident eleven years before. We bonded at once.

Here was another example of a kind, empathetic stranger randomly coming into my life. What was different, however, was it happened right after saying I did not think of Lacey so much at the basketball games. Suddenly, I was filled with all the familiar malaise. The woman then asked, "Have you ever met this couple behind us who leads the group Compassionate Friends for bereaved parents?" I looked behind me and recognized a lovely couple who had provided me with great comfort the three times I had attended this grief support group. They smiled warmly at me.

I suddenly thought about the odds that bereaved parents would sit in the first three rows of this section of the huge stadium. *Lacey loved to be the center of attention, and if I thought for one minute I wouldn't think of her at a basketball game, she proved me wrong.* I took it as my daughter kicking me in the rear saying, "Mom, I'm here, too!" It would have been just like her!

Chapter Eight: Grief Becomes
Isolation

Tears
The crystal rags
Viscous tatters
of a worn-through soul
Moans
Deep Swan Song
Blue farewell
of a dying dream.

"Tears"
~ Maya Angelou

A t times, I worried that if I thought of something terrible, it might actually happen.

Again, I found myself reflecting on the premonition I had of attending one of my children's funerals a few days before Lacey's death. I did not tell people about my premonitions, which are highly personal and difficult to speak about. I also feared scaring others if I were to disclose these episodes. Suddenly, I had become afraid of them myself.

Having premonitions became difficult and conflicting for me because I found myself feeling guilty. I berated myself for not stopping things from happening. At the same time, I was aware of not having any power over what transpires in this world. *If I did, Lacey would still be here.*

I felt impotent experiencing these premonitions. For example, within a year after Lacey's death, I had a premonition about a patient at Sierra Tucson Hospital drowning. I just did not know who it would be or when it would happen. In this case, I did communicate my fear to the staff in a general way, and the drowning did happen.

I also had a specific premonition about a friend and coworker having a heart attack but not dying. This also came true. I have had some incredibly positive intuitions, as well. A year or so before my son was born, I saw him in my wake-sleep exactly as he looked at two years of age. This visual came to me several times before I gave birth to Will.

Typically, my premonitions are highly visual images. They take me right into a scene that I experience as if it were happening at that moment. They are not hallucinations but rather clear, detailed scenes in my head. I become deeply affected emotionally when these occur. If I sense them coming, I consciously try to snap myself out of them, because they frighten me.

In retrospect, I think I always knew one of my children would die young; I just did not know which one. In fact, I often thought it could be my son. The more accident-prone of the two, he visited the hospital several times in his childhood, needing stitches from mishaps due to being a hyper, daring, and active boy and breaking his shoulder after jumping off something high. Will was very athletic, and I often worried about him getting hurt in a sports activity. And I believe he often drove too fast.

Lacey was athletic as well, but at sixteen, she had never needed stitches. She'd had no injuries, broken bones, or anything requiring other than routine medical exams and immunizations. And a few weeks before her death, I had told her how great a driver I thought she was.

☆☆☆

Many people say, "Time heals everything." In the case of losing a child, I disagree. Eventually, we adjust to life without our child. The perennial hovering cloud of angst becomes familiar, and we learn how to maneuver beneath it, but we do not simply heal. *Time does not heal; time goes by. It is not the solution to grief.*

Grief became woven into my state of being. I knew instinctively it made me feel different, burdened—yet I knew I could use my tragedy to help others. I also knew I had to find purpose and meaning in my loss and go on despite my mental and physical agony.

My training and experience in treating trauma taught me that typically those who develop severe PTSD had experienced complete helplessness at the time of the traumatic event, as I had. Over time, they would fare better if they could find meaning in what happened.

I had experienced complete helplessness in Lacey's death. I was not even *there* to take some sort of action.

When trauma occurs, it disrupts brain functioning and affects balancing emotion, memory formation and retrieval, the ability to make sound decisions, and more. For patients with unresolved traumatic experiences, the treatment is to help them regulate trauma-related emotions as well as the resulting negative cognitions and belief systems. Emotional extremes related to fear and anger are often prevalent in trauma survivors. Supporting these individuals in strengths identification (processing of traits that have effectively helped them transcend past challenges) with the intent of reducing feelings of powerlessness—along with education on the neurophysiological response during and after trauma—helps survivors understand that their actions and current symptoms are normal. All this leads to restoring homeostasis.

Working with the person's physical body post-trauma is also critical. Many survivors assume a rigid, unconscious posture or movement pattern that physically expresses the impact of the event but is not beneficial to sustain.

Despite knowing all this, however, I did not connect any of my knowledge to caring for myself. None of what I knew was even in my conscious thought! Rather, to feel relief, I connected with nature and tried to follow the advice I read in this line of a poem my daughter wrote at age twelve: *Look. Listen. Be still. Be hyper. Be you. Look at the sky. Look at the stars. Look at the sunrise and find peace.*

☆☆☆

During the holiday period that year, I had difficulty maintaining any bit of positivity I had accessed. The spiritual beliefs that previously kept me going waned as the months went on. In this struggle, however, I learned to discern what actions helped me feel a little better. These included being with my son anywhere, enjoying time in nature, spending time with Jack, walking with Jack's dog, working out at the gym, being at work, and being around special people. Still, I did not always take care of myself by doing them. Feeling miserable, I often turned down invitations from friends and isolated myself in my house. I was bad company; I could not spend time with people and be present. *They would be better off away from me.* This belief was silly, and I knew it. Sometimes, though, I just could not rationalize myself out of this thought pattern.

I began to notice Jack was distancing himself from me, and I felt very alone. One Saturday night when he hadn't called all day, I felt so cut off from him and everyone that I was triggered into an enormous emotional meltdown. I found myself sobbing in a puddle of pain on my living room floor. This happened often. I could not leave the house; I just wallowed in my misery on the floor or couch. *If I got in my bed, I would never get out of it.*

This was the most horribly desperate feeling I had yet experienced. Again, I called out to Lacey and to God for help. Suddenly the phone rang—Jack. I felt better after speaking with him and directly asking him if I had done anything to upset him. He said no, and I was aware he was having his own issues relevant to losses in *his* family. I also knew I could not fix him, and he could not fix me.

☆☆☆

I had taken the week of Thanksgiving off and realized that, without the focus of going to work, I simply could not get out of bed in the morning. I just kept falling asleep and avoiding the days until Will came home. This regression alarmed me. Looking back on it years later, I see it was a necessary part of my grief process—I had to let my body rest. I also had to stop being judgmental toward myself. Although I believed I had to keep bartering with God and even myself to stay in life, I knew I needed to stop isolating. Still, this was mostly all I wanted to do—be alone and try to connect with Lacey as I towed my pain around from room to room. *My house felt like a tomb.*

At times, suicidal ideation appeared, and when this happened, I knew I was in a bad place. My only reason to keep living was my son—*the* reason for my existence. And I feared losing him as well.

☆☆☆

I continued to visit the death site of my daughter and the memorial we had placed there. Of course, it was hard to avoid, as I had to drive by it whenever I went east out of my subdivision. I made a point of regularly placing a few things there and filling the vases with fresh flowers every week. From across the road, the site looked like a lambent mix of color amid the sere November vegetation. The surrounding mesquites and palo verde trees seemed to bow over the lively site, competing only with the azure sky that blanketed us from above most days.

One afternoon while in one of my dark periods, I exited my gate and noticed what I assumed to be a homeless man walking down River Road. His worn and tattered clothing, shuffling movement, and well-used plastic grocery bag influenced my assumption. I knew that if he kept walking, he would pass my daughter's memorial. At first, I quietly hoped he would not take anything from it, then I berated myself for even thinking this. *How unfair to judge an unknown man who was simply walking down the side of the road.* Yet, it was not just *any* road. It was River Road. *I considered myself to have ownership in a small sector of the road.*

As I returned home that evening, I passed the site and saw a blue bandana hanging off the boulder there. Someone had also placed a bottle of water right in the middle of the memorial. I stopped and walked over to it, but because it was dark, I could not see well (despite my ex-husband having placed a solar lighting system at the site). I again noticed the bandana and water, and I instinctively knew it did not come from someone who knew Lacey. Then I remembered seeing that presumably homeless man wearing a blue bandana.

In the morning, I returned to the site and quickly scanned the area. I had every item and its position memorized and always felt joyful when I discovered new gifts people had brought. Two days before, I had noticed the Buddha statues that my ex-husband's girlfriend had brought to replace stolen ones were gone. I was glad my Virgin Mary statues were still there, although that morning, I noticed the hematite bracelet I had placed around the neck of one of the virgins was gone. This bracelet had been taken once before, when the Virgin Mary statue from my childhood disappeared. It was later returned and had disappeared again.

I then looked down once more, and there, in a glass candle holder surrounded by purposely placed plastic flowers was the *head* of the Virgin Mary statue I had owned as a child. Stunned, I was also surprised I felt happy the head had been returned, even though its body was still missing. The person who placed it did so in a respectful, caring manner. I wondered if the homeless man was behind this, and if he had left his bandana and water in exchange for the missing hematite bracelet.

Unusual, inexplicable, and puzzling things like this happened almost daily. But rather than be angry, I decided to choose gratitude. After all, the memorial site had become a place of comfort and fascination for many. It reflected not only my daughter's life but the substantial number of people she affected—and how they were coping with her loss, too.

Before Christmas arrived, I began to find more peace in going to my daughter's memorial site by decorating the area like a Christmas tree. Lacey was always exuberant about the holidays. Although I could not bring myself to celebrate Christmas in my home, I could still take Christmas to her memorial.

I brought ornaments to hang from the trees along with stars, battery-powered lights, angels that lit up—all kinds of beautiful things. Others also stopped and brought gifts. Although some of the vandalism continued, I came to accept it and not let my emotions overwhelm me on the days I discovered something missing.

Over time, I became accustomed to my tender torment as I walked side-by-side with longing and sorrow. They were always with me, sometimes felt more profoundly than other times but always there. I continued to feel as though someone had yanked a vital organ from my body. *How could I be living without this body part?* Yet somehow, I was. It seemed so dissonant.

I also wondered, *How could I still be walking on this earth?*

Four deaths occurring before my daughter's still had a significant impact on me. One was losing one of my best childhood friends when I was eighteen. Harriette died instantly in an automobile crash on her way home from college during the Christmas break. We had planned to meet in the town where our parents lived. As a result of this experience, I felt I knew what Lacey's friends were going through.

My oldest brother Tom's death was unexpected, and it shattered me. The news came via a call from a relative who said my brother was in a coma in Connecticut following a bicycle accident. He died three days later. Lacey grew up hearing about Tom's death and knew I did not attend his funeral due to giving birth to her any day. From that came the view that one of her roles in life was to take care of me and others—that she arrived to support me through a grim time, to cheer us up. She even told us frequently, "I'm here to cheer you up." Then she would say, "After all, my name 'Lacey' means cheerful." She had researched her name and learned it was a derivative from the Latin word lascivus, which means cheerful, playful, unbridled.

Both of my parents died the year before Lacey did. Before their deaths was a four-month period of escalating concerns regarding my mother's condition and next steps to assist both of them in old age. During this time, I traveled often from Tucson to New Jersey to help take care of them and meet with my two siblings to hear their concerns and ideas. My sister, who lived just a few miles away from them, was adamant they move out of their home to a small apartment on her property. With my brother, we went through my parents' home of more than fifty years. We made decisions about their belongings, prepared the house to sell, hired nursing care, and ultimately made funeral arrangements, then attended their funerals. I wrote both their obituaries and remember how surreal it was selecting a casket for my father, who died first. My sister and I pondered if we should order everything we bought through the funeral home in duplicate in preparation for my mother's imminent death. We did not but, in short order, repeated much of this process.

I was gradually moving through the grief of their deaths when Lacey died. When my daughter passed, however, these four earlier deaths felt like nothing but a skin prick in comparison. Choosing to experience them as positive, not negative, I regarded them as having helped prepare me for the ultimate and most traumatic event of my life. Unable to find people who could relate to my acute grief, I imagined a young mother who had never suffered the death of a loved one losing her child as I had. *She would have no experience of how to cope.* This thought allowed me to access more gratitude and courage in my heart.

In my situation, grief and bereavement had become all too familiar. Although I had several tools I could access, I still found myself in moments of self-pity—too often. I would then remind myself to suspend my self-judgment. In this state, my loneliness—initially an unwanted visitor—accompanied my self-pity and left me feeling entirely isolated in the world. In short order, however, loneliness served as my best friend and my worst enemy. Dichotomy was present again.

I was grateful that, most mornings, I could get out of bed and put together a day, although often I felt depersonalized—a nebulous image of the woman I once was. I went to work each day and did a good enough job. *How did I focus on someone else's issues and comfort them when I was suffering so greatly on my own?* Somehow, though, this ability helped me through. As the darkness descended on my house, converting it into a harsh prison, the relentless cruelty of the nights were excruciating. My wretched cries to my daughter tormented me; other times, it was all I wanted to do.

☆☆☆

As Jack and I no longer spent much time together, I focused on being grateful for the months he had been there for me. Even though I felt angry and hurt at times, I realized he had given me all he could. Over the holidays, our relationship unraveled more. I was never clear what was going on with him, because I perceived him as shut down and closed—something I felt coming the week of Thanksgiving when he did not reach out. Even my son asked about his whereabouts.

One day, Jack sent me a genuinely nice e-mail saying he had to cancel our dinner plans to spend time alone with his daughter. Laura was twenty-six years old, a delightful person, and I adored her. I knew they were having problems, so I supported his decision.

But when he did not contact me again for three days, I was hurt and felt abandoned, angry, and sad. I felt I was being punished. *How could God take away my daughter and then the man who was my main support, too?*

Life seemed dismal. The accumulation of even small experiences seemed more than I could hold. So I went again to therapy as I had done before although not regularly. My therapist seemed genuinely concerned about me. The metaphorical dance Jack and I engaged in had become a familiar pattern: I felt he danced a smooth, calculated waltz while I swirled around him in a frenetic polka. Even before Lacey's death, there had been periods when he would fly off the radar, weaving in and out of my life. This inconsistency triggered my abandonment issues.

Following Lacey's death, though, Jack had been there for me wholeheartedly—a gift from Lacey. But when this old behavior emerged again, so did feelings of bitterness. I was certain I could not go back into an inconsistent relationship.

Safety is a basic human need. As humans, we all need connection with others to sustain life and thrive on this earth. Safety encompasses *physical* safety as well as *emotional* safety. Although I didn't always experience safety in relationships, I felt safe with Jack. But that too seemed to be gone. It led me to decide that if my destiny was to be alone in my house for the rest of my years, then somehow I would manage it.

At fifty years old, living alone, losing a child, and having a son in another state, I felt destined for a lonely life. Yet, living alone would not have felt so horrific were it not for its suddenness and the circumstances. This defeatist attitude seemed histrionic at times, but I had little ability to thwart it as I was often cloaked in shame and guilt. Pangs of my Catholic upbringing whittled away at my previous drive to battle any unproductive thoughts. My shame shouted at me, "You did something wrong, Nancy, and this is what you get as a result!" *We reap what we sow, right?*

Some days, these negative cognitions scared me as much as my fear of being pulverized by the grief. I worked hard to curtail them.

☆☆☆

Near the end of 2006, more things disappeared from my daughter's memorial site. The head of the Blessed Virgin Mary statue was again taken, along with angel wings a child had hung from a nearby tree. The continuing need to fight my pain through translating my experiences as either positive or negative was wearing on me. So when items disappeared from the memorial, the effect on me became pernicious.

No sooner had I accepted the recurring theft at the physical memorial on River Road than I shifted again into a constant state of vigilance. *Who entered her site? How many times? What was being taken from it?*

Still, new objects kept appearing and others disappeared.

Chapter Nine: Kids Became
My Lifeline

Daughter may you turn in laughter
A candle dreams a candle draws
The heart that burns
Shall burn thereafter
May you turn as roses fall.

"Burning Roses"
~ Patti Smith

It occurred to me that I did not live life; I just existed. I was going nowhere. *Was this God's plan?*

As I grappled with this question, I thought God's plan for me was some sort of flippant joke or cruel test. Eventually, I believed, I would lose due to not being able to take on any more. After all, God is the supreme ruler. I could not compete with this.

Increasingly I recognized how I was groomed to believe what I was taught in Catechism and Catholicism. Despite my denial of subscribing to religion, I could not escape the dogma that imprisoned me. I had never left my religious tenets at all; I had never made peace with this part of my past. After Lacey's death, my religious beliefs did not just creep back in; they landed in my soul like a tsunami. That meant I needed to reckon with my sins, believing they were the reason I lost Lacey. The old adages came back to life as I remembered phrases such as "this is your cross to bear."

At this extremely low point, I began to divide my days into six-hour blocks of time. As a member of a Twelve-Step fellowship, I was familiar with the concept of "one day at a time" and its benefits.

So I used this tool to help me set small goals for myself *and* to forgive myself if I didn't do what I thought I should.

Why did I pare it down to six hours at a time? I knew that, when I was asleep, I was okay, so I really needed to deal with my agony only eighteen hours of each day.

On weekdays, I woke up at five o'clock and told myself, "Okay Nancy, you just need to get through until eleven. You will be at work then, so you will be all right." At eleven, I would then say, "You just have to get through until five." Again, this didn't seem too bad since I usually stayed at work at least until then.

However, the evenings were the most difficult. When I came home to my empty house, I would isolate and go through Lacey's photographs and poems, or I would reread the newspaper articles about her death. The weekends activated more fear of the pain. Although I knew I needed to have plans to help me through each day, I struggled to make them. Not only had I lost a child, but with it came an unusual form of empty-nest syndrome—an intense and unfamiliar separation anxiety. I walked through an abyss of distress within which I found no stability.

I desperately wanted someone to be there when I came home at night. Yet did I? I did not want "someone"; I wanted Lacey. I wanted to see her bright smile, hear her mirthful laughter, observe every nuance in her expressions, feel her hugs, discuss her tears and fears, or just know she was somewhere in our home chatting on the phone. I longed for *Lacey*. As a result, I felt starved for affection, comfort, and safety, even though I was not. So many kind hearts were reaching out to me, supplying me with love and supportive hugs, gestures, and words. Whenever I found myself circling the toxic pit of my depression, I called on Lacey for help. Almost at once, I would hear from someone saying they loved me. *Yes, I had to remember my fortune in having a large circle of people around the country who checked on me and expressed their love.*

I wondered if having my family in Tucson would have made this time less painful. *Would it have been easier to grieve with a husband than to be physically alone so much of the time?* I will never know the answer. This approach didn't help; there were no answers for these questions. Again, I needed to remind myself to seek the least disturbing thoughts.

✩✩✩

One night, a friend I'd known since I was four called from San Francisco. Worried about me, she wanted to comfort me. During our conversation, she told me she remembered how strong I was when we were kids. She had witnessed me bear a sometimes-brutal childhood, standing up to my father and defying him until he finally took his angry attention away from me. She said she had never known anyone so self-sufficient and capable of taking care of herself.

I appreciated the compliment, but at the same time, I wanted to scream, "I am tired of taking care of myself! Please bring someone to help me!" I never *asked* for help, though.

Over the years, I have admired many people who seek support when suffering from addictions, trauma, mood disorders, and other mental health issues. In my perception, asking for help is courageous and represents strength. Yet hearing compliments from friends and then refuting their words brought me face to face with all my negative self-cognitions and the erroneous self-appraisal system I had developed as a result of my childhood and life experiences. Beliefs such as "I am not worthy" and "I am not good enough, smart enough, pretty enough" crashed down on me in one enormous wave.

Looking back on the early years after losing Lacey, I came to see how every unresolved issue of my past presented itself, forcing me to tackle all my demons head on. And by doing so, I consequently increased my capacity for resilience.

✩✩✩

As I developed Lacey's Myspace site, I saw that people could request to be her friend and I could turn them down or accept them. I frequently did not know who many of them were, so I would do some research and then accept or deny. I denied only a few. This told me how many people Lacey had known and made an impact on during her short life. People felt connected to her through this website, sharing their love, their stories, and their grief. Amazingly, five months after her passing, I had accepted two hundred and forty-four friends and noted almost seven thousand visits to her site.

Many of her friends called me often to check in. The kids were so sophisticated, impressing me with their love and deep thinking.

Lacey's death forced them to confront the possibility of their own deaths, and this topic made for many a long afternoon's exploration. I valued these discussions in my living room, listening as a small group of youth tackled the fundamental question of existence. Many of them made videos in Lacey's memory. If I posted on Myspace that I felt particularly sad that day, they would try to comfort me, and I did the same for them. They understood that my grief was different, but that their grief was significant as well. Just one line a young person wrote about Lacey, or even about me, would temporarily relieve my depression. These precious moments became therapeutic for me.

I developed a large network of young people from ages fourteen to twenty-one who reached out to me—an incredible gift. I came to know my daughter better through their stories of her kindness, her going above and beyond to help others. They helped me feel more comfortable believing that my child was not suffering.

Shortly after Lacey's death, my son and I discovered a small piece of paper that said, "If I die, give my cell phone to Andy Schlicker." Finding this in her room was eerie. We were puzzled and unsure who Andy was, although I had some memory of a boy she talked with on the phone who attended a different school. She called him her brother, and he called her sister, as he was an only child. We found other small pieces of paper in her room noting things she liked, what clothing she loved, and whom she wanted close to her. *Did she know her death was imminent?*

Then one day five months after her death, Andy contacted me through the Myspace site. He wrote a great deal and told me he did not find out about Lacey's death until a month after it happened. Deeply affected, he wrote long tributes and expressions of love to her on the site.

In one note to me, he shared a dream in which my daughter came to him and told him she was happy in Heaven. She said she now had the true ability to make people smile and help heal their pain—what she had always wanted to do—and had instructed Andy to tell me this. He said he awoke feeling relief.

I cried when I read his words, as the language he used read exactly like my daughter's words. I recalled a similar conversation we'd had about how she wanted to heal others. This message was coming to me through a web of her friends from different areas of town and different schools, many of whom had never met each other before.

People continued contacting me to share stories about Lacey or dreams they had about her. Their dreams consistently indicated Lacey felt content. They felt compelled to share them with me, and I felt immense gratitude.

☆☆☆

Although I often felt Lacey around me, at times I did not. When this happened, I chose to think she was helping others who needed her more than I. By six months "post Lacey," a definite pattern was emerging—that is, every time I fell into the bottom, something positive happened. It was as if the pale, lapis sky opened up over the desert, directing me toward relief. The synchronicity of events was at times staggering. *What astounding magic.*

☆☆☆

One day after sharing about my struggle regarding helplessness with my sister, she gave me good advice: to make a seven-day plan for myself. Under this plan, I could schedule myself to drive around aimlessly and avoid going home, or I could have options to keep busy. Planning to spend special time with friends pulled me out of my very dark place, at least for several days. Any day I had moments of freedom from my deep cauterizing pain—or could smile or even laugh—was as valuable as gold. I also asked Lacey for a reprieve from the constant, pressing pain that scared me—those times when I would think about dying. *How I missed her smile. How I missed seeing her trot up the stairs like a sunflower opening each morning in the garden.*

Despite recognizing what helped me feel better, or at least distracted me from my anguish, it was extremely difficult to access the motivation needed to effectuate these activities. I cited coping behaviors that included hiking, walking, calling a friend, going to a comedy movie, and more, which I started to do at a snail's pace. Although all these things soothed me, I rarely had the stamina to do them. I still felt as if I were the living dead. *Everything I saw, felt, found, or heard was about Lacey. She consumed my life—and I loved and hated it.*

I was reminded to be gentle on myself if I could not pull it together. Even though I disliked being in the house without Lacey, I had a tough time leaving it. I continued to look through her things expecting to find a message from her. I did not, although I knew she was around. I still felt her presence strongly.

Any chance I got, I'd stop by her memorial site to rearrange and decorate. I found contentment in taking care of it, buying new things to enhance its beauty—items I would give her in life. *I could no longer take care of her, which is what I loved to do, so I was left now to take care of her memory.* This was torturous at times, but mostly I felt contentment seeing the many gifts others had left for her, too. In fact, when I discovered new mementos, I felt like a child who'd just found a new Christmas package to open. I rarely saw who stopped by.

I also spoke about Lacey incessantly, obsessively at times. Although it was not in my conscious thought, I knew that telling stories—sharing the trauma narrative—can help survivors gain understanding of what happened and begin to make sense out of an incomprehensible experience. Those narratives support affect regulation and stabilization of mood.

By verbalizing the story of Lacey's death, I was subconsciously decreasing my emotional sensitivity to the event and attempting to gain a semblance of control over my psychological state. It also kept her alive to me.

Chapter Ten: A Conversation with God

Remember me when I am gone away
Gone far away into the silent land
When you can no more hold me by the hand
Nor I half turn to go yet turning stay.
Remember me when no more day by day
You tell me of my future that you planned
Only remember me; you understand
It will be late to counsel then or pray.
Yet if you should forget me for a while
And afterwards remember, do not grieve:
For if the darkness and corruption leave
A vestige of the thoughts that once I had
Better by far you should forget and smile
Than that you should remember and be sad.

"Remember"
~ Christina Rossetti

I was learning that one of the most destructive behaviors for me was to recount all the things I did *not* do for my child, the times we were argumentative, or any other way I perceived failing as a parent. I became adept at stopping myself from going there. It served no purpose. If I learned nothing else, it was this: *I have no control over my life or the life of anyone else.* If I had, then my daughter would still be here.

At some point in my weary trudge through grief, I stopped my "poor me" stance and became more selfless. I began to experience days when I could embrace my loss and not try to heal it. Instead, I reached out to others who were suffering to give them comfort and love. This helped. Somewhere along this unenviable journey, I became a completely grown-up woman—someone with courage, integrity, and grace.

My pain, however, was constant. *How could I permanently maintain freedom from being in a victim role?* This thought waned and then surged again. Once I accessed freedom, however, avoiding self-pity became easier despite the ruthless grief that filled every space.

Through the holiday season, increasingly I found myself needing to be a good mother to my son and more available to him. I agonized over seeing him in emotional pain. I realized how often I would dissociate with wandering thoughts and lack of presence. I considered how other bereaved parents might behave if they had other children and wondered if they would focus so much on their deceased child that their other children would feel emotionally neglected. Realizing that, I prioritized making Will feel loved and important.

One day, I made a deal with God, saying I would take on more pain and suffering if Will could be spared from some of it. I think my prayers were answered. I had periods of feeling worse as I watched him resume his social life, enjoy basketball games, and make exciting plans with his friends. Mostly, I felt grateful to see this.

I continued to receive phone calls from kind, supportive people, and I still struggled to answer the question "How are you, Nancy?" I could not tell people "fine" because I was not. What's more, explaining my condition was often difficult and, with some people, I only wanted to talk about Lacey. I still received e-mails from her friends and others, and there were new stories unfolding that all revolved around Lacey. For example, her soccer coach told me she was still the center of attention at St. Gregory School. In many ways, she seemed very much alive.

Around Christmas, the deacon who delivered an incredible eulogy at Lacey's service called to see how I was doing. Dr. Joe King, a psychiatrist from work, had also served as a deacon at St. Phillips

Church. When I approached him asking if he would consider presiding over Lacey's funeral, he was touched and honored. He was a dear, kind, and loving man. "Nancy," he said in our conversation, "there is nothing worse than suffering the loss of a child." That certainly felt true in my life, for I had never experienced anything so debilitating and disorienting.

However, I knew I had to avoid thinking that because I'd lost a child, nothing else as crippling would ever happen to me. Actually, I *could* think of something worse—the loss of *two* children, which brought up worries about my son and his overall safety. A phrase I read years ago about the painful arithmetic of the human condition had stuck in my mind: With every loss, I was given the opportunity for spiritual *gain*. This thinking helped me—but never in great enough capacity to replace the physical presence of my daughter.

The idea that I needed to help others to help myself was not foreign to me. In Twelve-Step recovery, Buddhist teachings, the Bible, spiritual teachings, and more, the principle of reaching out to another who is suffering is recommended as a path to self-healing. As I read heartbreaking stories in the local newspaper about teenagers dying in accidents, I reached out, writing a comment on the news article that let other bereaved parents know I could and wanted to help.

Every day was a compelling emotional experience. Sometimes I felt intensely focused on a task; other times, I checked out, inattentive. The inside of my body felt extremely chaotic—like a decorative Christmas globe you shake to watch the snow fall.

During this time, my position at work required I give out awards and attend certain Christmas parties. To cope, I had to numb myself. I did not consciously do this, but somehow my brain chemistry took over and walked me, seemingly undisturbed, through what could have been agonizing events. Going numb is a common response to traumatic experience—and it was the only way I could tolerate what seemed intolerable.

Celebrating Christmas—laughing and eating with others—felt completely incongruent to me. Christmas was Lacey's holiday. She loved it, and we made a big deal out of it. *I did not want to do Christmas without her. It was just all wrong.*

One week, I felt a strange but strong and inexplicable sense that something wonderful just happened for Lacey. It came suddenly and was an instinctive understanding that brought me to a memory of my childhood when my grandma told me a story about a little girl passing on. She would go to Heaven and work as an angel. Grandma described this as a glorious, happy event. The child simply needed to take a few tests to acquire her wings in Heaven. I had grown up believing this notion was true, so with this sudden feeling I thought, *Lacey just received her angel wings!* This belief undoubtedly came from the many sweet stories my grandmother imparted to me, and it surprised me to sense it again as an adult. Still, something noticeably clear and unquestionable was occurring for Lacey in the moment. I sensed this at a depth that was undeniable.

Later that week, I went through a few things people gave me the first week after her death. I found a CD from her photography class from her teacher. It was a compilation of photographs that Lacey had posed for in class. I had seen many of them before, but while browsing through them, I unexpectedly came across one beautiful photo of her in angel wings.

I nearly stopped breathing. The photo was taken in April; she died in July; and I found it in December. This photo gave me great comfort, and I shared it with many of our friends and family. Genuinely moved, they continued to honor her memory through online tributes. They also continued to add stuffed animals, letters, clothing, and decorations to her memorial site. These actions—and believing Lacey was an angel—helped mend my fractured soul. To me, she had always been an angel from Heaven.

☆☆☆

A week after that, I had a disturbing experience with a woman at work who claimed to be in communication with Lacey. When she shared this with me, I became transfixed by the surge of emotions that flooded me. I had no belief my daughter was communicating through this woman she didn't know. And I barely knew her. In her efforts to connect with me, I believe she thought she was helping me, but her sudden approach and statement of "I have been communicating with your daughter" and the resulting physical sensations warned me to be guarded. After taking a moment to breathe, I accepted one of her statements that my daughter wanted *me* to find ways to communicate with *her*, to not rely on Lacey presenting to me first. A new thought!

Another time, this same woman came to my office and told me my daughter was crying because I was not communicating with her. Her allegation felt self-serving and unkind. I reacted with anger as she smiled and spoke about how she and Lacey would help me "get it." At that point, I dissociated to some degree but became present enough to politely ask her to leave. I thought about this encounter for days. This woman likely did not intend to hurt me, but her insensitivity wounded me in whatever part of me was left to harm.

Then one morning I awoke to the thought that I frequently talked to Lacey out loud and nonstop without allowing time for her to answer me. In the early months after her death, I could hear her voice in my head saying things she used to say. For example, I would look in the mirror and question my size, and she'd say, "Oh, Mama, you are *not* fat. Don't be ridiculous!"

That particular morning, I decided to say a few things to her and then wait for an answer. I did not exactly hear her voice, but I could see images in my mind. One image was of flowers. The message I picked up from her was "Be attentive to flowers today." I thanked her for the communication and went to work. Just before lunchtime, an employee I didn't know well came to my office with a large planter of white flowers she had grown herself. The arrangement was a stunning mix of amaryllis and narcissus. I was stunned. She said she woke up thinking of me and put together this arrangement. White flowers were my favorite. Lacey *must* have been involved.

A small smile creased my face.

As the end of 2006 crept closer like a black ominous cloud over the desert, I found myself desperately stuck. My great idea to help other bereaved parents had not taken shape. I struggled with engaging in the actions I had identified as helpful and often felt debilitated. When I started to admonish myself for my difficulty in decision-making or motivation, I had to reaffirm I was doing all I could—and remind myself of how much I *was* doing. *Progress.*

One thing I avoided was shopping, but I knew I had to attempt finding presents for my son and a gift for Jack. I would often go out but, having no plan, I would drive aimlessly. Paradoxically, once I was out of the house, I did everything I could to avoid going home. One Sunday before Christmas, I found myself at an outdoor mall in which I knew most of the stores because Lacey and I had shopped there. I knew exactly what I would buy for *her* but had no idea what to buy for Will or Jack. *I was in the wrong place.*

I left feeling afflicted by my failure and spent six hours wandering through other shops and came home with nothing. Again, I had to convince myself this was acceptable.

On December 19th that year, I had two dreams of Lacey. They pleased me, because I rarely dreamed of her—or so I believed. The truth was I frequently dreamed of her but longed for *so much more* that I perceived the frequency as "seldom."

In my first dream, she came back to life, and I was advising her on how she needed to be careful about her return. It would have an enormous impact on many. I remember telling her, "After all, you know Jesus now, and that is a very big connection to have." The next morning, recalling this statement amused me.

In the second dream, Lacey came back and told me she had decided to live with her father. This was surprising and hurtful because, in life, she did not spend time at her father's home. Buddy was a source of pain for her due to his ongoing struggle with alcohol. He also traveled frequently and did not have a stable home environment. In the dream, she invited me to go to his house with her, and I watched as he cooked pancakes for her and two other children before school. I was impressed he was taking such diligent care of Lacey, but then fear emerged when he told her she would have to walk to school *eighteen miles away.* I reacted and said, "No way is my daughter walking eighteen miles to school!"

All day, I fixated on the number "eighteen." What does it mean? I am attentive to numbers and often look for meaning in those that present arbitrarily. Late in the day while taking a break at work, it suddenly hit me—*today, I was eighteen years sober.* I had forgotten! I then interpreted the dream to mean Lacey was letting me know that *she* knew the significance—and that she was congratulating me.

My son was scheduled to return to Tucson on Wednesday, December 20th from Boulder. That morning, he had packed his bags, only to learn that a blizzard had shut down Denver International Airport. People were stranded everywhere, and he was told he could not fly out for two more days. On the third day, he showed up again at the airport and, after waiting five hours, was turned away from his flight. This was all he could take. Frustrated, he called and informed me he would drive home. The trip is fourteen hours by car, and I was understandably nervous. He expected to be home sometime Saturday afternoon.

By four o'clock that Saturday, I had not yet heard from Will. I called his cell phone and to my horror, an unfamiliar male voice answered it. I asked who he was. He said he was Clark Nelson from Garland, New Mexico, and he and his wife had just found my son's cell phone on a frontage road along I-25.

My heart sank. I shakily asked if there had been an accident in the area. No, none that he could tell. I then told my whole story to this kind stranger, explaining Lacey's death and my son's travel uncertainties. Suspecting Will had accidentally left the cell phone there, Mr. Nelson assured me he would send it to me. He promised to call me if he discovered anything that would assist me in locating Will.

For three hours, I waited and waited to hear from my son. Had he been abducted—or worse? Knowing how upset I was, Jack invited me over for dinner to relax. I declined his invitation as I could not leave the house until I heard from Will. I remained frozen on the couch.

I had two thoughts: *Someone will come to my door that evening* and *It will either be the sheriff or my son.* I flashbacked to the horribly fateful day I felt fastened to my desk chair waiting to hear from Lacey Jane.

This time, however, I experienced a moment when I was not engulfed in fear and, briefly, anger at God materialized and escalated to a lather. Being angry with the Father was not a feeling I broached much. With my Catholic upbringing still haunting me, I remembered the abusive message from the nuns that I "would burn in Hell." I took a risk, though, because I often felt I was already in Hell, so I yelled out loud to Him: "How much more do you want me to endure, God? Why do you need my son to have such a challenging time? Do you find our suffering amusing?"

I told Him I had strived to be compassionate toward others, but it had become clear His plan was quite different than mine. I resigned myself to Him, stating angrily, "I guess I have no choice but to accept Your plan for me, which seems to be one of continual heartache and suffering!" In my fury, I became aware I was again feeling sorry for myself, the state I so abhorred. I also felt shame that I was not managing better. I would swoon at recognizing all the childhood messages that had groomed me to accept myself only as someone who presented as strong and capable. After all, I had always been told I was "the strong and capable one." This belief had been woven throughout my being, silently dictating so much of what I did and did not do in life. For the first time, cloaked in all my pain and shame, I was letting go of this self-perception that no longer served me.

I had to remind myself to breathe. Often, I would become aware of holding my breath while in terror. Breathing assists with the process of oxygen flow to the brain, enabling us to think more clearly. Breathing consciously can deter the physical response to fear by reducing the heart rate, lowering the blood pressure, and slowing the release of adrenalin. Taking slow, deep inhalations and slower exhalations sends our body a physical message to calm and relax. *Breathing is an easy-access coping tool we all possess. Remembering to do it is the most difficult part.*

Following that "discussion" with God, my escalated emotional state abated, and my son arrived home safely. I cannot describe the relief I felt when he walked through the door. He explained that he had stopped on the side of the road to check a tire and did not realize until hours later he had left his cell phone on the hood of the car. At that point, I contacted the Nelsons, the kind strangers who found his phone, to say he was safely home. They had walked me through my panic earlier in the day by staying in touch and speaking words of comfort to me. Two days later, Will's phone arrived in the mail. The Nelsons, like so many who came into my life, were unexpected angels appearing out of nowhere.

Will and I did our best to have a tolerable Christmas Eve by going to church and having dinner with Jack and his daughter. On Christmas Day, we went to a friend's house for brunch. I had no idea how either of us would get through this dreaded holiday without Lacey, but thankfully our precious friends carried us through.

In fact, that day, I experienced a reprieve from my deep and searing pain. During this difficult yet precious time with my son, Will shared what he was going through emotionally and how he behaved as a result of Lacey's death. I was amazed at how similar our coping experiences were. He talked about struggling with a need to isolate in his apartment, feeling conflicted if he agreed to go out with friends, wanting to stay in bed all day and hide. He was describing the classic symptoms of traumatic grief. As a coping method, we both used busyness: He dove into his studies, and I dove into my work.

Yet, Will deserved to have his mom feeling stable. He never complained to me, criticized me, or asked anything of me. He was and always had been exceedingly kind and loving toward me. Because I was so focused on Lacey, I wondered how this felt to him.

Meanwhile, Buddy, Will's dad, had begun to disintegrate emotionally. He announced he was not celebrating Christmas and had not bought our son a present. With his substance use disorder escalating, he escaped into travel. He planned to be in Tucson for only one day, then fly to Thailand. I imagined Will might feel he'd lost his father, too. *I hurt for my son.*

Despite these moments, my ability to smile periodically was coming back slowly, but very slowly. I can remember laughing a few times with people and again feeling as though I had betrayed my daughter by doing so. This was part of my distorted thinking, a result of undergoing so much shock and trauma. What I really knew was this: Lacey was a happy and joyful child who played, sang, and danced. I once did these things with her. We laughed a lot. I knew she would want me to enjoy myself now. For the most part, though, my world was only about surviving, not living.

Chapter Eleven: New Year,
Same Pain

Why is Truth silent?
Why does she not send her doctrine forth?
As rays from noonday sun
That all the world may see
And thus believe?
But, no, she gives her confidence to stars
Which twinkle faintly in a night of doubt
And scarce are noticed
By a sleepy mob.

"Silent Truth"
~ Irene Daly (my mother)

On New Year's Eve, I found myself home alone, often tearful, because I did not want the last year Lacey and I shared in life to end. On New Year's Day, I had been alone for so many hours that by two o'clock, I felt compelled to leave the house to intervene on my fear that I might resort to taking a nap. *What dispiriting company, even for me!*

For many years, I viewed napping during the day as shameful behavior. When I was a child, my mother napped daily. I remember the verbal scoldings my siblings and I received from my grandmother or housekeeper telling us to "be quiet" so Mom could sleep. *But why did Mom need to sleep in the day? Why wasn't she doing something with us?*

Something about this did not seem right. Years later, in adulthood, I learned about my mother's depression, her thyroid problems, and most profoundly, her broken heart. After her death, I found letters and photos of the man she still pined for decades after being married to my father. This man had fought in World War II and, while in Europe, impregnated a French woman. He wrote my mother an honest, heart-wrenching letter saying he needed to do the right thing and marry this woman. My mother wrote him back and placed a copy of her letter in her diary. Her words clearly demonstrated her taking the high road, congratulating him, wishing him well, and stating that she understood. Deep down, she was shattered, though, and found escape through sleep.

☆☆☆

Early in January 2007, I noted that although my tears continued daily, they had subsided some. My crying became unfamiliar to me; I did not sound like myself anymore. My cries turned into weak whimpers—guttural, but not long in duration. I often walked around the house whimpering for hours, recalling how I told patients who feared their tears: "We have tear ducts for a reason."

That New Year's Day, I drove toward the east side of Tucson with no plan but went toward the part of town where we lived when Lacey was born. I drove to our old house and tried to recall good times, but all my memories seemed too painful and tender to think about. Even if they were joyous, it hurt to remember a time when she was alive and, at least for a brief period, we had belonged to a happy family.

My grief resulted in the morose thought that I was *not* destined to be happy. *So much for not wanting to feel or behave like a victim!* I had developed a catastrophic view of the world, at times expecting people to die or thinking I would be the recipient of unwelcome news. Still feeling raw, my misery showed like an open wound.

I asked Lacey for direction that day and found myself in Saguaro National Park East and decided to go for a hike. As I passed couples and families, it felt uncomfortable hiking alone on New Year's Day. *Will I ever have such relationships again?* I felt starved for companionship and was confused by why this question appeared so profoundly after Lacey's death. *Had she fulfilled so many needs in me? And was I really feeling the void of aloneness, or was it the separation anxiety?* I knew no one could ever fill the space she held in my life.

Because the aloneness and loneliness I felt in the world engulfed me, I vowed I would not spend New Year's Day alone again—the only New Year's resolution I set for myself. I also resigned to a developing belief that I could only take this journey *alone.* Therefore, I reasoned, I should no longer expect relief from another person.

Distress avoidance is a basic psychological need. All humans adopt specific behaviors to avoid painful and/or terrifying experiences. When I forced myself to admit it, I knew any desire I had for a relationship was actually a desire to reduce my emotional pain. I had used this method before to avoid distress. It was an ineffective coping mechanism to medicate my difficult feelings through life. A steady relationship with a man would not and could not provide this, anyway.

In fact, I was groomed for this dysfunctional coping method through a repetitive message from a few female elders in my family and the culture I grew up in. I had been told, "Find a man, and your problems will be over." Of course, this was not true. I can remember joking about this with girlfriends and saying instead, "Find a man, and your problems will just be starting!"

As I continued my hike that day, my mind was an unceasing chatterbox of doom and catastrophic thoughts. This was in sharp contrast to my typical temperament of positive thinking and my belief that good things happen if I make them happen. Again, I felt I no longer had control over my life and reflected on the thought, *If I could not save the life of my daughter, I definitely had no control.*

☆☆☆

Returning to work after the holiday season was, in many ways, a relief.

My tears continued, and I kept calling out to my daughter from the depth of my whimpers. I talked to her in the car, and I could hear her sweet voice respond in my mind as if in live conversation. At those times, I felt she was with me.

I frequently found it difficult to maintain my concentration, and the traumatic loss of Lacey rendered me easily distractible. I turned to my psychology background and my emerging interest in neuroscience as well as the neurobiology of the brain. I knew that, in the case of overwhelming threat, fear, and trauma, neuronal connections in the brain are disrupted. Neurologist Dr. Robert Scaer has written about how, after trauma, some of the brain's processes (e.g., thinking states and emotional states) begin to function independently. They no longer have the previously connected relationships.

Dr. Scaer, who defined this unconscious process as dissociation, wrote: "People who report symptoms of shock and numbness after a traumatic event, and exhibit symptoms of dissociation, are actually in the freeze response at the time."[11] When assessing patients for trauma symptoms, clinicians described patients as being "in the freeze" if they presented as distracted, unable to track a conversation, feeling detached from others, suddenly blanking out on what they were saying, or exhibiting spaciness and slow movement. Knowing this, I was puzzled by how well I was performing at work, easily making sound decisions and generating creative ideas. Outside of work, though, I struggled to plan, articulate my thoughts, and stay focused. Often, I was indecisive and inconsistent following through on my intentions.

Trauma affects both the brain and the body. When there is perceived threat, the body prepares for an emergency according to the brain's instruction. When the amygdala senses danger, this brain structure mobilizes the stress hormone system. The result is adrenaline, cortisol, and other neurotransmitters are released to give us the greatest chance of survival under threat. Adrenaline and cortisol increase blood pressure, heart rate, and rate of breathing to prepare our bodies to be able to fight or flee. Conversely, the brain shuts down any unneeded processes when under acute stress. As an example, when faced with danger, the body does not need the functions of digestion or reproduction to be active. Instead, processes best suited for the moment are activated for the short term. Increased blood sugar and blood pressure provide extra muscular energy as well as strength. The increased release of endorphins helps us counter feeling physical pain. The body and brain adjust to provide quick movement, decision making, and more. Once the danger has passed, depending on the nature of the traumatic event, how one experienced it, personal history, and other factors, the body returns to its previous state—homeostasis. For some, however, the aftermath of a traumatic experience and the changes that can occur in the brain are extremely challenging. These changes affect our thinking, our assumptions about the world, our ability to trust, and (for some) our sense of safety. The brain's job is to keep us safe. To do so, it responds to patterns of behavior stored in memory.

In previous years, I had the privilege of attending conferences around the United States to advance my knowledge in my field and earn continuing education units as required by my license to practice. In the late 1990s through 2005, I was inspired by exceptional keynote speakers such as Dr. Dan Siegel, a psychiatrist from Harvard and pioneer in the field of interpersonal neurobiology. An interdisciplinary field, interpersonal neurobiology integrates input from many areas of science to better understand the human experience from varying perspectives. Dr. Siegel developed the Mindsight Approach, which promotes kindness, compassion, and overall well-being.

As I was attending lectures by Dr. Siegel, Dr. Cardwell Nuchols, and Dr. Emory Bremner, I was fascinated with the information regarding the brain and behavior. In particular, I was intrigued by neuroplasticity, the brain's ability to change itself based on experience in the environment. I realized I was subconsciously calling on this learning to better cope with my loss of Lacey. On my journey continuing past Lacey's death, I wanted to formulate a new model for treatment for addiction, trauma, and other mental health issues. I would base it on my understanding of what the brain's plasticity could do to improve treatment methods and outcomes. These seeds of knowledge silently germinated as I continued in my walk of grief.

☆☆☆

On January 4th, while driving to work, I received a call from Jack. After the typical "how are you" conversation, he casually mentioned he had placed his house on the market and was planning to move to Colorado by June. I almost ran off the road. He initially minimized this event, but within a week and several conversations later, I learned he had placed his house on the market January 2nd! We had *not* had a recent discussion about this. I felt surprised and hurt.

Jack frequently told me he wanted to move back to Colorado. Because it had not happened in the almost three years, I had known him, I didn't expect this news on January 4th. *Who would be left in my life in a year's time?* An unproductive question.

After Lacey's death, my ex-husband and his family made little contact with me. It was just too hard for all of us, and no one had dealt with a death like this before. With my sister in New Jersey, my brother in Florida, and my son in Colorado, I began to lose faith that my life would improve. This had become an obvious pattern: loss of faith and then hope again, loss and gain, loss and gain. *Is this not typical of anyone's life, though? Isn't it part of the human condition?*

Yes, suffering is part of the human condition. There is no zip code where all residents are exempt from life's waves of joy and pain. We cannot have one without the other.

I questioned myself over and over. *What was my lesson to stop this pummel of pain? How could I find at least a brief time to experience happiness?*

Mostly, I felt little familiarity with my life. I increasingly believed I must have done something terribly wrong in this life or another. To interrupt this pernicious influence on my psyche, I began to practice meditation. I started slowly by lying prone on my exercise mat and attempting to focus on my breathing. But the rumination continued, so I stopped trying to focus on my breath and imagined my body being filled from head to toe with a beautiful, warm, energized yet soothing golden light of contentment. This helped me momentarily.

As I continued this practice several times a week over the next months, I was reminded of my work with patients who presented as being attached to their emotional pain. My efforts helped them gain insight into how they replayed their past suffering in a subconscious attempt to make the negative event come out differently. I became aware of this emerging, unspoken belief telling me: *If I can just figure out what really happened the day of her accident, who was responsible for it, and what to do about it, then all my pain and suffering will end.*

This thinking represented another paradox. I knew this from working with patients who, in attempting to eliminate emotional pain, actually held it tight. They consumed themselves with a kind *of "why this pain?" thinking. Was this what I was doing? Was I engaging in unhealthy attachment to my pain? Was I seeking pain?*

When these questions arose, I had to let go of them. This was agonizing to do. At a primal level, letting go seemed akin to abandoning my daughter and could even threaten my identity as a loving mother. Abandoning my pain, therefore, was not an option for me. So I continued sporadically with my meditation practice and did find it beneficial. Just ten minutes of quiet time resulted in increased clarity and restfulness and less obsession with toxic thinking.

☆☆☆

Still, no words could describe how much I missed Lacey. No practices could stop this. I longed to hear her sweet melodic voice, to see the nuances of her facial expressions and body language. Despite my longing, I was still receiving spiritual gifts though. For the first time since Lacey's death, I experienced a decent Sunday.

Going back to early childhood, Sunday had never been my favorite day of the week. Our house had always been somber on Sundays, and that mood had stayed with me into adulthood. I frequently dreaded that day.

On this particular Sunday, I had agreed to meet my friend, Debbie Peck, for lunch, followed by shopping. That's when I realized I desperately needed someone to talk to—in person and female—who had known me for years. I cried several times with her speaking about Lacey, and she listened to me, which helped me enormously. Even though we were in an outdoor mall where my daughter and I had spent time together, that Sunday passed quietly. The memories still wouldn't allow me to go into several stores. This Sunday, though, I did well to be in this mall with my precious friend, although Lacey was very present in spirit.

That evening, I went to a movie with Lacey's friend Emily Heintz. I thought it sweet that her friends still contacted me to spend time together. Of course, seeing Emily could never replace being with Lacey, but it helped me feel connected to her. Her friends were still grieving enormously.

☆☆☆

Overall, I was crying less, but I sometimes felt guilty if I did not cry as much as before. I knew this was irrational. Tears are not a measure of love. The truth, of course, is that nothing—not today, tomorrow, or ten years from now—would ever take away the pain of the loss. I knew this, and in my more rational moments, I also knew there would be more days in which I would again feel joy, laugh, and eventually have full days without this stabbing pain.

I also knew that *not* missing Lacey or thinking of her daily would always be impossible for me. That was okay. I never wanted to forget a single thing about my beautiful daughter.

☆☆☆

When I saw Emily, she told me a story about another friend who thought of Lacey as a big sister. His name was Nico, the brother of Ernie, who was in the car with Lacey on that tragic day. Nico loved Lacey dearly, and he had written to me about her on Lacey's Myspace site. Apparently, Nico and three other boys were in a car accident that resulted in a rollover, with the car landing upside down in a field. The boys were trapped in the car for a brief period, but all were wearing seat belts, and minimal injuries resulted.

When Nico was freed from the vehicle, he reported knowing that Lacey had saved his life. He said he felt her standing next to him and pointing her finger at him the way she always did. With a half-cocked smile, she said, "Now Nico, you know you can't be doing this. I saved you this time. No more crazy driving with anybody."

Stories like this abounded. I was constantly astounded each time I heard one.

To counter my melancholy, I told myself that, although I could not see Lacey, she was definitely around doing important work on earth. Many people, adults and youth alike, claimed having connections with her. I was also reminded that I had passed out the three hundred fifty green bracelets engraved with *Lacey Buckle For Me*. Several stories had come back to me in which the green bracelet saved someone's life, such as a driver seeing the bracelet and then buckling his seat belt. I felt a sense of triumph. *Although I could not save Lacey's life, just knowing that one person might have been spared because of the loss of my daughter was salvation itself.*

I continued to feel up and down—hopeful one day and then falling into a bottomless wretched space the next. Jack's decision to move to Colorado, whenever that might happen, left me feeling distressed about the Lacey Jarrell Foundation I was setting up. He had come up with a lot of the ideas behind it and had also begun to work with an attorney to set up the 501(c)(3) nonprofit status. With Jack gone, thinking of the six months to follow left me feeling apprehensive about even going forward with the foundation. I questioned my ability to develop the foundation without him.

Jack was the highly accomplished business executive, and I did not have all the knowledge needed for this project. *Without Jack, could I do it at all?*

I asked Lacey for help. *Please let me know how to proceed.*

Chapter Twelve: The Medium

I find you now in feathers white
In cars, in homes, in the night and in the light.
Remnants of you in your brother's eyes
And even my face at times can't disguise.

"A Mother's Lament"
~ Nancy Jarrell

In three days, I was scheduled to have my first session with a medium. Never having done this before, I was both excited and anxious. I had spoken with a psychic, but not a medium. I hoped I would hear from Lacey.

A few nights before, I had a dream that Lacey was at my parents' home sitting on my sister's bed. Although it was sold and renovated following my parents' deaths, in the dream, the house looked the same as when I grew up in it. Lacey did not say anything to me in the dream, but one of our favorite dogs, a large, gentle pit bull named Cracker, who had died years before, was lying on the other twin bed. The message I received from Lacey was that she was with our dog. Buddy and I had often marveled about how Cracker was so gentle with our children despite his generous size and their crawling all over him attempting to ride him. I felt great comfort in believing he and Lacey were reunited.

The next day, one of our medical doctors approached me at work. She was a mother who had also lost a child. Her son was in his thirties when he was diagnosed with cancer and eventually died. Although the ages and circumstances around our children's deaths were quite different, we both described remarkably similar experiences around our individual grieving processes.

She came into my office to announce she had visited with a medium over the weekend. I did not know she planned to do this. She said that while communicating with her son, the medium told her a girl was also there, and her name was Lacey. She said Lacey had died in a car accident, and she wanted her family to know she was okay.

I stood frozen, then burst into tears. My friend was highly intelligent and rational as well as extremely kind and compassionate. She said she had not told the medium anything about Lacey nor anything about her son because of her skepticism. "I was completely focused on my son and did not have Lacey in my mind at all," she told me. We were both amazed. The rest of the day, I chose to believe this and again felt solace.

☆☆☆

The next two days, I was filled with an incipient state of anxiety. I could not relax. I often felt as though I would shed my skin like some sort of reptile, leaving me exposed and no longer able to manage the intensity of my emotions. I knew this was connected to my approaching appointment with the medium.

I had waited four months for this hour-long phone appointment. I called at the designated time, and a woman with a foreign accent but exceedingly kind voice answered, and we quickly moved into the session. I did not tell her much. Like my friend, I also felt skeptical—and I knew that if she had googled my name, she would know many things about me.

The medium identified my mother first, saying she was behind me, and that a child was coming in behind my mother. This child was Lacey, although the medium did not state her name. She told me Lacey had died in a car accident and was completely surprised by her death. I knew the accident had been reported in several Tucson newspapers, so I continued to feel skeptical.

As the session went on, the medium was able to name three specific people important in Lacey's life. She said Lacey wanted to give them hugs and tell them she was okay. My daughter hugged everyone.

The medium also told me Lacey saw me wearing her bracelet and wanted me to know it looked good on me. I was stunned. When Lacey died, all I received from the coroner was some of her hair and a silver bracelet she was wearing at death. Her clothes had to be destroyed. I had not taken off her bracelet since then, and I often wondered how Lacey would feel about me wearing it. Because we were the same size, we often wore each other's clothes and jewelry. We'd even tell the other, "Stop taking my clothes!" At that point, I started to believe Lacey was truly communicating through this woman.

The medium also asked me about the name Steven, bringing up the name several times, but I still could not make the connection until later.

Toward the end of the reading, I asked what I called a "test question" to test the accuracy of the woman's report. Could she tell me about the last conversation I had with Lacey, one I'll never forget? Lacey had asked me if she could get her nose pierced, and I resisted. Since her passing, I often thought I would have let her pierce her nose a hundred times if I could just have her back. The woman did not identify this conversation. In fact, she said something else that did not fit. Days later, however, I remembered we also talked in brief about the topic she mentioned.

At the end of the communication, she told me this: "Validation of Lacey's presence today will come to you in the form of a rose."

At one point during the reading, the medium said that Lacey was telling her that she loved purses and had many. This was true. She described a purse that had writing on it and said I needed to find it, because I had missed some things in it. She also said I would find a lip gloss. So after the reading, I went to where I had stored Lacey's purses, feeling positive I had gone through every one of them. However, I did find a purse with French writing on it that I had overlooked. It was full of Lacey's things, and yes, I found a blue lip gloss inside.

I pried further into the bottom of the purse. My hand grasped something cylindrical and small. As I pulled it out, I realized I was rocking back and forth. In my hand was a small red rose encased in a glass container. *Was this the rose the medium mentioned?* What followed was a sense of calmness and comfort. That's when I chose to believe the session was cogent. I walked away from it with curiosity and many more questions.

Talking to this medium had not changed my life. I'd had many communications with Lacey in other forms more powerful than this. I recognized that Lacey was always with me. *I did not need a go-between to feel her presence.*

I continued to ask my daughter for help directly and received immediate intercessions, which helped mitigate my ravaging, all-encompassing, soul-shattering pain and depression.

Chapter Thirteen: Emergence

If I can stop one heart from breaking
I shall not live in vain.
If I can ease one life the aching
Or cool one pain
Or help one fainting robin
Unto his nest again
I shall not live in vain.

"If I Can Stop One Heart from Breaking"
~ Emily Dickinson

My son returned to college in Boulder around the middle of January. Over the Christmas break, he and I became closer, forging a new bond that left me feeling deeply connected to him. We talked more, and he told me he loved me every day. I did the same. Somehow, he helped me get through the holidays, and I prayed I had helped him. When he left, I missed him terribly.

Around this time, my brother and sister made contact about my parents' never-ending estate settlement, and we began to argue via e-mail. I was disgusted. I barely cared about any inheritance; I only cared about making it through each day. I spoke my piece and let them argue. Especially troubling was that, since I had lost so many family members—particularly Lacey—I had little family left. Really, I felt my only family was my son. Growing up in a large Irish Catholic family and then having a family of my own for so long, I seemed lost with how to deal in the world by myself. *There was much to do, but I could not possibly do it.*

On one of those days of feeling particularly lonely and unable to function, Jack called from Colorado to ask how my day was going. He was on an ice climbing trip and would likely also look for a home to purchase. I told him I was doing well. My silent self-assessment, however, was that since I had thrown myself on the couch and cried for half an hour, I must *not* be doing well. In fact, I never knew how to answer the question, "How are you?" The typical, "Fine, thank you," never fit. I could not even pretend to say that! I held back, though, and did not tell people how crippled and devastated I felt.

Jack asked me what I had done all day. "I met two hours with a reporter," I started. "Then I went with my real estate agent to look at houses and, after that, to the gym to work out." Suddenly, I realized I *had* done a lot. Actually, I recognized I did a lot every day, and I frequently pushed myself to the maximum. Although I thought of myself as stuck and lethargic at times, I was actively moving forward with my life. The part that left with Lacey, however, was my zest and spark.

Earlier in January, I had read in the *Arizona Daily Star* about special people who had passed away in 2006. I loved this culturally diverse piece. It featured several adults who had done special things in their lives to benefit others. I felt compelled to write the author and let him know how moving the article was.

The thought came to me: It might be inspiring to have a similar article written about children who had died in 2006 and how they affected the world in their short lives. So I wrote to the reporter, Tom Beal, and briefly verbalized my appreciation for his story. Then I shared my idea, mentioning Lacey. Not long after that, we scheduled a meeting to talk. Tom was not sure if we had a story, but after we spent two hours in my kitchen, he said he'd like to get some of Lacey's friends together and interview them. His focus would be on how teens coped with loss, how they had helped *me*, and how I had helped *them*.

I felt excited and incredibly grateful to this man. I was also aware of feeling an almost immediate sense of comfort with him. After asking around about him, I learned he was a well-respected writer in Tucson and clearly a man of integrity.

This blessing came at a valuable time. I had begun to perceive that many people no longer wanted to hear about Lacey based on observing their body language and interpreting the unspoken. But I still needed to talk about her. I knew people were not being unkind; they cared about me and wanted me to feel better. Yet I also understood they were weary of comforting me. The truth was *nobody* could comfort me.

I made arrangements for Tom Beal to meet a few of Lacey's friends at my house. I also gave him the phone number of Michelle St. Rose, the remarkable woman who had witnessed the accident. He then spoke with Alan DeKalb, the paramedic on the scene.

I had not talked to Alan in weeks but chatting with him was easy. We marveled at how we never knew each other before the accident, yet we've become connected through this tragedy. Several people I had never known came into my life. We shared the history of being touched and changed by a beautiful girl, my Lacey Jane. They were all good, good people.

Thus began an interview process that would culminate years later in an amazing and surprising result.

After a serious bout of depression and having succumbed to the pull of the darkness, I noticed one day, again, how much good existed in my life. Many things that had been insignificant or not especially memorable before Lacey died had become enormous parts of a chain that linked me to her and got me through the day. I received so much love from so many people, and I knew the healing effect of strong interpersonal relationships. Research I read cited those who are socially connected and experience daily loving touch fare better than those who are isolated after being exposed to trauma.

A woman at work, Kathy, whom I did not know well, had an office down the hall from me. Kathy would come to my office every day, wrap her arms around me, and say, "I am here to give you your daily hug." I would get out of my chair smiling, and she would give me the most comforting of hugs. Her daily offering was precious to me.

One week, a Sierra Tucson marketing representative from Connecticut came to Sierra Tucson for a planning meeting. She and I had become close before her move to Connecticut, as we had carpooled together for a few years. She was a young, married mother of two children. One day at lunch, I was feeling overwhelmed, and she easily detected the struggle on my face. She got up from the table and said, "Nancy, let's go to your office for a minute."

We walked silently to my office, and there, I broke down. *Finally, I could take off the face I wore throughout my workday.* Then she told me I'd had an enormous impact on how she is raising her children and her own life. Several months before, I had told her about my joy in knowing that my last words to Lacey were, "I love you. Good night." I had talked with her about how I believed we should treat our children, and how much easier it was for me to discipline mine without any physical reprimand. I was always conscious of never letting myself lapse into rageful behaviors such as cursing, throwing things, or shaming them. These had been done to me as a child, and I knew, even as a fifty-year-old woman, that I still carried the scars.

I also spoke about how I talked things through with my children and listened to them, even when I did not agree with them. Ultimately, I felt fortunate I had reared two lovely children who spoke their minds, behaved appropriately, and knew they were loved and special. She thought of me every day, she shared, and as a result of our conversations, she behaved differently with her children. Hearing that was such a gift to me.

☆☆☆

I cannot give adequate accolades to the staff at Sierra Tucson, who carried me through many inconsolable days when I thought I'd implode from the enormity of my grief. I was well aware how fortunate I was to be working with some of the finest clinicians in the world and surrounded by therapists, psychiatrists, psychologists, nurses, and others in the helping profession. All of them expressed sensitivity and warmth toward me. In some ways, they all carried a piece of my pain.

Even more, the hospital planted a tree on the grounds and installed a beautiful plaque. It bore both Lacey's words and mine and quoted one of Lacey's poems that implores others to look for the beauty in their lives. The tree became known as the Lacey Tree. Jack donated a bench for the site, and counselors took patients there to process their grief. Soon, precious items of love and respect showed up hanging from the tree's branches. A few counselors even conducted ceremonies there.

I stayed connected to the idea that many good things came my way each day. The night after the tree was dedicated, I received an e-mail from one of Lacey's friends. Her brother's friend, a fifteen-year-old boy, had just died in a rollover car accident. The boy's family and friends were in horrible grief, and the girl requested some of the Lacey bracelets to wear. She also asked for my support in talking about the loss.

I quickly responded. One thing I could do as a therapist, a bereaved parent, and a mother was to help others who suffered the same tragedy. I immediately provided the bracelets. But I never spoke with the family—the opportunity did not present itself.

I didn't know it at the time, but this proved to be a blessing. *In no way was I stable enough yet to assist another bereaved parent.*

Chapter Fourteen: Seeking Life's Lesson

I wandered lonely as a cloud
For oft when on my couch I lie
In vacant or in pensive mood
They flash upon that inward eye.
Which is the bliss of solitude
And then my heart with pleasure fills
And dances with the daffodils.

"I Wandered Lonely as a Cloud"
~ William Wordsworth

In the new year, my work schedule changed. I was asked to go in and revamp our evening and weekend program to provide better patient care. This involved supervising additional staff and creating new group content to support patients in their continuing therapy and also provide them coping skills for relapse prevention.

With this change, working some nights and weekends, I became aware of isolating more when not at work. Although I still struggled with living alone and being alone, I made little effort *not* to be alone. When Jack left town again for two weeks, I worked even longer hours. When I was home, I spent most of my time involved with something connected to Lacey.

I had accepted my tears as normal, knowing that crying—a biological expression or shedding of distress—helps remove pain from our bodies. A colleague of mine often said the way out of experiencing difficult feelings was to *go through* them. That meant facing the feelings head on rather than stuffing them, which only prolongs them, as they will periodically reappear until fully processed. By letting our feelings flow, they can then pass through our bodies allowing us to reach the other side of the feelings and then move on.

☆☆☆

At this point, I was well into conversations with the reporter, Tom Beal. I invited three of Lacey's close friends to my house to tell him their stories. None of these girls knew each other, but they knew of each other. Lacey had many circles of friends. It seemed she had pockets of them everywhere.

"There was no one like Lacey," one of her friends shared. "She gave love to everybody. She was the kind of girl you wanted to like you. She was always the one any of us could talk to for advice, and we all walked away feeling better, special, and loved by her. She was so wise."

☆☆☆

I talked again with Alan DeKalb and Michelle St. Rose. I valued both of them and the compassion they showed me. I was grateful that Michelle and two other loving women had been touching Lacey's foot, feeling her pulse, and praying as she left this world. Michelle and at least one of the paramedics had PTSD as a result of the accident. Both said Lacey had changed their lives. Michelle said she became more attentive to her children and told them "I love you" each day.

With each interview, Tom became more fascinated with our story. I hoped his work might gain attention for the burgeoning Lacey Jarrell Foundation, but mostly, I hoped it would help others going through loss and grief.

After I spoke with my accountant that week, things came together for Lacey's foundation. We finally had something we could present to the Internal Revenue Service for nonprofit status. I started to feel hopeful. For months, I had been writing the application to the IRS for approval of a 501(c)(3) nonprofit organization to support young artists with educational and counseling needs.

The application process proved grueling, requiring written answers to many critical-thinking questions. When I completed the answers, the application exceeded eighty pages. I could not fathom that I had done it. As I reread parts of it, some of my writing seemed "other" directed—optimistic, clear, and fresh. I intuitively knew it would be accepted.

☆☆☆

While Jack was gone, I tried to prepare myself for the time he ultimately moved to another state. *Would he really do this?* Knowing his house was on the market, I knew I needed to move on. We did talk on the phone every day, and nothing had really changed between us, but I was beginning to back off.

I desperately missed the daily "I love you" from Lacey. Both of my children were comfortable saying this to each other and to their Dad and me. We verbalized this every day, too! This was not comfortably done in my family of origin and neither was hugging. This did improve, though, particularly after my brother's death.

I had always wanted comfort and touch in the family Buddy and I created. And it came naturally. At some point, I had learned about the health benefits of hugs. Oxytocin, a hormone released by the brain's hypothalamus, plays a significant role in social bonding. It facilitates the attachment between a mother and her infant, floods the brain with feelings of contentment and security when we are falling in love, and is released when we engage in loving touch such as a hug. Some experts recommend we all engage in at least five hugs a day.[12] I felt grateful I received that number of hugs most days.

All humans also have attachment needs. Dr. John Bowlby, a British psychologist and psychiatrist, pioneered in developing the attachment theory. It defines how, as newborns, we innately seek proximity to someone we perceive as stronger, wiser, and more capable to provide us safety and thus survival. We come into the world as dependent, helpless beings. As infants, we require maternal (or other) care to keep us safe, satisfy our hunger and thirst, and provide basic human needs. In the first three years of life, our brains grow more rapidly than at any other age and begin forming healthy, integrated, and functional circuitry to survive and thrive. When a mother (or other) is attuned to our needs and responds to them consistently, we learn to regulate our emotions and develop social intelligence, healthy rewarding play, language, self-care, and more.[13]

- 139 -

Dr. Bowlby believed that relationships or "attachment schemas" were the accumulation of thousands of experiences with our primary caregiver in early life. These experiences predict or build a template we unconsciously follow in later years, leading us to either avoid or seek proximity. Early relationships with our caregivers that result in physiological and psychological changes in the brain are activated unconsciously in us, even before we interact with another person. Thus, our early life experiences become our guide for how we engage in our future relationships.

Much research has been facilitated on what is called "secure attachment" and "insecure attachment." To those treating mental health concerns, insecure attachment naturally holds the most interest. Three types have been identified: avoidant, anxious–ambivalent, and disorganized. Many believe that addictions and other mental health issues are merely symptoms of attachment disorders.[14]

☆☆☆

Around this time, the number of dreams I had about Lacey increased. They were a gift to me; at least I could *see* her. I also received the tape from the medium and listened to it several times. The more I listened, the more I believed Lacey had come to me through this woman, at least to a degree.

Again, I began to formulate my spiritual beliefs. Specifically, I believed that each of us had many lives, and that we returned to earth however many times it took for us to advance our souls and move to a higher place. I believed we all needed to conquer certain lessons, and that Lacey had been taken because she had completed the lessons she needed to learn in this lifetime—how to love, forgive, and truly let go with love; how to suspend all judgment of others; how to work through enmeshed relationships with males; and finally how to transcend her dependency on males and take care of herself.

As I witnessed her doing this throughout her short life, I was amazed that a person so young had such ability. She was a role model for me in how little judgment she expressed of others—and how she defended people with all of their faults in tow.

Initially, she believed her father's alcoholism was about her. *If he really loved her,* she thought, *he would stop drinking.* His disease was the cause of our divorce. Lacey loved her father deeply but also became terribly angry with him as she grew older. She ultimately came to this place of acceptance: "I don't like it, but I know I can't change it, and it is not about me." At that point, she took the reins in their relationship and set boundaries with him in a loving way. She would not be forced into seeing him if he were under the influence or if she felt uncomfortable. I was so proud of her wisdom.

Lacey had also passed through her teenage love with Ernie. She had come to understand they needed to go their separate ways, as they had disparate goals in life and differing levels of ambition and motivation. Lacey learned to move on with love for him and end the relationship. Sadly, her choice to end it was challenged over and over, as Ernie seemed obsessed with her and would not accept her decision. His persistence led to the two of them being in her car that fateful day.

I focused on not blaming him. Still, my anger was like an ever-present burning ember that could ignite at any moment. Although my daughter had been dead seven months, Ernie continued to come up in my world—through her friends, through my friendship with his mother, and through stories I heard around town.

I treasured my times with Ernie and, at the same time, felt repelled by my conflicted state. This paradox of wanting to stay close to him and being warned to stay away tormented me like a subtle but chronic physical pain. I asked him over and over what happened that morning, and every time he willingly shared the same chain of events. From that, I thought I understood what lesson Lacey had to learn and wondered at what point mine would be revealed to me. I hoped I could learn the lessons, because I was clear I did not want to return for another life. *I still believed Hell was on earth, and I was in it. I wanted out.*

Fortunately, I did feel a tiny spark of hope flicker deep inside. It was not much, but I tried to capture and kindle it so it would grow. I waited. And the pain continued.

✰✰✰

I remember speaking with some of my staff members as they repeatedly made assumptions about policies. Some believed a policy was the same today as it had been in years past, even though a new company had purchased the hospital and revised the policies and procedures. I overheard one of them say to another, "Well, I did it this way because that's how we did it last year." When I heard that point made again in a staff meeting, I spoke up. "When in doubt, remember this," I offered. "Absolutely nothing is the same. Anything that was, is no longer." As I said these words, it struck me how this was completely true for me not only at work but in every aspect of my life. *Absolutely nothing was the same.*

I felt as if I lived in two worlds. One was my busy working life, which I knew I used to medicate the worst of my horrific pain. The other was my time in Lacey's world visiting with her friends and reading comments and writing on her Myspace page. But mostly, I isolated and talked to her, dreamed about her, looked at her pictures and her artwork, visited her accident site, and tried to develop the nonprofit organization in her name. She consumed me.

Some things were a little easier, though. I was becoming accustomed to her absence from the house and experienced longer periods in the day between my gut-wrenching tears. The night was a different story; I would just wail out loud. No one could hear me. *Maybe* she *could!* That thought would take me out of it. *I would not want her to see me in such agony.* As in life, I still protected her in death.

It was important that I continue to fight for her memory and for the story of her life to be one of truth. On rare occasions, I would hear something from one of her friends indicating her life had been all about a teenage romance. Some even claimed her attraction to green stars was about them, rather than her. At first, I felt compelled to correct these inaccuracies, but I would remind myself that my daughter's friends were still kids, and that they loved her. *No need to correct anything.*

I was amazed how many Myspace comments kept coming, and that Lacey's adoration seemed to grow to near-mythic proportion. That January, it snowed one day in Tucson, an exceedingly rare occurrence. The Myspace comments poured in with people thanking her for bringing the snow. Some of the girls took on her persona, doing their hair, nails, and clothing just like Lacey. I continued to learn about the incredible impact she had on so many—in life and in death. *She was a precious spiritual being sent to us for sixteen years to change our lives.*

Certainly, Lacey changed *my* life beyond recognition. Her life and death brought up all the pain, suffering, joy, angst, insight, and lessons that one could ever experience in a lifetime. I worked hard on acceptance. I saw how I had changed in terms of dropping expectations and envisioning the future as I moved through life one minute at a time.

Although I continued to isolate myself, people kept coming into my life. I read the obituaries daily, and when I saw a story or heard of another child dying unexpectedly, I wrote to the family through the newspaper's online diary. I would pray for them and offer support. By then, I had passed out six hundred green bracelets to encourage people to buckle their seat belts. As the word spread, I was often asked for more. Many people wanted to speak with me—to support a safety program and promote safe driving, to provide grief counseling and to help me with ideas about my foundation to heighten awareness of artistically talented kids.

Some days, so much was happening, I could not get organized. Although I spent my free time alone, I was often on the phone or pulling together and organizing all the ideas coming my way. Although Lacey had left this earth, she continued to feed me with energy and daily doses of love through these connections. I also continued to receive cards, calls, and hugs. I so missed her hugs and her daily "I love you, Mama," that I took this comfort from others and gave it back to them, as well.

Chapter Fifteen: The Meaning

of Family

*In family life, love is the oil that eases friction,
the cement that binds closer together, and the
music that brings harmony.*

~ Eva Burrows

The first months of 2007 were full of energy as though an enormous number of electrical sparks were flying through the universe and touching everyone around me.

As this continued, daily life improved slightly in that I was able to hold the love coming my way rather than staying consumed in grief and depression. Then two of my cousins called and offered to come out and do whatever I needed.

I wept uncontrollably at this offer. I had been longing for someone to just say, "Hey, we're going to help you get things organized, and we will do whatever you tell us." Chores and responsibilities overwhelmed me most days. I wanted to move, to change my will, to set up the Lacey Jarrell Foundation, *and* to keep working. Work got most of my attention.

I also continued to feel gratitude for the many nights I came home in a state of dark despair, only to find loving cards in the mailbox or receive a comforting phone call or a request from someone wanting to visit. *People did not forget.*

I continually heard from people who had been afraid to share with me in the early months following Lacey's death. Now, they were telling me amazing stories of things that happened to them after she died and how the experience had changed their lives. Many talked about seeing her in dreams. The most profound experiences centered on other mothers—those who reported fractured relationships with their children and repairing them as a result of Lacey's death. More and more people stopped by to share their tears and tell me how Lacey had influenced them, even seven months after her passing.

As Lacey's network of friends continued to visit, one of the many perceptions about my daughter was that she never judged anyone and had kind words for everyone—whether it was the "geeky" kid in school or a child who was extremely overweight. Many of them said to me, "Who will I talk to now that Lacey is gone?"

At first, I couldn't understand this. Then I realized they didn't have anyone to talk to at their most vulnerable level and feel safe in doing so. The overweight girl who Lacey befriended, for example, was in the popular crowd because Lacey had embraced her. Through Lacey's death, I discovered she was exceptional to many, not just our family. *It takes a village to lose a child.*

☆☆☆

In mid-January, I went to see another psychic in Tucson. Despite my earlier resignation about not needing psychics, I still sought information in varying ways. Always a skeptic, I did not expect to believe what this woman would tell me. Yet on the contrary, for almost ninety minutes, I felt as though I were having real communication with Lacey. I was elated when she conveyed information that was personal and private—that only Lacey and I could know. Some of the language contained phrases typical of how Lacey and I spoke to each other. I was addressed as Mama, for example, which is what Lacey called me. The psychic described several of Lacey's possessions and told me what to do with them—which piece of jewelry to wear and which to give away and to whom. I was impressed and roused.

Perhaps most important, Lacey sent advice on how I should live my life without her and even identified my writing this book. She said she was helping me write it, that I must continue. Thus, I have kept writing.

I was also given practical advice, allegedly from my "guides," who helped me write a list of what I needed to do in the remainder of my life. This was immensely helpful, especially as I had been going to therapy for months and never felt I received the right tools to help me cope. This session with the psychic gave me coping skills such as stretching, involving physical movement with specific instruction to open my heart, maintaining a healthier posture, allowing silence, and creating a daily time to read a brief meditation or repeat a mantra or prayer.

Once again, I genuinely believed my daughter was only a short distance away—I just could not see her.

☆☆☆

The resolution of my parents' estate came into sight again. As the final settlement moved forward, my sister misinterpreted my answers to questions the attorney asked regarding certain checks written from my parents' account after their deaths. My sister Janey had control of my parents' checkbook, but I knew the answers to the questions, as I had been with her when she paid for our parents' caskets and funeral home expenses. The attorneys had made errors that, without my clarification, made it seem my sister had mismanaged some funds. I also knew of checks that were not appropriate, in my opinion. So in my e-mail reply to the attorneys and my siblings, I stated, "I am willing to look the other way on these checks."

What ensued was unconscionable. I believe the attorney deliberately misconstrued my words and sent an e-mail to my sister stating I had accused her of embezzlement and she should hire an attorney immediately. This was completely false. The accountant, in fact, confirmed the accuracy of my clarification of errors made by the attorneys. This validated that I had protected my sister from their mistake that had made it seem as though she had misappropriated funds, which I knew she had not.

My sister did not hire an attorney but in her response stated she did not want to be contacted ever again by me, my brother, or the attorney. I was dumbfounded. Had it been a different time in my life, I would have picked up the phone and asked my sister to reread my e-mail. I found myself numb and frozen. I had no energy to manage any additional dejection. My solution? To empower myself by affirming agreement with her no-contact request then taking the high road by detaching with love. I did this via e-mail, and my sister became another loss for me. Ironically, I felt some peace after this. It hurt, but I accepted losing my relationship with my sister, and this acceptance extinguished an ember of familial tragedy.

Time and time again, I was learning how life improved if I took the high road. This lesson was muted at times, but at other times was as pronounced as the Arizona sky.

☆☆☆

How I expressed my grief changed its path once again. The whimpering decreased, and I began to cry robust tears that left my body quivering. This emotional release shook me to my core.

One week, I had an appointment with my dermatologist, whom I had visited two weeks after Lacey's death. When I had walked in then, the office seemed to stand still. The women there all knew about the accident, and no one had expected me to keep this appointment. I hardly know how I did; I just knew I had an appointment and that I should keep it. Months later, I was back again, and the dermatologist who treated me the first time saw me again.

We talked a little about how I was doing with my loss, and the woman shared about losing her father two years earlier. It was having an enormous effect on her still. As she said that, she became tearful and had to leave the room. When she returned, she apologized and said she needed to tell me something. She shared that the first day I came in, she had been terribly upset. She had traveled the day before, and when she got home, she discovered her jewelry missing from her luggage. I remembered hearing the women talk about this when I was in the waiting room and thinking, "I wish all I had lost was my jewelry." Of course, I did not tell her this.

She proceeded to tell me that, after hearing my story during the first visit, she had to leave the room and cry. (I was not aware of this at the time.) While out of the room, she'd had a profound spiritual experience—that is, her father came and spoke to her clearly. He told her, "Forget about the jewelry. There are more important things. Look at what *this* woman is experiencing." After hearing that, she said she found immediate peace. At the end of her workday, she went home and looked one more time for her jewelry. It was in her luggage where she claimed she had looked multiple times! And in a drawer, she found a pair of earrings her father had given her, ones she thought had been stolen on her trip.

The woman told me she believed Lacey was responsible for all of this, and that my visit to her office is what connected her to her father. I listened and believed her. Whatever this woman experienced that day was real and true for her, which I always keep in mind when talking to anyone. I never want to discount anyone's stories or feelings, knowing their perception is reality to them.

Two days later, I came home to a comforting card from this kind woman, letting me know how much she was thinking of me and admired my strength. *What a remarkable person!*

That night, and I do not know why, I experienced a big meltdown. I went down to my daughter's bed and cried and cried, lying on top of her bedspread smelling her scent. I could not eat and needed to go to bed at seven-thirty to escape the searing pain.

Although I had increased periods of emotional respite, my profound misery still came back and usually in a colossal way. I felt lost in a vacuous funnel. Exhausted from doing life, I did not think I could ever find the key to unlock this ball and chain I dragged around. I had no words to describe my condition. However, I found the fortitude to forgive myself. *What else could I do?*

☆☆☆

The calendar turned to February, and Jack returned from Colorado. I was happy he was back in Tucson, although our relationship continued to confuse me, but I didn't dwell on this. My priorities focused on how to live day to day, not on how to maintain a relationship.

I missed my baby girl beyond words. I thought of her pure white skin, unmarred; her peering, large green eyes; her wavy, waist-long auburn hair; her slight body, pressed into the tiniest jeans; her wide smile; and the way she welcomed me with her strong hugs each morning and evening. To me, there was no female more stunningly beautiful, both inside and out. I thought of how we laughed when I told her women actually paid to have full, pouty lips like hers. I remembered her cocky walk, her dance moves, and her expressions. I never wanted to forget anything about her. Then I realized I could not, anyway; Lacey was eternally etched in my brain, a permanent memory cell in my body.

My friend, Mel, told me that "energy never dies." These three words soothed me, and I fell back on them many times over the ensuing years. Believing Lacey still existed in some form, somewhere, provided me hope that I would be with her again. I dissolved any consideration I gave to thinking she was forever gone. I did not want to believe any interpretation my thoughts might wander to about "for dust thou art, and unto dust thou shalt return." (Genesis 3:19 King James Version).

As I looked back over the seven months since her death, I was starting to form memories of my life *after* Lacey—and some were good ones. This felt shocking and incongruent to me. *How was there even any life after Lacey passed?* Still, there were more days I felt hopeful that I could adjust to my new life. I experienced periods of great acceptance in which I could resign myself to the suffering and feel connected to a higher spiritual place. I continued to believe that everything led my soul to greater growth. Would that happen fully in this lifetime? I didn't know.

At other times, though, I felt disconnected and different from those around me. I often "faked it" around people I saw consistently, pretending I was all right. I felt fragmented—a shard of broken glass, purposeless. I carried a knot in my stomach, and as I continued to overwork, I became aware of appearing and feeling more fragile. When a friend called or I ran into someone I had not seen for months, I burst into uncontrollable crying. I knew that release of emotion was positive, though. Again, stuffing my feelings would only prolong the gnawing agony.

☆☆☆

I also experienced periods when I privately struggled with what actually happened that terrible day. *How did Lacey end up in the car with Ernie? Why did the phone logs not match what Ernie had told me? Why did she leave the house with no shoes, no purse, the television still on, the door unlocked, and her art project lying on the table waiting for her return?*

Periodically, I became plagued with these questions, and the torment often set me back. I had to remind myself repeatedly to choose my thoughts carefully, selecting the least painful ones while bringing up a buffet of more positive thoughts.

To deal with my depression and grief, I began to research week-long treatment programs. I was becoming frustrated with my grief therapist because I often felt "opened up" and then left to process the feelings by myself. In the past, I could do that with incidents in my trauma history. The loss of my daughter, however, felt greater than any tragedy I had ever known. *The grief seemed insurmountable.*

Once again, I found myself taking a risk in getting angry with God. *Was it amusing to Him to see me struggle? How far could He push me before I would crack?* I was not afraid to die, but I did not want to completely fall apart and have no one to pick me up.

Despite the love and support I often felt around me, no one could relieve my grief. Knowing I was on my own overwhelmed me beyond description. I sadly began to expect more pain and experienced moments of absolute hopelessness about having a joyful future. During these times, I relapsed into distorted thinking while wondering how many days I could keep going . . . and yet the calendar pages kept turning.

☆☆☆

One day, my friend, Cyndy Neighbors, called with an offer to help the Lacey Jarrell Foundation. She had been hired to take over the advertising and promotion of an area in Tucson known as Gallery Row—the exact place I had dreamed of having an art gallery for Lacey's foundation. That she was working there and wanted to support a charitable organization to also help promote the row of art galleries there, seemed like a Godsend—or, as I began to conceive of it, a *Laceysend.*

Thus began my thinking about what was a Godsend versus what was a Laceysend. To some degree, I was aware of turning my daughter into my personal deity. I trusted her to help me and care for me. I did not have the same trust in God.

While in my car where I held many conversations with Lacey, I decided to get her out of the middle of God and me and talk with Him directly. Again, I was angry and let Him know that. I felt like he had targeted me, that he had done an excellent job of fracturing my life and seeing to it I was miserable. I experienced a sudden struggle to access gratitude and maintain my positive attitude. Honestly, I was tired of making the effort. It felt like a game and I was a pawn on the chessboard.

Although I had never desired death as much as I did at this time, I was not ready to give up my fight. I had no desire to take my life, but I knew that when I visited my daughter's roadside memorial, I continued to play with death by parking dangerously or crossing the street in traffic at the deadly curve. Holding me back from walking into traffic were thoughts of the poor stranger who would have the misfortune of hitting me. *I could not do this to anyone.* And given my intense love for my son, *I could never do this to him, either.*

Gratefully, I still had this forward-thinking ability to process possible consequences of my potential actions. Shortly after, I met with my trust lawyer to make sure Will could acquire my assets in the easiest way possible.

Chapter Sixteen: A Tentative Vision for the Future

You may not control all the events that happen to you, but you can decide not to be reduced by them.

~ Maya Angelou

*L*ife can change in a blink of an eye. This aphorism applied to me, and I reflected on it often. After Lacey died, Will and I searched our computers for photos of her, and we found a drawing she did of a beautiful, piercing hazel eye. Underneath was the saying *"in a blink of an eye there lies eternity."* Like so many other notes and poems we found, it was eerie. Also, the drawing was unquestionably of her own eye.

At times, I managed to access the cognitive behavioral therapy belief that some of my misery related to my mindset, that if I heeded my own advice on choosing positive thoughts, I might improve my outlook. I decided to try this again for one day, although I doubted I could do it.

The previous weekend found me fragile and quick to tear up, so I resumed dividing my day into six hours at a time as well as reframing my thoughts. Whenever I was conscious of a negative thought such as, "I will never get relief from this pain," I reframed it as, "I will get relief from this pain." Even if I did not believe it, I kept chanting the thought.

Where had my humility, my focus on gratitude, and my spiritual composure gone? All I knew for certain was I suffered from crippling loneliness and a deep, gaping emotional wound that could not be described. Words such as "pain, sadness, hurt, and grief" in no way captured what I endured. The only way to describe what my losing Lacey felt like was through the use of metaphor such as feeling as though a vital organ had been yanked out of me or that a storm had invaded my body and rearranged the location of all my nerve cells.

The morning I wrote this, I went to work and again began my practice of choosing the thoughts that made me feel better. On the drive in, as I cried over a memory of Lacey, I realized things were not going well. Throughout my workday, I frequently felt overwhelmed or detached from what was happening. I could not do this for long. In this highly demanding job, I had to be "on" to support my staff and process with patients.

Sierra Tucson is a beautiful, spiritual place that is also filled with angst, tragedy, trauma, and crisis. I had gravitated toward this kind of work as a "wounded healer." I had lived through adverse experiences, many of which were similar to our patients. I once medicated my pain and shame in unhealthy ways, so I understood their suffering. That's why the work called to me. It was no accident I worked here. I loved the work and the crisis. It energized me. Ironically, however, I did not love my own life at all, which embodied trauma and crisis.

As the day progressed, I somehow shifted into a more positive frame of mind. Although I had been asking God for tools to deal with my loss and grief, I did not recognize this shift until later. That afternoon, I met with my supervisor to discuss budget issues. I liked her very much and always enjoyed our conversations.

That day, we talked about our personal situations with money. She told me about a "vision plan" she created for herself more than a year before and described how all of it had manifested. I recalled having done something similar years before: being specific about what age I wanted to be married, own my own home, have children, and even pay off a mortgage. Miraculously, all these things had come about by the ages I had envisioned. I took this conversation as a message that I could manifest a future for myself. Without Lacey, it was excruciating to think about the future at all. I hated that I felt that way. However, the thought of manifesting something positive appealed to me, and it slightly elevated my mood.

When I returned home that evening, I wrote down my vision for the future. I noted what type of people I desired to have in my life, what kind of house I wanted, how long I would stay in my job, and when I wanted to complete the setup of Lacey's memorial foundation. Added to the plan was a timeline for publishing this book.

I felt grateful for this planning tool. I was ready to take up the battle—to live a spirited life and not behave as a victim. I pledged to focus on how blessed I was to have had Lacey in my life for almost seventeen years.

That night, I received a message on Myspace from a male friend of Lacey's who wanted to make contact but was afraid of his feelings. He described missing her and said how much he had loved her as a friend. Although we had never met, this boy had been watching the Myspace communications and read everything I had written. He had also heard about me through Lacey's long chain of friends. On the site, he wrote that I was his hero. Seeing that, I burst into tears. *It's tender moments like these that allow me to navigate the darkness.*

☆☆☆

While I was in the medical director's office at work one day, he told me about a friend who had sent his daughter to a treatment facility back east. He said the young woman had stayed in treatment for a few weeks, then walked off the campus. No one knew her whereabouts, so her family hired a private investigator. Days later, she was found in a motel room with several other young men and women.

For safety, the police were called to the scene. As the officers were about to break into the motel room, a flurry of kids came running out screaming. A young woman had just died of a drug overdose. Her father sat in the parking lot waiting for them to bring out his daughter safely. Instead, he witnessed her body being carried out.

My heart froze and my head reeled as I heard this story. I could vividly picture this anguished father watching as authorities carried his daughter's body out of the motel.

The doctor then told me that, weeks later, that same father asked to have his niece who had a drug problem admitted to the same treatment center from which his daughter had fled. Initially, this behavior puzzled me until I understood how he must be compensating for not being able to save his own daughter. At least he could focus on saving his niece.

I felt that father's pain. If my daughter's death resulted in the saving of one life, then at least it created some sense and hope out of a horrific tragedy. I thought about organizing a group of "angels" who would help families that had suddenly lost a child. Having felt the need for help myself, I could think of a hundred things a family might need. I often wished I had an assistant to organize my life but more so to *reorganize my brain*. I perceived that my nervous system was dysregulated and struggling with the unfamiliar changes caused by losing Lacey.

☆☆☆

Sometimes guilt gnawed at my soul. *Should I have insisted we change Lacey's phone number sooner? Should I not have suggested we do it on Saturday, the day that never came for her? Should I have stayed home from work that day because of my premonition?*

When the guilt began its slow creep, I learned to stop it. Otherwise, believing that I *could* not and *did* not keep my daughter safe would plague me into my grave. I still had to desist from these terrorizing thoughts.

I also became aware that I medicated a great deal of my pain by being on my computer. Checking Lacey's Myspace site and reading the loving comments from her friends revived my spirit. Many of the writings brought me to tears, but as I have noted, tears had become a completely normal part of my life.

I was also aware that many people thought I was doing well. I held a leadership position at Sierra Tucson and, yet, as my workload increased, I felt more fragmented and knew my emotional stability was waning. It seemed as if a multitude of thorns pierced my body and I suffered from invisible sores. Sometimes my entire body felt crippled with grief. Yet I smiled externally through the relentless pain.

On one particularly rough Sunday, I let God know again I was quite sure He had made a mistake. "You got it wrong this time," I told Him. "I can't handle this, and I'm not going to get through it. I really can't survive without my daughter." Again, the idea of dying hung around on the sidelines as an option. I spoke to no one about my thoughts.

As those thoughts loomed, the phone rang. On the other end was a friend of forty years, Ginny, who lived in Wisconsin. We had met in the fifth grade and stayed in touch ever since. Ginny was loyal, solid as a rock, and always there for me. Despite my difficult life experiences, including my younger years of addictions, she stood by me. I knew she most desperately wanted to help me but did not know how.

When we were young and Ginny first came to my school in New Jersey, she was not initially accepted by some of the girls in the "in crowd." This did not matter to me. I liked Ginny and accepted her as a good person. I knew this at the age of ten and picking her as a friend was one of the good choices I had made in my life. I felt grateful for her constant acceptance of me. Ginny, too, had picked me as a friend even though I was not in the "in crowd" either. I was also grateful to her for seeing something worthy in me.

As we talked on the phone forty years later, I was in tears, and she wanted to fix me. In her good-hearted intent to quell my sadness, my friend thought moving to a different city might help me. She suggested moving to Madison, saying I could live in her downstairs apartment and be close to her. She reminded me I had three other lifelong friends who loved me and also lived in Madison. Perhaps I could go back to school at the University of Wisconsin, Ginny suggested. I already held a post graduate degree, and I found myself feeling exasperated with my inability to convey my needs to her.

I did not even know *what* I needed. I also did not *want* anyone to try to understand my experience. *The only way to understand was by becoming a member of this abysmal club that did not want new members.*

Ginny did not understand that moving to Wisconsin—a cold and foreign place to me—and living in her apartment would be more depressing than staying alone in my home. After all, she would be upstairs with her husband and kids. Plus my three friends there also enjoyed solid, close family relationships.

Finally, I told Ginny why this plan would not work—that sometimes it took all my strength just to drag myself out of bed. I simply could not make plans and follow through on them. And I definitely did not want to move to Wisconsin and go back to school.

Then I told Ginny something I needed to say to a lot of people but had not dared. I explained how people kindly called or wrote, saying I could come and live with them or visit them. But if they really wanted to help me, I needed them to come *here*—to pack up this huge house because I needed to move, go grocery shopping for me. In my grief, these were all equally enormous chores to me!

As always, Ginny was patient and said she would come whenever I needed her. And she said I deserved people to come to me, because I had been so good to many people. For the life of me, I could not figure out how I had been good to her. *Why would she say that? I did not see myself deserving of this.* I believed it was she who deserved a lot for being consistently kind, accepting, thoughtful, and caring. I often felt inferior to her.

Later, I realized our mutual acceptance of each other long ago was a gift that helped her, too. I felt proud of myself, knowing this was exactly what Lacey would have done. In fact, she *did* do it; she accepted so many people exactly as they were—without judgment.

Suddenly it made complete sense why so many of these young people asked me, "Who will I talk to now that Lacey is gone? Who will help me?" Lacey's full acceptance and love of people gave them a gateway into feeling acceptance with others. *If Lacey liked them, then they felt okay. And she loved everyone.*

Chapter Seventeen: Priorities

Do not live in pain or sorrow for me.
Live your life, conquer your fears.
And don't be afraid to forgive, but not forget.
Don't be afraid to accept help when needed,
And life will be good.

"My Poem"
~ Lacey Jarrell, 12

Big things became little things and little things became big things. One night I was home alone asleep, and my security alarm went off about two a.m. Typically, the alarm sounding would have been a terrifying experience for me. I do not know why it was different this time, but I calmly got up and retrieved my gun. I went into my kitchen to check the readout on the alarm keypad. *Was a door open? Was motion detected?*

Operating on automatic pilot, I called 911 and spoke to the sheriff dispatcher, who told me the deputy sheriff was not close by and would not arrive for some time.

With that information, I decided to search the house myself—I did not want to wait anxiously, doing nothing. I covered every room and door and found nothing indicating a break-in. I felt surprisingly void of fear and ended up calling off the sheriff. Not knowing why the alarm sounded, I was still able to go back to sleep. Months before, this would have prevented me from doing so.

Conversely, little things became big. For example, I attended a weekend strategic planning meeting for Sierra Tucson involving two long days of consultations and brainstorming. At the end of the meeting, our executive director bid us goodbye and said, "Let's get you all home to your families now."

This was a truly kind, appropriate statement and certainly benign under any circumstance. For me, however, it triggered a large emotional response. I kept it to myself, but I looked around the room and counted my eighteen co-workers. I knew all of them—who was married, who was divorced, and who had kids. As I scanned all of them and thought about their circumstances, I realized I would be the only one not going home to a family. *I would be going home to no one.*

Feeling hurt and sad, I began my nonproductive thinking. *Why, out of nineteen people, was I the one who had suffered so much loss?* Driving home, I tried to reframe my thoughts but again found it a challenge.

☆☆☆

After all these long months, I was still consumed in thought about Lacey every waking moment, and her loss still felt recent. My makeup, streaked with ashen tears, proved a poor cover for my chronic distress. I knew the loss had altered me—all the way to a cellular level. I did not feel the same emotionally, physically, or spiritually. Yet, I could still look out at the world and find positive experiences. I came to learn what gifts strangers could bring me, and I encountered many who kindled a glimmer of hope in me, promising that better times were possible.

One morning, I saw an article in the newspaper about a group of women. They were all cancer survivors who made and sold angel earrings to support a foundation set up in memory of a friend who had died of ovarian cancer. I called one of the women, intending to buy earrings for my daughter's friends and support this cause. I ended up speaking with a lovely woman, and we quickly developed an easy conversation discussing her losses and mine.

Although she had never lost a child and I had never had cancer, we connected quickly around how we felt when people would tell us "you are so strong." She stated it made her angry, and I replied, "Me, too. I know exactly what you mean."

We talked about how we appreciated people's good intentions but were both tired of being strong. *Couldn't someone step in and help us?* We laughed a little during our thirty-minute conversation, and this unexpected "meeting of the souls" brought some relief into my day. I was reminded of how helpful it is to reach out to strangers and accept their outreach, too. For that day, I was not alone in my grief.

☆☆☆

However, this awareness was extremely hard for me to maintain. I was approaching eight months post Lacey and believing things were not getting *better* for me. They were simply *different*. When the crying increased, I found myself less able to get out the door and do things with others. Even more, I had trouble doing things such as walking or exercising that I knew would help me. Like an insect suspended in amber, I felt frozen in grief.

My short-term memory impairment continued to flare. I would lose my train of thought and be acutely challenged to retrieve it. Many times, I'd finally get to the grocery store to buy milk and arrive home without it. *Did I leave it in the store? In the shopping cart? Did I even buy it?*

This was disturbing but rather small when I considered the bigger picture of life. Because I knew this behavior was dissociation, a symptom of traumatic grief, I did not pummel myself over these minor inconveniences. Instead, I learned to accept the dissociation as normal.

Amid all this, I received a phone call from Andy, a boy Lacey had known and who sadly learned about her death a month after it happened. He and another boy, Corey, who was also very close to Lacey, asked to visit me. They came over one Sunday evening around five-thirty and stayed for three hours. I could tell they were worried about me and did not want to leave me alone. *They were very precious.*

I was stunned by the outpouring of emotion these two boys displayed. It staggered me. They clearly loved my daughter, and like so many others, talked about all the reasons she was so special: how she made everyone feel welcome; how she did not judge anyone; how she took time to listen; how fun she was to be around. They were both in tears throughout the evening, and of course, I was, too. They wanted to see everything they could about Lacey— her videos and pictures—and they asked to read her poetry.

They also wanted to hear how I was managing. Being incredibly careful not to be intrusive, they made attempts to cheer me up and take care of me, which moved me beyond words. I had never met these two boys, and yet I felt so close to them in such a brief time. They even offered to come back and do home repairs for me.

Again, another unexpected visit carried me through the night, and I thanked Lacey for bringing me the gift of these two boys. *What wonderful friends she had!* She had attracted, and been attracted to, good people with big hearts and lots of love to give and receive.

Knowing that giving and receiving love is key to wallowing through the grief, I tried to give it wherever I could. I was continually described as "compassionate" at work, and people complimented me, saying they did not know how I had the capacity for so much compassion. *Compassion becomes easy to give once you have experienced suffering.*

☆☆☆

I do not know of anything more disorienting for a parent than the loss of a child in a sudden and tragic way—or in any way I could imagine. Life no longer has an order to it. I can live in the same house, drive on the same roads, and go to the same job. Yet nothing, absolutely nothing, remains the same. I felt as if my life compass, which used to point in one direction, had suddenly gone haywire, the needle moving frantically all over its face. This had become my life—frenetic and chaotic. Often, I felt I had no direction.

In later years, I came to know and help several bereaved parents who suffered a stigmatized loss. Parents whose child had suicided, died of AIDS, a drug overdose, or in an alcohol-related automobile accident found themselves carrying shame over how the child died. Sadly, many do judge parents who have lost children in these ways. The stigma prevents these parents from sharing with others, and the resulting bottled-up effect and isolation further challenges them to confront the loss and develop coping skills to move forward.

As a therapist, I know we must confront our grief in order to transform it. Grief cannot be measured in depth or value; it is deeply personal and unique to each individual. We can find soothing through interpersonal processing. But many of those with a stigmatized loss struggle with the battle of shame and guilt. They avoid processing with others, which is critical to move us forward after a tragedy.

Day by day, I learned to tolerate the intolerable, and I had many setbacks. My motivation ebbed and waned. Everything was back and forth, upside down and inside out. Nothing felt stable. Years later while studying the brain and behavior, I gained insight into how the brain has a bias toward negativity and perceived negative thoughts and states. Knowing this, the now obvious pattern of mine made sense. Since the overall purpose of our brain is to help us survive, the focus on negativity serves to assess for threat.

☆☆☆

As I sought help from all directions, I attended a psychic fair one Sunday and engaged a woman reading Tarot cards. She talked to me about how doing my best was all that I could do, that if I got out of the house twice in one day, then that was my best. If another day I could not leave my house at all, then that was my best for that day. She encouraged me to let all of that be okay, that I did not need to compare my actions from day to day. I could wake up with the best of intentions to go out and end up making no movement at all. I learned from this woman that however I was, I was okay.

She reminded me that Lacey had become my guide, and that I could call on her for anything. For a long time, I had struggled with this idea with a good bit of guilt. I still held on to my role as her mother and did not want to ask for her help. Instead, I felt I needed to help *her*. This day, however, I did ask for Lacey's help. Immediately, the phone rang, and someone invited me to go out—the now predictable pattern. These were Godsends, or as mentioned earlier, Laceysends. But my Catholic guilt made sure I included God in most of my cries for help.

☆☆☆

One particularly dreadful night, I collapsed on the floor in Lacey's bedroom. I fell down on my knees with my head in my hands, sobbing uncontrollably. I called out her name and proceeded to walk around the house yelling for her. Feeling like a complete crazy woman, I eventually cried myself to sleep.

In the morning when I awoke, I went outside to get the newspaper. There on the front steps were three fluffy white feathers—just like one I'd found before. Immediately, I smiled and thanked Lacey. I found white feathers for the next two days. The next morning, there was one on my kitchen table. That same day when I went to the gym, there was a short trail of white feathers leading from where I parked my car and along the path to the front entrance. I marveled at this. *If I had this kind of experience, then others must as well.*

This taught me a great deal about keeping my eyes and ears open while not dismissing the many serendipitous experiences taking place around me. By doing so, I could find my way through the living darkness simply by keeping attuned to my heightened senses. I also gained a strong, growing belief in how the world was connected—whether it was a human connection, a plant and animal connection, a divine connection, or something else.

I became aware of having many images that were metaphoric in describing my experience. For example, one was seeing myself swimming underwater in murky, pea-green water. This vile water did not envelope me in complete darkness, as there was just enough light in the putrid color for me to discern that I had no way out. Being underwater meant I had no ability to clearly see or find the surface to get air. I could not even tell if I was going up toward relief or down further into the turbulent darkness.

These arduous days continued eight months post Lacey. One evening, I gave into my impulse to call Jack and shared what had become a repeated, private statement I had only shared with God thus far. "God has made a terrible mistake," I cried to him. "He really did get it wrong this time."

Jack, who always maintained his patience, said in a soft, calm, even-keeled voice, "Nancy, I do not know what you mean."

"What I mean," I responded, "is that I really can't live without my daughter! I just cannot keep doing this! He picked the wrong person for this role! I really can't do it!"

Hysterical. I went on and on, naming all the dreadful things in my day. I was then even more horrified, because I had worked so hard to *not* let Jack know how much I suffered. He had already seen enough, and I knew it was difficult for him to hear me in such raw, unfiltered agony. I felt great compassion for him. He had been a part of this tragedy from the beginning and stayed with me throughout, helping me in any way he could. I knew, too, that he was deeply

affected by my daughter's death. He never had an opportunity to grieve because he was always attending to me.

I went to bed that night and when I woke up, I was able to see that, once again, I had made it through another rough twenty-four hours. As the pattern seemed to be, the miracles and magic picked up again the next day.

✩✩✩

The magic continued with a woman who worked in my dentist's office. She recognized me from my name and had also seen me visit my daughter's memorial site. She came over and introduced herself, hugged me, and told me how sorry she was. She then shared with me that, in December, she had lost her twenty-nine-year-old daughter who had lived in Phoenix. I was shocked, and of course, sad for her. I hugged her back and asked how I could help. She told me the authorities still did not know the cause of death. Her daughter had died in her sleep amid questions about drugs and alcohol.

That's when I realized I had lived longer in this new existence than this woman had—almost eight months compared to her two. I shared with her some of my personal experiences, such as how long it took to get Lacey's autopsy results and what I did to contact the medical examiner and keep in touch with the investigating sheriffs. Suddenly, I realized I sounded like some kind of expert on what happens after the sudden death of a child. *How did it come to this? I never wanted to be an expert on this topic.* We exchanged contact information, and later I sent her a card.

That day, I saw another doctor and received a thorough assessment about my back pain. For years, I had struggled off and on with my back, the result of a few horse-riding accidents. At this point, my body bore the burden of all my emotional pain, as well. The compassionate doctor spent time educating me on why my back did not improve. At the end of the appointment, the doctor touched my hand and tearfully said, "I am so sorry about the loss of your daughter." I lay on the examination table looking up at the ceiling in tears.

I also saw a woman who had been providing me acupuncture treatments. Jack had been receiving acupuncture from Cary to treat his pain from multiple injuries as an athlete and mountain climber. He encouraged me to see Cary, too, believing the acupuncture could

help me. I felt out of sorts, and Cary listened while I cried. Jack was right, however. Just lying on the table in a dark room in Cary's office as she cradled my head in silence was soothing. The thirty minutes of relative calm was enormous to me at the time.

By that evening, I recognized I was surviving despite describing some days as "the worst" or "unbearable." The following day, I stayed connected to knowing how fortunate I was to have received genuine concern and validation that my depleted state made sense. This helped immensely. To have someone listen while I spoke about my loss and *not* try to fix me was the best care I received. The people around me became my lifesavers.

☆☆☆

One evening while visiting with Jack, I told him about the woman I had met in the dentist's office. I said I was amazed at how cheery she was, even while sharing that her twenty-nine-year-old daughter had been found dead. I remembered her sweet, prosodic voice, mostly because I was surprised she said she was managing okay and why: She loved her job and the dentist was especially nice and wasn't it a great day out and all sorts of incongruent statements. I felt sorry for her, knowing she really did not feel okay—that her denial was still extreme.

"Was I like that?" I asked Jack. He immediately responded, "No." Then I asked him how he perceived me, both then and now. I could tell he was uncomfortable, but this began a new line of questioning I had not yet dared approach. I really wanted to know how I presented in my grief, and Jack was the perfect person to give me feedback.

He said I moved terribly slowly, that everything about me seemed sluggish. He described my movements, my walking, and how my speech became measured. He said I frequently became so focused or obsessed about something that there was no way to reach me. He recalled many times seeing me hunched over the computer and completely detached from what was going on around me. He described me as lost in thought looking out a window and disengaged from conversation. He said I did not hide my grief, that I talked incessantly about Lacey, particularly in the first six months.

I knew these things were true, but I had little awareness of this in the moment. His feedback was kind and careful, presented without

criticism. *It really helped me to hear this.* I let him know that, and I also asked him if I still behaved like that. He hesitated, but said, "No, not so much anymore." I knew he answered this way to avoid hurting me. He was polite and wanted to feed me positive support. I realized, however, that I had really become slow. My movements and my words were carefully measured. I processed events and feelings hours later, no longer in the moment. Although he did not know it, what Jack described was genuinely acceptable to me. *I wanted this truth. I had asked him for it.*

I knew as well that I took people aback when I openly shared how I was when asked. Sometimes I answered with, "I'm really in a lot of pain today, missing my daughter. Thank you for asking." At the same time, I tried to be sensitive to the effect my honesty had on others. But I also was aware I had to be completely authentic as often as possible. I could tolerate my emotions and thoughts with increased ability when I shared them with complete honesty.

Chapter Eighteen: Letting Go

of Expectations

The raining from the eye,
The laugh of the earth,
The explosion of the soul,
The tug of war with the soul,
The giggles of a baby,
The cries of her mother.

"My Poem"
~ Lacey Jarrell

Andy Warhol once said, "In the future, everyone will be famous for fifteen minutes."

Tucson is what I'd describe as a big small town. Although strung out across the Tucson basin with a population of 900,000, Tucson is still a place where everyone seems to know one another. Stories spread like wildfire in the Catalina Mountains.

With my daughter's death, I recognized I had developed a "name." People often recognized me by seeing me at Lacey's site or by hearing about my tragedy. It was bewildering to have my fifteen minutes of fame because of a horrific tragedy. *Who would want to have a name based on being the mother of the beautiful girl who died on River Road?*

My daughter also had a great deal of fame. Her name was mentioned all over town, and so many had heard something amazing about her. Cards and supportive phone messages continued to arrive.

Despite Jack's feedback, I had little clear perception of how I presented to the world. People often told me they admired me. On a good day, I could take in that praise as a positive. On a difficult day, though, I thought, "Admired for what? For still living, working? What warrants admiration?" It was during one of those morose moments I realized I was looking for some sort of reward for my suffering. In that instant, I knew the only path to grace, dignity, and humility was one in which I had no expectations. When I focused on letting go, I felt better.

☆☆☆

At eight months, I still could not say, "I had a good day today." That I expected anything different in a short eight months speaks to the level of my impaired thinking. I did, however, have longer periods in which I felt this day was more tolerable than other days. As time passed, I realized I was formulating good memories after my precious darling's death. Any mention of my daughter still brought me to tears, but they were tears not solely immersed in misery. I had to tell people, "I still persevere with the pain, and I need to talk about and hear about my daughter. Please don't walk furtively around me." At these times, the loneliness would subside.

I continued to search in books, go to therapy, visit psychics and mediums, have my palm read—anything that might connect me further to my daughter. I found some relief in these activities, especially when the psychics and mediums and other healers all said the same thing—that Lacey was happy now, and that I could call on her and she would provide help until I adjusted to my life without her. At that point, she would need to move on.

I tackled my guilt daily and debated whether I should call on Lacey or not. Some days, my misery took me beyond these doubts, and I asked my baby girl for help again. Often it was simply to say, "Please guide me through this day and stay close. I am not doing well." My day would always get better after I requested her guidance. I also asked her questions, and often I received answers. I still could frequently hear her voice in my head.

I continued to question my sanity, but then I shrugged it off. *So what if I'm crazy?* I felt better if I believed my daughter was communicating with me. One night, I came home from work and walked from my car to the mailbox. In the dark, I could see something shiny in the driveway. I knew right away it would be a wrapper from a Hershey's chocolate kiss.

I do not know how I knew this, but I did, and I was right. I picked it up and read the word "Kisses." I had just been talking to Lacey, telling her how I missed our hugs and kisses. We always said "hello" and "goodbye" that way. When I picked up the wrapper, I believed it was Lacey sending me kisses. A year before, I never would have even noticed this wrapper. Again, I was reminded of how nothing had opened my senses, my internal radar, and my noticing of the world around me more than the loss of my daughter. I looked for her everywhere, and she was there.

☆☆☆

I was still, however, detached from the reality of my situation. Some days, I thought I only went to work and then came home and slept. On other days, I recognized how much I'd actually done in a fleeting time to manage my pain and keep my daughter's memory alive.

Many exciting things were going on around me. Tom, the reporter, was still interested in writing a story about Lacey and bereavement, and he stayed in touch. By this time, he had visited me four or five times, spent time at my house with three of Lacey's best friends, and brought in Jeff, a photographer. One afternoon, both Tom and Jeff came over, and we walked together down to Lacey's memorial site. Jeff took photos as we talked and walked.

The memorial site had become an astounding place. Every few days, different cards, handmade objects, pictures, love notes, candles, and other items were added to her site. By Valentine's Day, the site was so full of color, it was impossible to miss it if you drove on River Road.

I had never seen a roadside memorial like it! From a short distance, it appeared as a colorful carpet, designed with items of azure, magenta, violet, emerald, and jade, and glittered with viridescent trees—palo verdes, mesquites, and desert grasses. I asked Tom and Jeff what they thought about it. They, too, found it to be profound and were touched by my explanation of all the objects there. On another day, Jeff came back and walked to the site with me again to take more photos.

The boulder we were given, to which we added her name and dates along with the green star, showed up like a throne governing the blanket of color at its foundation. The rock itself pulsed with vibrancy. Its wheat color shimmered with sand rubies and specks of quartz, all accentuated by the sea green star. The protruding white cross spoke a message: *This is sacred ground to us.*

The photographer wanted me to just do what I'd normally do there on a Sunday, the day I always added something to the site. I also brought a trash bag to clean up the area, if needed.

Although I never liked to see cigarette butts or other trash tossed on the ground, I did not mind it here for that indicated someone who loved Lacey had been there. I was happy to be the site's care-taker. *It was another way I could continue taking care of my daughter.* After all, I had been doing it for almost seventeen years, and I was still her mother.

Tom and Jeff told me to call anytime if I had visits from the kids, so Jeff could come and take photos. One evening, I found out some of the girls planned to visit in the morning, so I called Jeff and he came. I was touched that he stayed for two-and-a-half hours while the girls and I told Lacey stories. We cried a little but also talked about everything from boys to makeup. His picture-taking was not intrusive at all.

The next day, Tom asked for another meeting with me. I never knew where this story was going and found it easy to trust these two men. I told them both that if no article ever developed, I was grateful that they just let me tell my tale, that they listened and conversed with compassion and kindness. It meant so much that something involving Lacey, especially something that could help others, might happen. *What a gift they gave me.*

These visits and interviews also brought hope—and something to look forward to—into my life. My only concern, which I was truly clear about with Tom, was that no one be harmed.

☆☆☆

The formation of the Lacey Jarrell Foundation was moving for-ward. Jack had contacted a lawyer with whom we had all sorts of connections. The lawyer's children had gone to St. Gregory's School, and he had been on the board of directors there. Also, one of his daughters had worked with me at Sierra Tucson.

By the end of February, the attorney had completed the paper-work to set up the corporation. I had been in contact with my accountant, who was guiding me on what I needed to submit to the IRS to get nonprofit status. Both the attorney and accountant knew my story, and the accountant had even attended Lacey's funeral. I knew that my vision of setting up a nonprofit to benefit other children would become a reality.

My dear friend, Cyndy Neighbors, gave me a push one day and said, "Get out your calendar. We're planning the first meeting of the board of directors for the Lacey Jarrell Foundation." In mid-March, a few weeks before the meeting, Jack, Cyndy, and I met at my house to focus on our mission statement and see what direction we wanted to take. I wanted to support artistic youth, and Jack's creative vision helped me see the possibilities. Cyndy was a vision-ary as well, and her input helped enormously.

Lacey was an artist. She wrote poetry, painted, drew, danced, played the piano and drums, and engaged in photography. She loved creative expression, and with that, Jack and Cyndy helped me to refine my mission statement to heighten awareness of young art-ists aged twelve to twenty-one. We sat at my dining table for two hours one Sunday and mapped out a plan for our first board meet-ing. Focused on our mission, we came up with concrete ideas on how to promote young artists so we could help them realize their pas-sion. We also talked about helping young people sell their art by holding an "Art Slam" in Tucson, for example, and bringing artist mentors into schools. We also wanted to provide scholarships as well as counseling sessions for these young people and their families.

We decided to start with one fundraiser and use the money to provide educational scholarships. This was only a first step from a preliminary outline, but we had proudly begun. The corporation was in place, and I was waiting on the IRS approval for nonprofit status. I felt grateful for Jack and Cyndy's support. And I felt blessed. *My dream was coming to fruition!*

☆☆☆

During this time, I was able to see how much I had done in only eight months to save my own life, to find meaning in Lacey's death, and to turn the tragedy into something that could help others. All this gave me another reason to keep living. I knew Lacey would be proud of me. And I hoped my son would get involved someday.

I became conscious of the potential for so much focus on my daughter that I neglected my son, who was preparing to graduate from college and talking about law school. How could I support him completely in whatever he chose to do? He did not need to be involved with the Lacey Jarrell Foundation. I just wanted him to know I considered his expertise in poetry and all forms of writing to be important, as well as his strong ability for both critical and creative thinking. If he wanted to be involved, I wanted to assure him he always had a place in any of my endeavors.

☆☆☆

During this time, I thought a lot about loss and gain in terms of human suffering and joy. Looking back on the last eight months, I became aware I was finding ways to turn my loss into a gain to bear what still seemed unbearable pain. Nothing would ever take away the enormity of losing Lacey, but I could see that good things came into my life as a result of this horrible trauma. I was definitely living my life differently. I did not like my life script as I called it— being a bereaved parent. But I could find good in some areas of my new way of being in the world. My capacity for compassion and forgiveness had grown substantially. There was irony in this belief, however, as I was aware it was a self-serving coping skill to avoid any focus on my failures. Doing so exacerbated my grief.

Each day, I hoped to go to bed having cleaned up any conflict that might have arisen with anyone during the day. I told many that I loved them, and it was true. I felt a great deal of love for most people, whether I knew them well or not. It became easy to forgive people for their humanness and not carry resentment. I cared genuinely about what happened to those around me, whether they were friends, patients at Sierra Tucson, staff I worked with or supervised, or acquaintances passing through my life day after day.

☆☆☆

Over recent months, I had it in my mind to find some dazzling, green, battery-operated lights to adorn Lacey's memorial site. I looked for them every time I was in a store that sold decorative lighting. One evening, while shopping for a thank-you card in a small gift shop in the front entrance of a restaurant, I turned the corner. On display by the cash register was a large candle encircled by pink lights. As I checked it out, I noticed these lights were battery operated, so I asked the clerk if they had any green lights. Of course, they did!

I felt exhilarated. *Lacey will love these lights.* I purchased them and immediately drove to her memorial site. It was dark, but the solar lighting my ex-husband and son had placed there allowed me to set up the new green lights. I liked being there at night when my senses were heightened. Dark and quiet. I was vigilant about every sound or perceived movement and how the air blew—or didn't. Then I encircled the big boulder with the green lights. *Beautiful.*

A few nights later while driving home from work, I noticed the lights had gone out. *How disappointing!* I stopped my car and walked over to the boulder, but in the dark, I could not see well enough to find the battery packs and check them. So the next day I returned. As I crossed the road to the site, the area was very still and quiet. I easily found the two-battery packs, and to my surprise, the first battery I placed in both battery sets caused the lighting to work immediately. My disappointment turned to joy. *Such a simple thing brought me much joy!*

At that same moment, the wind chimes behind the rock where I stood chimed energetically. I turned to see them dancing and interpreted this as Lacey telling me, "Good job, Mama. I love them, too." The chiming did not last long, and the air suddenly became still again. *She had stopped by to offer her love and support, and then moved on.*

I walked back to my car and looked back at the site. My eyes filled with tears, and I knew I had done something Lacey would love. Then I drove to my lonely, empty house but cried no more that night. *The deep connection I felt with my daughter was everything to me.*

☆☆☆

Another week went by, but during that time, I felt a buzz in the air. It was February 28th, the day I received a significant salary adjustment *and* two checks from my parents' estate. I could hardly fathom the estate was finally closing. When I looked at the checks, though, I felt a minimal amount of relief but no joy. I was grateful to have the money, of course, but it did not repair my ruptured heart. *Despite my gratitude, these checks could not bring my daughter back.*

The money also represented a reason my sister and I were once again estranged. The reality hit me again that these pieces of paper could not bring back my parents. *I would have gladly exchanged the money to have my parents and my Lacey alive and in my life.*

I continued to question my ability to keep engaging in life. At times, I felt inconsolable. I was aware of broken heart syndrome, also known as Takotsubo Cardiomyopathy. The syndrome is caused by intense suffering from loss, which triggers the brain to distribute chemicals that weaken heart tissue. It can also lead to severe, short-term heart muscle failure.

With broken heart syndrome, one sometimes feels a pain in the chest that is vastly different from having a heart attack. Although I had no somatic symptoms, I felt only a small step away from dying from a broken heart.

Chapter Nineteen: Synchronicity

Her long hair loose and languid like her
A morning unlike the clear one.
When the sun was the only witness
As her body flew onto the burning pavement.
White skin opposed black car and tar.

"A Mother's Lament"
~ Nancy Jarrell

I had set myself up—pretending to be content and then feeling angry when people commented I was doing well. This became another paradox in my dealing with loss.

Around this time, I started researching weeklong programs to address my grief, but I could not find anything that appealed to me or I could afford. As my disappointment increased, I received an e-mail one day from a well-respected therapist I knew. In it, she told me about an intensive program she would be facilitating on a ranch in southern Arizona. Over five days, it would offer an opportunity to work on my grief and trauma within the modality of psychodrama. I signed up at once.

The workshop turned out to be intense emotionally. Psychodrama as a modality, being an action-oriented or action-modeled therapeutic intervention, differs from traditional individual talk therapy. It involves group participation, as a protagonist is invited to work on a personal issue through the use of drama.

For my psychodrama, I chose people to play members of my family of origin and, of course, Lacey. Two others played my horse and me. I went in and out of the roles, providing lines for each actor that approximated what my family members would say in a certain situation. I also instructed the actors on how my family members would move.

These extremely powerful sessions hit at the core of my emotions. For the first time since the loss of Lacey, I was actually able to stop performing in the presence of others, to stop trying to look good, and to stop pretending I was managing okay. I was *not*. At one point, I ended up on the floor in the fetal position like an infant. I cried and cried. I had not done this in front of anyone before. The position and my inability to collect myself in the presence of others was unlike anything I had ever experienced. I was as torn open as a butchered deer and could not self-soothe. The therapists identified me as having experienced severe trauma.

Humans and animals respond to traumatic events by fighting, fleeing, or freezing. Sometimes we do all three, with no order to it or any identified time and space among these three possibilities. We instinctively select whatever action will provide us the best chance for survival. The limbic system area of our brain is involved in this process to find safety, particularly the structure known as the amygdala. The amygdala—the alarm center of the brain—attaches emotional meaning to content it receives from the thalamus—the relay center of the brain. It alerts us to danger and sends information to the hippocampus where conscious memory is stored. The hippocampus further evaluates the threat and relays this information to the orbitofrontal cortex (OFC) for additional evaluation of the threat's severity. The OFC is responsible for the body's response to any threat of survival. The process results in instant physiological changes when we are confronted with terror to supply us the best chance of survival.

Fleeing or fighting are primary reactions and the freeze state, also known as toxic immobility, is often the last resort when we can't engage in the other two responses. The therapists saw me as being in "freeze" mode, and when I said I wanted to work on my grief, their agenda was to "unfreeze" me—get me to move. To pick up my pace, or even to move at times, was challenging for me. I held a rigid and stiff body posture, although I was not aware of this before having it pointed out to me. I held my fists tight and hunched over in a shame-like position. I carried a constant physical pain throughout my body but easily disconnected from it as the physical pain seemed minimal compared to my emotional state.

My "freeze" state was another contradiction. Despite being frozen, I also felt I was thawing. The volume of tears I cried—in fact, crying at all—was not typical for me, having been groomed in childhood to be stoic.

The therapists facilitating the workshop developed a plan for each participant's drama. The treatment plan for me was that Lacey and I would "dance," and then dance with the whole group of people in the workshop. I chose a woman I knew (she had children at my daughter's school) to play Lacey. Perfect. She happened to be dressed all in green that day, which was almost a sign. We were given long, silky, colorful scarves to wear as we danced. I felt like I was truly dancing with Lacey as tears rained down my face. I could not stop them, nor did I want to.

I experienced many powerful insights at the retreat. It became clear I had been in the frozen state for the last several months. I recalled how still I sat in my chair and was often dissociated—not fully present in life—as I continued to live in two worlds. I knew I needed deeper work to continue moving through this unrelenting pain. In the meantime, I concentrated on moving my body more to get out of the "freeze."

When I came home from the ranch to my empty house, I was acutely aware of coming home to that unfamiliar vacancy. Sadness overwhelmed me again.

Luckily, Jack took me out to dinner that night, and we reconnected. Our relationship, however, remained conflicted. I did not know how long he would be in my life, especially since he was still planning to sell his home and move to Colorado. I deduced that, if he cared about me, he would not leave. I knew this black-and-white thinking to be limiting, flawed. Yet, the simplicity of it seemed to be the best I could do when it came to my personal life.

In the prefrontal cortex, the frontal lobe focuses on assessment or figuring things out. But in terror when the reptilian brain is activated, little activity happens in the rational brain. I seemed to bounce back and forth between these two parts as I prepared myself for another loss.

The same night I came home from the retreat, one of my neighbors stopped by to bring me the mail he had picked up in my absence. He and his wife had been supportive of me during this time. I had forgotten, though, that he had badgered me about my lack of approval to have a speed bump placed in front of my home. It was a tedious "homeowners association" drama.

When he came over, I met him outside. Because it was bedtime, I was dressed in my pajamas and really did not want to visit with him. He gave me my mail, and I thanked him. As he walked away, he said, "Can I ask you something?"

"What?" I replied.

"Well, it is none of my business," he began, "but don't you think it's time to move your child's memorial site off of the road?" I took two steps back. He came toward me, and I put up my hand as I told him to back away.

Very clearly and with an expression of fury, I said, "That memorial site is not going anywhere. It is permanent. It will be there forever. It is cemented into the ground. And, yes, this is none of your business."

With that, I slammed the door and went into my house, breathing hard and shaking with anger and disbelief. I wanted to forgive people. If I considered what might be going on in their world and tried to understand their intent, it would be easier to forgive. In this case, I struggled to find anything I could remotely understand.

☆☆☆

During the times I perceived myself fragmenting, I was aware I felt like I was little, infantile, childlike, and often on the edge of collapsing. My body felt like a sieve that had filled and could no longer filter my grief. My co-workers commented that I looked sad. I *was* sad. I often felt like my body would explode from all the pain and sorrow.

I had started letting my feelings show more. For example, while at dinner one night with two of Lacey's friends, I cried through the whole meal. They cried, too. I was aware of how slow my speech was that night, and I remember talking to them from a place of wisdom. I shared my thoughts on life and death and what it's like to be a teenager and lose a friend. (As mentioned, I had lost one of my best girlfriends in a car accident when I was a teen.) I told them how being a mother was for me and talked of my continuing belief that *Hell was on earth*. I was in it.

I also knew it was vital to show compassion for others. Somehow, despite my own pain, I knew if I could still hold space for compassion, it might take me out of this Hell someday. Lacey's friends told me I reminded them of Lacey, that they needed to hang on to me because I was all they had left of her. I felt happy when they shared this. *I had become a mother to many.* But nothing could replace the love I felt for my two children.

☆☆☆

Then I received another reprieve. Once again, having reached the lowest of lows and feeling at my most vulnerable and fragile, encouraging things began to happen. My sessions with the reporter occurred more often. Tom spoke with many of the people I had mentioned. He interviewed Ernie; his mother Mel McBeath; the two paramedics on the scene, Alan DeKalb and Paul Smith; the main witness, Michelle St. Rose; three of Lacey's friends, Emily Heintz, Christina McAlpin, and Megan Shaw. He had also spoken with my ex-husband and my son as well as arranged photography sessions with me and Lacey's close friends.

One day, he asked if I'd be willing to be videoed for the paper's website. I was scheduled to meet with videographer Andrew Satter and also instructed to call Jeff, who had become "my photographer" whenever something went on that lent itself to the story. I said to Tom, "This is becoming a much bigger deal than I expected."

"Yes, Nancy," he replied.

☆☆☆

My story was scheduled to run at the end of March as a two-part series, beginning on the front page in the Sunday paper. It focused on the tragedy and the theory of six degrees of separation—how one event brought a group of people together who did not know each other but were all profoundly affected. The series examined how our lives had woven together in both positive and painful ways. One of the installments was headlined "Suffering Can Make Us Wise: Lacey's Gifts: In Her Memory, Lives Are Transformed."

Other things were coming together. One night, my friend Cyndy invited me to an art walk—a walking tour of the city's best galleries, museums, and storefronts. Cyndy was the friend who had called a month earlier and said, "You won't believe it! I have just been commissioned by the owners of Gallery Row to support the property with bigger advertising and attendance. I've spoken with them about featuring a nonprofit organization, and we've decided we'd like the Lacey Jarrell Foundation to be a part of it!"

Neither Cyndy nor I could believe it. My dream had been to have the Green Star Gallery—Lacey's gallery—in Gallery Row. This art walk was her first attempt at bringing more attention to the area. She had talked with many of the gallery owners about my story and received feedback on how they would like to have the not-yet-formed Lacey Jarrell Foundation be a part of what was happening.

I invited Jeff, the photographer, to the art walk where I met Cyndy and two of Lacey's friends. I had never seen so many people in this area, even during open exhibits in the evenings. Cyndy had done a superior job advertising the event.

Feeling particularly emotional that night, I cried a lot. Many people there knew who I was, including my neighbors who had given me the use of their property for Lacey's memorial. They owned one of the galleries and stepped out of their shop to greet me. *So much Lacey energy in the air!*

It became a night of hope, yet I knew I could not hold back my tears, even at a public event. I also knew that crying was okay, that my tears and pain had become more acceptable to me. This had shifted from having been groomed to hide difficult emotions. *"Big girls don't cry"*—words that no longer held power over me.

☆☆☆

Over the next week, so much synchronicity happened that I felt nearly overwhelmed. I had an undeniable sense that nothing in my life, absolutely nothing, occurred by accident. Everything around me was Other Directed or, rather, Lacey Directed.

The day after the art walk, I still felt dreadfully close to my pain, and I had been called into meetings throughout the day. That meant coming in and out of my office more than usual. At one point, I felt I was breaking. When I walked back into my office after lunch, I noticed a folded piece of white paper on the floor by my chair—a note written to me about six months earlier by a staff member at Sierra Tucson. It said, "I am so moved by your courage, and the way you carry yourself with such integrity and grace during this time of tragedy in your life. I know Lacey is very proud of you." That message filled me with emotion and comfort. *But how did the note get on my floor? Hadn't I taken it home long ago and placed it in my special box of kind notes and letters?*

That morning, I had been talking to Lacey (as always) on my drive to work and saying I was sorry I couldn't hold myself together better. I worried that my pain and tears kept her tethered to me and might prevent her from moving on. But once I saw the note, I interpreted it as a communication from Lacey telling me, "Mom, I am proud of you."

I thought about the people still in my life I had known either for a long time or in the few years before Lacey's death. Then I concluded that all the new people coming into my world had great meaning, and that none of them were here by accident. Every one of them seemed to have been purposely introduced to me, either to teach me something or for me to teach them. As souls, we're all woven together to form a greater purpose.

Sometimes, I felt crazy when I thought this way, but everything seemed magnified a hundred times. The universe was sending me messages from everywhere, all to help me heal *if I just paid attention.* And even though I knew I would never get over Lacey's death, I could see hope for engaging in life without her. Less and less, I was counting the days on the calendar until I died.

Chapter Twenty: Our Grief

Is Unique

Her absence is like the sky,
Spread over everything.

~ C. S. Lewis

One night when Jack came over to pick me up for dinner, he walked in adrenalized. He paced the floor rapidly and then handed me a DVD. "I don't know how this came to me," he said, "but this was without question meant for you."

The book and DVD The Secret was about to become an international sensation. By spring 2007, Rhonda Byrne's "New Thought" book had reportedly sold more than nineteen million copies in forty languages plus two million DVDs. The premise was that the law of attraction could bring people what they wanted—from happiness to wealth.

However, neither Jack nor I had heard of it. He just told me he found this DVD in his mailbox; it had no return address and no note. After viewing it, he said, "Nancy, all I can say is you *need* to watch this." He kept emphasizing that certain segments convinced him, without a doubt, the importance of watching it. He told me no more.

I put the DVD on the table so we wouldn't be late for our dinner reservation, and then I remembered I had not opened my own mail yet. I had received a small package as well, but it had a return address. When I opened it, I found a lovely card and a CD. At first, I did not know who it was from, but as I read the card, I saw it came from a New York psychologist whom I had met a year before. A group of professionals had visited Sierra Tucson to learn about our clinical work with patients. I had given them a presentation on equine-assisted psychotherapy, a process that utilizes the relationship with a horse as a metaphor for how people behave in life. This powerful, experiential therapeutic modality supports people in their healing.

I had spent many years as an equine therapist and had once managed the equine department. Equine therapy, which is facilitated on the ground, does not require participants to have any knowledge or experience with horses. They had always been part of my life in some way, yet after Lacey's death, I had dropped all my involvement with horses.

But recent messages I received indicated I needed to be around horses again. These came in a variety of ways. Even the previous month, one of the mediums told me Lacey said I needed to go back to the horses. And the theme of horses had come up again in my psychodrama work.

Just the night before I received the psychologist's package, I found myself in my bedroom, quiet and still, with my head in my hands. *I don't know what to do!* I stood like that for a couple of minutes. When I lifted my head, the first thing I saw was a line of stuffed animal horses on the top shelf of my dresser. They seemed to stare back at me.

"I need to go back to the horses," I heard. I acknowledged this silently, but replied, "I don't know how to do that." I didn't have the energy to do that, not understanding I didn't need to *do* anything with the horses—just *be* with them. That always made me feel better. *It was simply being with horses that I needed.*

The psychologist wrote kind, lovely words saying she knew of my loss and was thinking about me. She also recounted what a life-changing experience she'd had ("powerful, unforgettable") when I did an equine therapy session with her. Again, I heard the message about getting back to the horses.

She had lost her thirty-four-year-old nephew to suicide two years earlier. On the enclosed CD, she read some of her journal writings regarding his passing. I listened to it the next day while driving to work. The words were painful to hear, but the CD also incorporated some of her music and piano playing. The lyrics to one of her songs instructed, "Listen to things, not just beings." This made sense to me, for I was keenly aware that my experiences in the environment, not just people, provided me with guidance and hope. Clearly, she was using listening and playing music as a healing method.

I was encouraged to study the importance of sound as a healer. Although not conscious of it in the moment, days after listening to this CD, I researched the effect of sound on our brains and began incorporating sound healing into the neuroplasticity treatment model I was developing. I learned that certain rhythms and tones can calm our nervous systems and help us with emotional regulation. I also learned that slow music with a repetitive ten-second cycle calms the listener because the cycle matches the body's natural ten-second wave cycle of blood pressure control. That's when I knew I also needed to return to music in an attentive, conscious way rather than dismiss or avoid it. Until then, I believed my enjoying music was disrespectful to Lacey.

The psychologist described a series of events following her nephew's death that could not be labeled as coincidental. Rather, they seemed to be messages or communications from her nephew that helped her through the grieving process. They also supported her belief that when we die, our physical body stops, but our souls do not—that we remain connected. Her experience certainly mirrored mine.

☆☆☆

After dinner that night, Jack dropped me at home, and I watched *The Secret* DVD. It was about the secret of life featuring a blonde woman (Rhonda Byrne) who spoke about her grief after her father had died unexpectedly. *I am blonde, and my father had died unexpectedly, which made me feel a little apprehensive.*

She went on to say that's when she found the secret to life. The scene shows her searching through an old trunk, flashing to a note written on white paper that said, "Mama, this will help you. Xoxo."

My mouth dropped open. I grabbed my belly and began to rock forward and backward, trying to comfort myself. I was reeling. Jack was right. This movie *was* for me, even if it only conveyed this message. Lacey always called me "Mama," and she signed her notes to me with x's and o's. The handwriting even looked like hers.

The note had absolutely no relevance to the movie; it didn't mention this woman having a child or anything about the note. It simply showed up just at the beginning of the movie and then again at the end—only for a brief flash but long enough for me to read. *Astounding!* I broke into tears.

The film is presented in documentary style, with many inspirational stories and interviews of people who live their lives by the idea that "thoughts become things, so think the good ones." Although the concept was not new to me, I appreciated the instruction on how we can manifest what we want by visualizing it. The movie stressed living with a sense of gratitude rather than focusing on what we do *not* have. It was a good reminder of how *visualizing* positive outcomes often *result* in positive outcomes.

I wrote down some thoughts and ways to practice this, even though I had already started this process. The universe—or Lacey—was pelleting me with information to help me in my most desperate moments.

☆☆☆

The next day, I toured other art galleries with Cyndy and her son, Lee. It was wonderful to be with both of them as Lee was also my son's best friend of many, many years. We went to a different part of Tucson than I typically visited. I did not know this gallery area, modeled on the warehouse style, even existed. Everything I saw there related to our ideas for the Lacey Jarrell Foundation. *Fascinating!*

There, I saw young people working on art projects in one studio, and I spoke to two of them. One young man in his early twenties excitedly told me about his art, saying, "Art is about connecting body and mind." He was intriguing and obviously bright and talented. The other person, a fifteen-year-old girl, wanted to get involved in community art.

On the wall was a large mural, and people were invited to add to it. Both young people encouraged me to do so. Even when I explained I was not an artist, they still encouraged me, telling me I was an artist but didn't recognize it. Timidly, I added a green star to the mural as I shared my loss with them and told them I wanted to help young artists.

Then the young man handed me a piece of paper with his e-mail address, saying if I felt comfortable contacting him to do so.

"I'm a master's level student at Berkeley majoring in studio art," he said. "I will be back in Tucson after graduation this summer and would love to help you with your foundation." That touched me, and I felt I had made an important connection.

I heard that this young man had just lost his roommate in an accident three weeks before. While sharing this with me, he smiled and made statements I found confusing such as: "I am so happy for him" and "He is the greatest, he is soaring now, and I'm glad to know he is loving his existence." I asked him how he was able to access all this positivity in the face of loss. His affect changed suddenly as he made eye contact with me. With his head slightly tilted, he asked, "Have you read *Intra Muros?*" "No," I responded. He followed with, "You should read it. It will really help you." I made a point of writing down the title to research later.

✰✰✰

While I was walking through other galleries, my cell phone rang. It was Alan DeKalb. We had not talked in about a month, and I was happy and surprised to hear from him. He told me he only had a minute, but that he and Paul Smith—the other paramedic I had come to know—were at a hotel in Tucson for three days attending a program called Landmark Forum.

I had some familiarity with this program but not enough. Alan said it was helping them find direction in their lives, and that part of the program directed them to choose one person with whom to share what they had learned. They had chosen me, and Alan was calling to invite me for the last evening of the program. I was moved. Before saying yes, I wanted to check out this program on the internet. Although I certainly did not know everything, I already had sophisticated knowledge about group healing through my career and my own experiences in therapy. These men had become woven into my life. If I were to attend Landmark Forum, it would be because of them.

After I hung up, Cyndy and I headed toward the car. Suddenly, she stopped. She had spotted a woman in the distance coming our way.

"Nancy, I can't believe this," she started, "but the woman walking toward us was the mother of one of Lee's elementary school friends. I have not thought of her in years. Her son died at nine in a fire in their garage."

Cyndy looked stunned as she approached the woman and reached out to her. They hugged, and then Cyndy introduced us. I was quiet as they spoke, my thoughts full of compassion and pain for this woman as I envisioned her tragedy. We discussed neither her loss nor mine, but she did say, "I'm standing on two feet now, and I'm doing fine." I did not know if she was referring to her loss, but her statement gave me great hope.

As Cyndy and I went on our way, I knew that we shared the same thought—that all these things around us could not be dismissed as coincidence. Jack understood this, too. I did not know where all of this was going, but I did feel some peace as I left for home that afternoon. I also felt overwhelmed. I asked the universe to slow down for a minute so I could write about these things and return to my life's new pace to manage.

☆☆☆

Like a bolt of lightning, Lacey's presence manifested time and time again, startling my raw emotions right out of me. For days, I felt energy all around me, as if a series of electrical charges had gone off one after the other. Each of them seemed to represent my many serendipitous experiences. During these times, I was elated knowing Lacey was around me.

My life was moving forward. In one quick week, Cyndy, Jack, and I had developed a board of directors and agenda, found a meeting location, and held the first official meeting for the Lacey Jarrell Foundation. During the meeting, we planned a fundraising event for the following month. Suddenly, it was no longer just an idea we tossed around, but a reality. None of the people I selected for the board knew each other, but they connected quickly and well, and they complimented me on how I had picked just the right people with the right skills. I did not feel I had put it together at all; it just happened Lacey-style.

I knew the big newspaper series of articles was coming out in one week, mentioning our nonprofit organization. *I could not believe all of this was happening.*

☆☆☆

My session with the videographer, Andrew Satter, went extremely well. Andrew had won several awards for his masterful videos. He was adept at relaxing me, which made the videoing feel casual, with no pressure or expectation. Part of the shoot took place at my home and the rest at Lacey's memorial site. Andrew and I connected immediately and stayed in touch long after the piece was done. It was titled after some words I had spoken: "God Needed a Really Good Person."

I believed something extremely important would come out of all this publicity, and I anticipated major changes would follow. I hoped they would be uplifting, not just for me but for everyone around me who felt wounded in one way or another.

At this point, I began to experience some psychic change that came on abruptly. I suddenly found it difficult to look at some of her photos, placed all over the house. I did not go into her bedroom as often as before, and I even stopped visiting her accident site so frequently. *What was going on?*

As I continued in grief therapy, I was told that, to heal, I needed to complete my relationship with her. The way this was worded triggered me into a defensive thought. *You are asking me to end my relationship with my daughter? Never!* Of course, I did not want to finish any relationship with her, but I did understand that because it had been interrupted, I needed to do some work around what I missed about her as well as process the dreams I held for her. They would never come to pass.

As a therapist and clinical supervisor, I do not recommend suggesting to someone struggling with the loss of a loved one that she "complete the relationship." This is absolutely *not* a requirement for healing. And simply thinking about the dreams I had for Lacey's future was excruciating for me. I had not thought about what could have been, but rather who Lacey was and how her life ended. I did not complete this exercise.

Through my grief recovery program, though, I gained insight into the subjectivity of my process. I had long understood that engaging in comparison was unproductive. Why compare one person's grief to another? If two people lost their mothers, it did not mean they each knew how the other felt. If one had a strained and distant relationship with her mother, and the other had a close, connected relationship with daily involvement, the emotional responses to these losses would be quite different. We cannot generalize about death and how people feel. I only know how I felt. No one else could really know. Because each person's grief is unique, how we do it is simply that—how we do it.

☆☆☆

While researching different responses to grief and loss, I came across the work of Dr. Kenneth Doka, a professor of gerontology at the College of New Rochelle Graduate School. Dr. Doka wrote about how people responded to significant life upheavals. In conjunction with Professor Terry Martin, they identified two primary grieving styles. One they called "the intuitive griever" and the other "the instrumental griever."[15]

Doka and Martin described the intuitive griever as one who easily and openly expresses feelings, sorrow, and anguish with tears; does not fear seeking out others for support; and allows the time to experience the pain and angst fully. They described the *instrumental* griever as one who feels grief but is less comfortable with sharing feelings and expressing emotions, tending to rely on logic and problem solving as coping methods to loss. Further, they described the instrumental griever as seeking solitude to grieve, not wanting to emote in public, pushing aside emotions, using humor to cope, and tending to need physical means to express their grief. The two styles are each stereotyped as female and male, respectively. Doka and Martin further agreed that these styles occurred along a continuum and that blended styles not determined by gender also existed.

Regardless of these results, though, it seems evident that grieving depends on many external and internal factors, as individuals grieve differently.

Colombia Engineering and Colombia University Irving Medical Center published an article[16] in *Social Cognitive and Affective Neuroscience* about *avoidant* grievers and how they unconsciously block thoughts of the deceased during mind wandering. Avoidant grief is a coping mechanism some people use by making repeated, focused efforts to stop themselves from thinking about the loss.

This type of griever may not have any reminders of the deceased in the home, does not talk about the loss, and/or no longer goes to places where he or she will be reminded of the deceased—all conscious efforts. Until this Colombia University research came out, it was not known if these grievers could control their thoughts unconsciously about the loss, essentially blocking specific content. The researchers demonstrated that avoidant grievers are capable of unconsciously monitoring and blocking the content of their mind wandering. They were further able to identify how unconscious thought suppression occurs. According to the research, trying to avoid the grieving process is not healthy. "This kind of tailoring of mind-wandering likely exhausts mental energy and leads to time periods when the thoughts actually do break through."[17]

In addition, we know that experiencing earlier losses shapes how we manage grief. Aside from the loss of a loved one, our experiences with losing a job, relationships, health, divorce, relocation, finances, lifestyles, and more can all affect the psychological coping strategies we employ. Our culture, religious beliefs, ethnicity, and how we saw others grieve losses while growing up also influence our response to loss. Many psychologists and neuroscientists believe that our nervous systems have evolved to being vigilant about novel, unexpected, and surprising stimuli. Further, some believe the brain is wired to ignore repetitive negative experiences to conserve energy, which fits with the brain's purpose of continuing the species. Current research in war-torn countries in which death and loss of loved ones occur regularly show that some survivors have become so familiar with death, they are desensitized to the trauma surrounding them. For these people, losing a loved one is not new, novel, or unexpected.

In psychology, grief has been categorized into a variety of subtypes based on the length of time symptoms persist. I have found these definitions limiting and unhelpful. Grievers who continue to have symptoms after the defined time period may see themselves as having a disorder that, in turn, can exacerbate symptoms. Grief becomes pathologized. This, I believe, is a disservice for those like me who define grief as a normal response to loss.

To be specific, the term "normal grief" is defined as lasting approximately two months. "Complicated grief" is defined as lasting six months or longer, and "chronic grief" is permanent. Loss has also been described as "ambiguous." This describes family members who understand their loved one is physically absent but still believe that person is psychologically present. I fit in this category as well.

☆☆☆

In 2008, I saw a flier on the board at work for a conference in Phoenix called "Body, Mind, & Soul: Trauma and Mourning After A Child's Death." The conference was described as a unique multidisciplinary conference for grief and trauma professionals and bereaved families. I was intrigued.

The conference was organized by the MISS Foundation, a non-profit founded in 1996 by Dr. Joanne Cacciatore, who had lost a child. There, I was moved by the speakers I heard and also the bereaved parents I interacted with individually and in group sessions. One speaker, Dr. Stacy Teruya, a professor and program director at Charles Drew University of Medicine and Science spoke of his neuropsychological research relevant to grief. Dr. Teruya found that "chronic grief" originates in the dopamine area of the brain. He described dopamine as similar to adrenaline and, although we think of dopamine as a pleasure circuit of the brain, it also controls how we experience both pleasure and pain. Dr. Teruya spoke of chronic grievers as having a mindset of "I will not give up my deceased child or spouse." This refusal to let go may be activating neurons possibly giving this stance and memories of the loved one an addiction-like quality. The American Society of Addiction Medicine defines addiction as a primary, chronic disease of the brain; particularly involving the brain's reward, motivation, and memory circuitry involving dopamine pathways.[18] Boosts in dopamine from drugs as well as certain behaviors produce a "high" that compels some to seek that "high" feeling again, despite knowing the behavior places them at risk for severe consequences. The pursuit of a reward is pathological as an inability to even recognize significant problems with one's behavior results in a dysfunctional emotional response when others who care attempt to intervene. Those in chronic or permanent grief receive a payoff—that is, the brain experiences a reward when dopamine is released.

Although the dopamine pathway has mostly been associated with reward and pleasure, an experiment conducted in 2006 at the University of Michigan[19] first revealed that an extremely elevated level of dopamine was released in subjects who reported being in the greatest amount of pain. This tells us both pleasure and pain are engaged with the same brain circuitry.

Chapter Twenty-One:

Nine Months Post Lacey

And the stone word fell
On my still-living breast.
Never mind, I was ready.
I will manage somehow.

Today I have so much to do.
I must kill memory once and for all,
I must turn my soul to stone,
I must learn to live again—

Unless . . . Summer's ardent rustling
Is like a festival outside my window.
For a long time I've foreseen this
Brilliant day, deserted house.

"The Sentence"
~ Anna Akhmatova

At nine months post Lacey, I was clear that even as the one-year mark drew closer, it would not make an enormous difference in my grieving. The notion that all one must do is live through each anniversary and holiday for one year is nothing but a myth. I continued to feel encased in the utter and complete loneliness of missing her. Since my parents died, I had felt like an orphan in some ways. With my sister and I estranged and my brother's death some years before, I had less family I could count on to be here for me.

My other brother, who lived in Florida, would have come to my aid in a minute if I asked for his help. But I could not and did not. He had his own trials. His sweet little daughter, Hannah, had been born eleven months before Lacey died and approximately three months after our parents died. Lacey and I had flown to Florida to meet Hannah not long after her birth. My brother and his wife were always exceptionally good to us. It had been a precious time.

My son, of course, was my family, but he did not stay in close touch with me all the time. I often had to call him for several days before he got back to me, as he was studying with all the self-discipline he could summon. I knew he was determined to finish college, and I imagined that being around me was often more painful than helpful.

I had depended a lot on Jack but understood he still had his own emotional pain and grief after ending his long marriage. No one had done more for me to honor Lacey and take care of me in the immediate days and months after her death, but, of course, he had to move on and live his life. Also, I did not like feeling dependent on him to medicate my emotions, which he could not do anyway. I often felt conflicted. At times, I felt he was already gone. *Why spend any time worrying about being left again?* I imagined it had already happened, and I still survived.

Losing Jack seemed like a moderate inconvenience compared to losing Lacey. *Abandonment and rejection—one and the same, really, and perhaps our greatest collective human fear.* Although no one is immune from these happening, the way we experience abandonment and rejection can make all the difference throughout our lifetime. It often happens that we abandon ourselves. I see this in my work with addicts and recognized how I also did this when active in my addiction years before. As I often tell my patients, "If we have experienced abandonment, we will inevitably abandon, and sometimes this translates to abandoning ourselves."

☆☆☆

One late Sunday afternoon, I received an emergency phone call telling me about a serious patient injury at Sierra Tucson. I jumped in my car and headed up to the hospital. On the way, the nurse called back to say the man had been pronounced dead. She did not have all the details yet. I immediately went into my focused, take-care-of-business mode mentality. *Feel nothing, Nancy. Just do your* job. *You have a crisis here.*

I called any staff members who lived close to the hospital and asked them to go to the facility. I then called some of the other administrators, knowing chaos would ensue. When I arrived, patients were crying and screaming. Our trauma therapists were attending to patients and two staff members. The sheriff had already arrived and sequestered several patients as witnesses.

We met with all the patients and visiting family members in a large group, then broke into smaller groups to help people process their feelings. I took on some of the hardest cases—two young women in the throes of panic attacks. As a clinical administrator, I engaged the victim's family, an aunt, an uncle, and a girlfriend who had arrived for visitation. They were clearly in shock; this event was devastating for them.

I suddenly found myself in the same hospital where I had received the news about Lacey, but in the reverse role. *Why did the universe give this surreal experience to me?* Once again, I did not want it. I felt re-traumatized. I did a decent job with the family despite my own distress, and after three hours I was able to convince them to leave the property and head home to rest.

The deceased's girlfriend was particularly upset. Screaming, she let out an eerie, keening wail, and veered from anger to tears, trying to make sense of it all. I related to her completely. She wanted to see his body, just as I did with Lacey. She wanted to sleep in the bed where he had slept. After locating his clothing, I gave her his T-shirt and a pair of sunglasses, which provided minimal comfort.

Finally, although she towered over me, I was able to walk her down the halls and out the door to the uncle's car. That's when it hit me like an anvil in free fall. *Now I was in the caretaker role. I was walking someone else down the same hallways, to the same parking lot, that I had been walked down nine months before.* My body struggled, and I felt the trauma plunge into my back and skitter down my legs. I was in physical pain. I held back the emotional pain.

The next day, I stayed home from work with a significant degree of back and leg pain—the parts of my body that carried trauma. I felt heavy and burdened with this new layer of physical pain. I prayed for the patient and family members. One moment, they were happily coming to see their loved one and suddenly their world changed.

As I continued to research the brain and specifically the brain's response to exposure to trauma, I learned more about the trauma memory and how it is remembered through the senses and the body. Trauma finds a path into our internal physiological system and holds the story of what happened. Depending on the individual and past life experiences, someone exposed to a traumatic event may no longer be able to self-regulate (emotions and impulses). As the trauma memory is fractured and, to some extent, stored in the body, it's critical that those treating trauma survivors understand that verbalizing the story does not resolve any resulting symptoms. There should be no expectation by the clinician to receive a patient's complete and detailed trauma narrative in a logical, linear format. Asking the patient to do so can be re-traumatizing and shame-inducing as it is unlikely someone faced with terror could remember every aspect of the experience. Remembering is not required for beneficial treatment. What is frequently helpful to survivors is assistance in learning to self-regulate and to gain power over any flashbacks or intrusive thoughts, which can render the patient helpless as she experiences a past event as though it were happening in the present.

In 2007, I found a recently published book called *The Body Bears the Burden* by Dr. Robert C. Scaer. Dr. Scaer brilliantly describes the plight of someone in terror and the fight-flight-freeze response as he wrote: "People who report symptoms of shock and numbness after a traumatic event, and exhibit symptoms of dissociation, are actually in the freeze response at the time."[20] He further spoke to the freeze state as something that can last for years. "In fact, I believe that the most common complaint in current medical practice, that of persistent and unexplained chronic pain, has its roots in the persistent changes in brain circuitry associated with unresolved trauma, and the continued tendency for dissociation to occur in the face of stress or threat."[21]

I went to therapy a few days after this patient's death, and for the first time, I did some focused expressive anger work using a foam bat. I held it over my head and smashed it down onto two large pillows. I hesitated at first, believing it unacceptable to share so much anger.

But as my anger emerged, I dived into this exercise. As I let go, I suddenly realized I carried an enormous amount of anger in my body. I learned that I was extremely angry at the way I had allowed certain people to treat me in my life—that I frequently acted "nice," and that I was emotionally frayed from my efforts to always maintain positivity. In many instances, I had allowed myself to tolerate forms of abuse from others. I believed if I didn't act "nice," I would be left alone. *And yet I was alone anyway.*

I had tapped into an energy source that I knew had to be released. *Afterward, I not only felt stronger but almost invincible.* I could stop being a victim and fight for myself, even though I felt tired of trying to keep my head above water.

I became aware of the trauma release from my body. I had facilitated this type of focused expressive work with patients but never considered it for myself. I felt physically improved.

☆☆☆

Alan DeKalb had called the previous week inviting me to come to the firehouse and have dinner with the firemen. I was excited and happy about this. When he called later in the evening to confirm the time, I was aware again I was feeling a little better. I very much wanted to go to the firehouse, particularly because I had ultimately declined Alan's invitation to attend Landmark Forum a few weeks before. I had not seen my paramedic friends in months, and when I arrived at the firehouse for dinner, the entire department welcomed me with kindness. Alan proudly gave me a tour of the station, and the crew allowed me into their world with congeniality and pleasant jokes. I knew their lives needed lightheartedness, since they mostly faced hazard and trauma. I felt privileged to be in the presence of all these fine men who are challenged daily with saving lives and walking away with their own vicarious trauma.

That same night, I drove by Lacey's memorial and left her a silver bracelet with green stars. In the dark, with just the sliver of a moon to light my way, I wept a little. The wind chimes quietly said "hello" to me, then fell into silence. I knew I would be okay, and I let Lacey know that, too. This was my first experience of genuinely believing I would somehow find hope and peace in my life without her.

My son called later in the evening, upbeat and ready to visit. We laughed when he told me a funny story about being in Las Vegas a few weeks earlier. After this cheerful conversation, I felt more hopeful. I had been focusing on having a better relationship with my son, discovering a healthy way to carry on, and finding happiness within myself. That sliver of the moon was not the only little bit of light that night. *Perhaps my recent attempts to manifest change actually helped.*

At this time, nine months post Lacey, I recognized my grief had more intervals of space from its potential depth. The pain continued living with me, but its severity undeniably pounded me in waves now. Just as I stood tall on an island of hope, another wave knocked me over and dragged me back out to the turbulent sea. I often felt as though I were treading water in a vast ocean and would almost drown from my emotions. I was treading though, which required unremitting motion. I was exhausted from battling my painful perception of complete helplessness with my journey of grief, but I was finding hope. Moving through each day provided much needed proof that I was not helpless.

Chapter Twenty-Two: The Setup

*This is one of those cases in which
the imagination is baffled by the facts.*

~ Adam Smith

One day while at work just after eating lunch, I became dizzy and needed to vomit. I almost ran to find a restroom.

Because I work in a hospital and treatment center, I frequently see eating disorder patients who purge as part of their disease. That afternoon, I looked for a private bathroom to do my own purging. There was only one I could think of, which I could not get to quickly enough. So I went to a building that I knew to be the least busy that time of day and informed one of my female staff that I would be going into the bathroom and vomiting. I wanted her to know this, so if she heard me, she would not think I was an eating disorder patient. That could alarm her and result in her calling other staff members to investigate.

This thought amuses me today. *What unusual work I do!* To think I would have to inform someone of my vomiting tickles me, although not at the time. I became ill and was taken to one of the hospital's doctors to be checked. He examined me and asked if anyone would be at home to take care of me. As I said "no," I burst into tears.

Several others on staff were around, and I could not hold back. I shared that I would rather be at work than go home to an empty house. Then I told them how lonely I was, how much I missed Lacey, and how worried I felt about how to keep going. I received the greatest care and love from these people as someone took me to our Serenity Room to lie down. I stayed there for about two hours, during which I was constantly attended to by nurses, doctors, directors, and my assistant, Jan Robinson. Mostly, they just hung out with me.

I felt like a baby. I knew I was not doing well. The recent patient death combined with the anger work at my therapist's office, all contributed to my weariness. My body was telling me to take a break, and I knew I had to listen. A staff person drove me home, and two others followed with my car. I was so grateful to them. After they left, however, and I continued to be sick, I fell apart. I spiraled into one of my blackest holes and desperately felt like dying. I could see no way out of the pain and loneliness.

I also asked God for help. Once again, within moments, the phone rang. Jan from work said she was extremely concerned and was coming over to spend the night. She insisted. It was exactly what I needed that night—someone I trusted in the house with me. Someone who would take care of me if something happened. Janny was absolutely an angel.

☆☆☆

Later that night when I felt a little less dizzy, I went into the kitchen and briefly perused the newspaper. I love to get up to a cup of copper-colored coffee and the paper, but I had not read it that morning. By chance, I caught a small print story about a preview video to an article to be published on Sunday. The subject: a teenage girl who had died and touched the lives of many.

I went online and clicked on the website. I was overjoyed to see "Lacey's Gifts," and the short video featuring photos of Lacey and me. Tom, the reporter, gave a beautiful narration as he introduced the story. *Good things did happen.*

The next few days were full of excitement, though coupled with fear. I spoke with Tom repeatedly about the newspaper article, supplying last-minute information. I stayed home from work the day following my illness, and although still not feeling well, I kept my commitment to meet with Jeff, the photographer, for some additional photos.

☆☆☆

On Sunday morning March 26th, I walked out to my driveway to pick up my newspaper. I almost keeled over when I saw a photo of myself covering one half of the front page with the story also beginning on page one. I was not prepared for this. Despite knowing the article was coming out as a two-part series, I had expected to see the title "The Ultimate Loss" and then a reference to another page. The second part ran on Monday, and again, there I was on the front page. The entire series covered eight full pages of the newspaper with multiple photographs of me, Ernie and his family, and Lacey's three friends who had been interviewed for the article.

I remained overwhelmed for at least a week and had trouble absorbing much of the content. Initially, I had no true perception of its scope and ended up regressing in terms of feeling immense sorrow. I was extremely grateful to the reporter, however, as he had truly honored my request to write nothing that might harm another. In an uplifting way, he told the story with genuine compassion for us all. I received many heartfelt comments and compliments about it and was told how it inspired so many.

Despite this, however, it was all too much for me. I realized I irrationally thought the series would somehow relieve some of my pain and grief. Quite the opposite happened. Having set myself up with unrealistic expectations, I felt hurt. Also, because the series left out some points, I thought I could be perceived to be a poor mother. For example, one article mentioned that Lacey's school no longer had a driver safety program, so readers never knew I took Lacey to another driver safety program in Tucson. She had easily passed that course.

I also became aware that if I heard a hundred positive comments, I'd focus on the one isolated negative comment. Yes, exposing my life was risky, but I had never thought of the consequences. After reading comments posted online in response to the series, I was shocked when several people called me a bad parent for buying her a car. Some thought her accident was about her being a disobedient child. One mean-spirited person commented, "Boo hoo, little girls crying over a death. Who cares if Lacey died?" Tom had warned me in advance not to read the online comments. I did not follow his advice.

Then an anonymous letter came to my office suggesting I was an inept mother. Its writer described me as "privileged," going on to say I never had to work for anything in my life and I should have placed Lacey in driving school. This person also said she deserved *my* job, and could have been a psychologist, but that her father, unlike mine, she surmised, refused to pay for her education. At the end, the writer stated, "I don't know why you don't see that this is your karma for frankly having too much."

I felt devastated when I read this. I wanted to defend myself and tell this person about the abuse in my childhood, that I had worked since I was sixteen years old, that I did not just depend on my father, and that I *had* enrolled Lacey in driving school, which she completed the summer before she got her license.

Fortunately, I was again surrounded by work friends who read the letter and helped me get centered again. They reminded me of the psychological projection in this letter, said I should burn it, that an ill person wrote this. Many were highly protective of me. We ceremoniously burned the letter.

That's when I spiraled into deep agony. Although many friends stepped forward to pull me out of it, the comments still reeled in the back of my brain. I stopped sharing my feelings, retreated into isolation and silence, and spent several nights alone struggling. In this awfully bad way, I eventually reached out to one friend. She contacted several more of my friends to make sure I always had invitations if I wanted them to pull me out of my avoidance of life. I felt so blessed to have these women in my life, and I picked up a little. I began to focus again on the many positives that came out of the newspaper series. Strangers and friends alike contacted me and shared stories about how the articles changed their lives.

As I regained a positive focus, the countless e-mails, phone calls, letters to my work, and Myspace connections all added to my healing process. Each of these contacts told me how many people were moved by the articles. A father wrote, "I will now hold my seventeen-year-old daughter precious. I have been rejecting her." Someone shared a story with me about a Methodist church in another Arizona town who used both parts of the series in Sunday school. The ensuing discussions generated tears and commitments to safety from both adults and youth. People wrote me about how my level of compassion provided them with a role model.

Strangers called. Old, lost friends called. It became clear to me that my purpose in the article, which was to save one life or support one bereaved parent, had been achieved a hundred-fold. The wonderful comments continued.

The editor, I believe, had taken a risk in placing this story on page one of the Sunday paper. I made a point of writing the editor and complimenting Tom, Jeff, and Andrew. I knew I could never adequately articulate to them how much their interest in Lacey—and our story—helped me through many difficult days. I held all three of these men in the highest esteem, and often wondered how they themselves felt about the series.

☆☆☆

After the series came out, Jack said, "My biggest worry about this article has been that you would be hurt. You kept worrying about others being hurt, and my sole fear has been for *you."*

Hearing Jack's genuine concern for me moved me again into a conflicted state, fearing the loss of this relationship would put me in the ground with its timing of coming close to my ultimate loss. *All the emotions would choke me; how can I suppress any of them? Had I no filter to sift my feelings through and maintain a stable presentation in the world? Without the filter, would the flood of emotions drown me?*

Going out socially felt monumental. I knew I had to give myself time and not rush anything. Nothing could be rushed anyway. I was powerless over my daughter's death, and powerless over my feelings. "If only I could have my child back for five minutes!" I cried.

A week after the articles ran, I felt a sense of hope for a few more hours in the day. I went to church that Sunday with Jack, who invited me. We attended the same church where we had held Lacey's final service. The church where I had stood at the podium in front of the hundreds who came to honor her. The church where I spoke my tribute to my precious daughter.

It felt good to be here again where I felt closer to God and less angry with Him. And I felt infinitely less angry with Jack. I prayed for Lacey's soul and for peace for Will. I reluctantly asked God to please take care of my loneliness and turned it over to Him. Some of it was lifted that day.

Chapter Twenty-Three: Spring

Look up. See the sky. See the mountains.
Be still. Be hyper. Be you.
Let the blue light from the stars kiss your face
And lead you to peace.
For even in your darkest mourning
There is light to be found.

~ Nancy and Lacey Jarrell

A pril arrived, and I continued to make new discoveries. People continued to visit the roadside memorial, and the site was growing. I began to visit the site again and each time was greeted by added items: sixteen religious candles painted with the image of the Virgin Mary; multiple notes and letters to Lacey; and hand-drawn pictures of green stars created by children and hanging from wires strung through the trees. A new green hummingbird wind chime also hung proudly from a lower branch. New fresh flowers were also showing up and being attended to by someone other than me.

Sometimes at night, when I felt restless, I walked to the site. Friends thought this was dangerous, but I was not yet invested in my safety. I still felt defiant about anything happening to me. I would be damned if River Road would be my place of death, too.

When I arrived one particular night, even in the dark I could see a large gold cross placed in front of the memorial. It was radiant against the dark navy sky. I felt around it in the dark, trying to figure out who placed it. I reached for a Ziploc bag wired to the cross, stuck my hand in, and felt two small cards. I immediately headed home so I could read them. My heart filled with joy and pain as I read this one: "This random act of kindness was done in memory of our daughter, Nicola Arenosia. Please do an act of kindness for another and pass this card on when doing so." The card carried a picture of a beautiful young woman.

There was also a business card that gave me instruction to find a website. When I did, I discovered that other bereaved parents who had lost a daughter in a car accident left the cross there. They knew about my loss from the recent newspaper series. The website did not share the daughter's age, but her accident occurred about one week before Lacey's. *What they were doing impressed me!*

I decided to do a random act of kindness and pass on the card left in memory of Nicola Arenosia. Since returning to work in September, I had noticed a well-kept memorial site with a cross and flowers on Oracle Road. I drove by it every day on my way home from work. I always breathed a little prayer for whomever had died there. This particular day in April, I tried to get the name of that person and see what types of things were left at the site so I might add to it.

When I stopped there, I read this name on the cross: Mandy Smith. When I got home, I googled the name, as well as Nicola's. I discovered that Nicola, at nineteen, had died first as a result of a car accident. Lacey, at sixteen, had died next, exactly one week later. In a similar car accident, Mandy had died one week after Lacey at the age of twenty-one. I got goose bumps.

I was astounded how this circle of three beautiful young girls taken too suddenly came into my life. I then wondered how many other children died in accidents in July 2006, just in Tucson. Though I first reacted with immense sadness, I also felt connected to a shared experience. I came to believe that Lacey might be in Heaven with these young women. That led to my envisioning a group of local young women and girls who greeted each other as they entered the afterlife due to car accidents. I could see them supporting each other and hanging out.

A few days later, I stopped by Mandy's site and left a small stained-glass angel with the random act of kindness card. The angel was approximately three inches high and two inches wide—not intrusive at all. The memorial rested on the west side of the road. As I looked down at my humble offering, a thin, radiant emerald green and white light shined off the angel—another gift provided by the setting sun. I walked away feeling gratified, believing my addition to Mandy's memorial was fitting.

Also, after the newspaper series came out, I made a point to get in touch with all the people mentioned in it. That included Jack, my son, Ernie, his mother, the two paramedics, the witness, and several of Lacey's friends. We all shared a camaraderie and a common bond of having been a part of a horrific tragedy that day in July. As I talked to each of these people, I realized that, while all of them had been deeply affected by Lacey's death, few knew each other. I was the center of this connection, just as Lacey had been the center for so many people who had never met one another. She had loved them, just as they loved her.

So I arranged to connect the witness with the paramedics and spent time with Ernie's mother, Mel McBeath. She generously wanted to help me as she witnessed my pain and depression. She unquestionably loved Lacey, and when I had the courage to go to their house one day, I saw a shrine they'd built for her. They had also hung green stars in the garden.

Speaking with Mel as well as Michelle (the witness), and Alan (the paramedic) helped me retrieve more information about the accident. I learned that Mel collapsed at the scene and had to be placed in the ambulance. Ernie had called her immediately; she had arrived while Lacey's body was still on the roadside. She also told the sheriffs my name and where I was employed, insisting I not be notified via phone but in person.

Most important, I learned that Ernie had crawled under the car. He touched Lacey and spoke to her, but she did not answer. *Already gone.* Knowing this helped me, as I had needed assurance that Lacey was not trapped under the car alive. The paramedics, I also learned, had lifted the car off her within minutes. As more details of the traumatic scene came to me, I realized how dramatically all involved were affected.

Over the years, I would learn a great more detail about what happened for Alan and Paul the day of Lacey's accident. Alan had agreed to a recorded interview with one of my editors, Alanna Nash. He shared being particularly affected by Lacey's death as his son was the same age. He also had recently experienced a personal tragedy that resulted in feeling more vulnerable than was typical for him. Specifically, his wife had left him after he discovered she was having an affair with someone he worked with. His son had also just moved out, so he was dealing with his own shock and grief.

Alan had discovered his wife's long-term affair by reading an e-mail exchange. It took him by complete surprise! He described himself as breaking down and then questioning his ability to function well enough to be responsible to his "entire engine company." How could he support his team in their personal safety while on calls?

He then went to see his primary care provider and took three months off through the Family and Medical Leave Act (FMLA). During his time off, Alan attended the Landmark Forum and reported: "I learned more about death at the Landmark Forum than I had in the fifteen years I had been a paramedic." As a result of attending it, Alan increased his skill base by becoming more conscious of his communications with people who have just lost loved ones. He better knew what to say in the presence of someone who was dying, saying, "Research confirms that the last sense one loses is the sense of hearing." That made it critical for him to be more attentive to how his words affected others in all situations, not just on the job.

In his interview with Alanna, Alan further described how his senses changed during his three-month leave. "I went to Texas to visit my brother, and it was twenty degrees outside and snowing. But I did not feel the cold, and colors seemed different—like I had gone to a different place. Even when I returned to work, I was just more in touch with everything around me—the sights, the sounds, everything," he said.

It did not escape me that Alan was having a parallel experience to mine, although his occurred prior to Lacey's death. Regarding Lacey's death, he said, "This call just did it for me. I was done. I remember driving on Sunrise Drive, and I could not function. I could not even drive. I was an absolute mess. This was five days after Lacey's accident, the day of her funeral. I knew when the funeral was, I knew where it would be and what time, and just as that time was approaching, it was getting worse, and here this song comes on the radio about somebody who's lost somebody in a car accident, holding their hand, and seeing them in the next life—and that was it. I just pulled over. I thought, *I've got to do something.* That old '60s song—Where, oh where, can my baby be, the glass shattering . . . I'm trying to cope, and this song comes on and I say, 'Okay, that's it. I can't fight it anymore. I need to be there. I will not be able to function tomorrow.' I had to go to the funeral. I had to go for *me.* And I had to go for everyone else, too. So, I went home, put on my uniform, and drove to the funeral. If that song had not come on, I wouldn't be sitting here right now."

The song is called "Last Kiss."[22]

☆☆☆

Around the same time, I became aware of subtle changes within myself. Each week, I gradually felt more and more peace. But after work, when I was home alone, my suffering came down like a heavy curtain, shutting out all hope. At some level, I was slowly accepting the pain and loneliness. That concerned me, however, because I did not want to get too comfortable with this life script. Yet, I also knew I was still frozen in grief.

☆☆☆

Easter Day came, and I was alone. Ernie's mother, Mel, had invited me to join the family for dinner, but I could not go. I felt compassion for Ernie, but I was afraid that sitting across the table from him, looking into his face and thinking only of Lacey, would cause me more anguish. I planned to isolate myself.

It was the first time in twenty-one years that I had not prepared an Easter basket for one of my children. I wept, remembering the previous Easter as though it were an hour before. I had put together Lacey's basket and waited for her to get up and be surprised by it. With Lacey being older, the basket held fewer chocolate bunnies and more gifts such as CDs and clothes. She knew I absolutely loved her without question, and I could picture her coming out of her room and acting like she was too old for an Easter basket, yet loving it at the same time. This memory resulted in a pang of pain and joy.

Yet again, just as mysterious surprises came up when I felt extremely low, small miracles occurred on that first Easter without her. To my surprise, I received many phone calls, and one of them was a friend of Lacey's I had never met, a twenty-two-year-old woman named Carthelle Moore. She knew Lacey through Joey, the young man Lacey had started dating just before her death. In fact, Carthelle was dating Joey's older brother. After she had written beautiful things about Lacey on the Myspace site, we had planned to meet, and the time seemed right. I met her at a Starbucks, and we had a delightful exchange.

This lovely, kind young woman told me stories about Lacey that gave me more insight into my daughter's social world. One time, Lacey heard Carthelle comment that she would love to have her nails done but could not afford it. Lacey responded by saying, "Carthelle, when I get my first paycheck, I'm going to take you to get your nails done." Right then, a large part of me wanted to take Carthelle to a nail salon and carry out Lacey's plan. Carthelle graciously and adamantly refused this, however, and I did not push it. Lacey's first paycheck arrived in the mail some days after her death. I still have it in one of the many keepsake containers that hold many special items relevant to my precious girl.

Suddenly, I realized I had more invitations that Easter than I could accept. I became aware once again that when I prayed to God for help, He brought me people to be with; I just needed to accept the invitations. This pattern continued and yet each time I was given a reprieve I felt astounded by it and equally grateful. I had a full day that day, with many loving people whom I didn't take for granted. My grief, however, remained constant and continued to fill every space.

☆☆☆

When I prayed at this point, I asked God only for knowledge of His will for me and to please let Lacey be in the highest of places, feeling loved and happy while also giving love. I started off slowly with this, as I did not like asking for help. A friend told me I should "rock the heavens," meaning I needed to raise my voice. Initially, that felt uncomfortable, but in no time, I yelled out to God and Lacey, lifting my arms toward the ceiling. I had little problem shouting *at* God during my bouts of anger, but raising my voice without the accompanying anger was a new experiment.

"God, please let me know your will for me!!" I shouted. "I miss my precious baby girl! Please let her be okay and help me find direction!"

I did this ritual in the morning before work and in the evening before bed. I yelled it in the car while driving. At first, I was embarrassed, even though I was alone. I quickly adjusted, however, and for some reason, I always felt a physical and emotional sense of relief afterward. Yet I also felt completely crazy. I imagined Lacey could see me, and I could picture her laughing at me in a loving way. "Oh, Mama," I imagined her saying. "You are such a nut."

I also committed to maintaining a few positive daily rituals. Twice a day, I spoke out loud about everything for which I was grateful. Sometimes stretching it, I'd say things like, "I am grateful for my pain, because from it I know I grow and learn." I did not always believe my own words, but it felt restorative just to start a sentence with "I am grateful for . . ." and then fill in the blank with something I could find in my environment. It is hard to escape seeing a mountain view in the Tucson basin, so my first statement of gratitude was "I am grateful for the mountains."

This helped! Each day, I was able to add to my gratitude list. Eight years later, I came across research confirming that simply *thinking* about gratitude activates the dopamine system in our brains, which results in feeling pleasure. Being in gratitude also boosts the release of serotonin, a neurotransmitter. This results in experiencing improved mood and helps connect us to a higher emotional intelligence.

I did not know about this research when I first practiced the daily ritual of citing things I was grateful for. I did recognize, though, that the periods in the day when I felt somewhat okay grew longer. Laughter came a little easier.

When spring came, I made an unconscious decision to change my wardrobe. Going out to shop was still too painful for me, so I brought out clothes from my closet and creatively put together stylish, colorful outfits to wear to work. That was after nine months of wearing only blacks and browns. I wasn't consciously choosing drab colors, but I had stopped my habit of accessorizing with lots of jewelry and color. I wore the same jewelry every day, and mostly it was Lacey's. When I revived my old style, carefully dressing for each day, many noticed the change. More people gravitated toward me, and many of my co-workers were hypervigilant around me, wanting and hoping for me to get well.

As another result of the newspaper series, I began making new contacts and meeting or hearing from people who had also experienced tragedies. They all seemed very loving and genuine. For example, I developed a relationship with a woman in Massachusetts whose daughter died just days before Lacey in a similar accident. This mother was heavily involved in legislation to change seat belt laws in her state, and she and I agreed to join forces at some point.

As part of this whirl of attention, the Lacey Jarrell Foundation was coming closer to reality. People continued to donate money or goods in support of artistic youth.

With so much happening, I realized I did not have to be lonely; I *chose* to be alone and isolate, feeling separate from others. At the same time, I accepted the reality of it and became accustomed to often being alone. I was surprised by the days when I actually wanted to come home and be by myself after a long day at work. I stopped trying to get away from my house. I was starting to embrace living alone.

☆☆☆

Depending on how I counted it, nine-and-a-half months or forty weeks or two-hundred-and-fifty-two days had passed since Lacey's death. I had cried every one of these two-hundred-and-fifty-two days, although I was aware I cried less than before. At some level, this scared me. I was so familiar with the deep pain and tears. I *expected* them because they represented the measure of love I had for Lacey. Or so I believed at the time.

I was engaging in simplistic thinking again. I knew I loved Lacey and Will more than I had anyone. A mother's love is unparalleled. However, I also knew my thinking could be distorted, and I was moving toward a time when I would have one full day without any tears at all. I told myself that would be okay.

What is true is this: *Love cannot be measured. And the number of tears one cries in grief or sorrow does not prove how much one loves.*

Chapter Twenty-Four: Moving On?

We only part to meet again
Tho' mighty boundless waves may sever.
Remembrance oft shall bring thee near
And I will with thee go forever.
And oft at midnight's silent hour
When brilliant planets shall guide the ocean
Thy name shall rise to Heaven's highest star
And mingle with my soul's devotion.

"To Emily Virginia Chapman"
~ Edgar Allan Poe

Speaking my emotions out loud seemed to help me immensely. My difficult emotions had less power over me once I identified what I was feeling and verbalized these by name aloud. At times, I felt I was in a battle with some of our most primal emotions such as sadness, hurt, fear, guilt, shame, anger, and loneliness. I experienced longer periods in a day where I could think and talk about Lacey but not burst into tears. I still cried privately at home and in my car. I was surprised how I could speak of her to others in a loving, gentle way and not always cry. Yet many days, I still could not believe that any of this had happened.

I continued to struggle with not knowing what day it was. It still felt like Lacey would come bouncing up the stairs from her room at any moment. While home alone, I called out to her: "I love you, Lacey Jane!" I shouted, my arms raised up to the heavens. In my imagination, I could hear her laughing at me and see her smiling. *How could Lacey be gone?*

Again, I was amazed that, after ten months, Lacey's friends continued to call me and asked to come visit. They also still posted comments on her Myspace site. Some of them asked her help with a particular problem, then wrote about how Lacey had granted their request, and they thanked her for her intervention. They continued to pray to her as though she were a goddess.

Some of this worried me. Probably fifty of us were praying to Lacey, and I, too, often had my prayers answered. It felt as though she really was with me, that she orchestrated events to back me off the metaphorical cliff just as I was about to jump. I imagined her being so busy helping all of us on earth that she had little time to do what she needed on the other side. Yet, I wanted her to be able to advance her soul and move on to a higher place. *Were we all keeping her tethered to earth? Would that be in her best interest?*

We would have to let her go soon, I believed. So I began thinking of ways to help the kids loosen their ties to her and not encumber her soul—a conflicting thought at best.

More and more, I recognized the many unusual occurrences that happened just before the accident and signaled her death was near. There was no doubt in my mind that, at a subconscious level, both of us knew she would die soon. As these thoughts and memories persisted, I did not want to shake them. With intense clarity, I recalled every conversation we had in the days leading up to her death and exactly where we were in the house when they occurred.

To Ernie's credit, I remembered that, five days before the accident, he called me one evening out of concern for Lacey. He told me he had learned from Lacey that one of her girlfriends had ingested two black capsules to "get high." The girl had taken these before and was encouraging Lacey to do the same. Apparently, she told Lacey they would "make you feel happy." Ernie further stated he did not know what the pills were, but he was afraid for Lacey and any further exposure to drugs. I believed him and assumed the substance was some kind of amphetamine.

Lacey arrived home about an hour after Ernie's call. I invited her to speak with me and I told her what he had said. I did not need to ask her if what he shared with me was true. She immediately said, "He told you the truth, Mama." She burst into tears and repeated, "I'm sorry, Mama, I won't take those pills, but I wanted to." I held her and told her she was not in trouble and that I appreciated her honesty. When I asked her about the pills, she wasn't clear what they were. She then told me she had smoked marijuana. This led to a detailed communication around drugs and alcohol and their dangers, risks, and consequences. Although it was not our first conversation on this topic, it was the most emotional and personal one rather than being only educational.

At the end of our talk, she said, "Mama, I promise I will never do drugs again."

I replied, "Yes you will, honey. I need you to know, though, that it terrifies me. I could not live if something ever happened to you." *Yet, something did happen, and I am still living.* That she kept her promise, too, did not escape me.

I loved this child so much, but I could not save her, and I could not prevent her death. I again flashed back to that evening speaking to her as she walked back and forth from her bedroom to her bathroom, changing her clothes and fixing her hair and makeup. It was the evening she did not provide details but alluded to being afraid of Ernie's inability to let her move on. For a moment, this scene came back to me as though it were happening in the present. I relived the fear, feeling as frightened as I did that night. I could again feel how I stunned myself by telling her I was afraid something awful could happen, something that could even cause her death. I saw myself suggesting we change her cell phone number and prepared for a quarrel about it. I felt the surprise when she did not argue with me or refute my fear of her dying. I could not forget that this conversation took place that Tuesday evening. We ended it by agreeing to go to T-Mobile the next Saturday—the Saturday that never came for Lacey.

☆☆☆

The experience of having a memory return and reliving that moment is a symptom of post-traumatic stress disorder. Even innocuous reminders of a traumatic event can result in psychological fear and physiological reactions years later. Treatment for flashbacks and emotional reactivity requires first establishing both physical and emotional safety for the trauma survivor. The sense of safety allows for building trust and for the limbic brain and the body to relax. Providing education about the brain's response to trauma and normalizing the survivor's response is paramount. When one experiences trauma and the result is post-traumatic stress disorder (PTSD), it is likely the individual felt completely helpless at the time of the event. Assisting that person to gain a sense of control in the present can help erode the negative cognitions and self-blame often acquired after such an incident.

The most effective trauma treatment approach recognizes the need for a holistic process—that is, caring for the mind, body, and heart. It involves a multi-disciplinary, multi-sensory approach that comes from genuinely compassionate and empathetic providers. It's a treatment team approach with professionals who are open to utilizing a variety of modalities in addition to talk therapy. For example, it's most effective to add body work such as massage, yoga, acupuncture, and more, as well as artistic expression, drama, sound, music, and education about the brain and behavior.

Most appreciable is having supportive relationships. Using a gentle and comprehensive approach can assist a grieving person to bring unconscious memory to the conscious level. That neutralizes its power and intensity, allowing for some understanding and a return to normal functioning.

☆☆☆

As I gained perspective on the world around me, I saw how so many parents were also losing their children, whether in car accidents or other tragic ways. My fractured heart ached for them. When the tragic killings occurred at Virginia Tech that April, I was angry at the news stations for repeatedly showing the crime scenes and the killer. Those images had to be beyond devastating for the families. My loss felt enormous to me. Still, I wanted to help others, so I continued to reach out through e-mail or in newspaper comments, offering my support despite getting little response back. I understood this, though. After losing a child in those early months, it's all a parent can do to speak to those who are close, let alone complete strangers.

Physiologically, what is happening? The terror parents experience upon learning their child has died temporarily shuts off their prefrontal cortex. The computation of what has happened during this time of trauma is corrupted. That means we lack access to full consciousness due to the intensity of the fear we feel.

☆☆☆

I was worried about the safety of my son, Will, at the University of Colorado. So, on April 14th, I did something I had never done before—I flew to Colorado to be with Will in Boulder on his twenty-second birthday. He did not like a lot of attention on his birthday, but I thought it important to be with him on this special day. And when I arrived, I could tell he was excited to see me.

On this short trip, I took Will and his girlfriend out to dinner, gave him gifts, spent one night at a hotel, and flew back to Tucson the next day. What a jet setter! I was extremely happy we had spent this precious time together. I cherished every moment with Will, and I think he felt the same.

Will was still hurting deeply from the loss of his sister and only sibling. I knew he felt lonely despite having a circle of remarkably close friends. Before I left Boulder, he gave me a literary magazine that featured one of his poems. Creative expression was his therapy, his love, and his talent—the true poet in the family. A skilled and gifted writer, he's a natural and has been since he was a child. The poem was about seeing Lacey in the coffin the day we had the private family viewing. My heart accelerated while reading the poem and then normalized as I reached the end. Then I exhaled, recognizing Will's writing was therapeutic, and the fact that he allowed it to be published indicated his willingness to reveal and release his private anguish. This was a positive action.

☆☆☆

During our visit, he told me of his plans to graduate in June and move back to Tucson. I said he could come home any time and not worry about the rest of the lease on his apartment in Boulder. Through conversation, though, it became clear Will did not want to move back into our house. Of course, I understood a twenty-two-year-old man would *not* want to live with his mother, and I supported his decision. However, I learned he did not even want to stay at our house one more time. After Lacey's death, it was just too painful for him.

This made me think more seriously about moving as I vacillated between staying or leaving with glimpses of how staying here had been a blessing, but it also exacerbated my depression. Lacey's energy was everywhere in our home, and although I did not want to leave this place of many memories, I knew I would have to move on.

In fact, downsizing had always been the plan, even before Lacey died. My house was way too large for me. There was also the matter of the unfenced yard. My beautiful yard backed into a branch of the Rillito River, and wildlife abounded. I loved the wild desert, but a family of bobcats sometimes shared the area, and a herd of javelina roamed around at night. I desperately wanted a dog to provide me steady companionship, yet without a fenced yard, I had no safety for a dog.

I planned to get more serious about looking for a new house.

Chapter Twenty-Five:
Getting Answers

It is not the answer that enlightens, but the question.

~ Eugene Ionesco

Wandering through my home one night, I picked up some family photographs and counted how many relatives had died and how many were still alive. Of the twelve of us in my sister's wedding picture, four were gone. Lacey, a flower girl in the ceremony, was the youngest person in the photo at age eight.

I could not believe the multi-generational mix of those in the photo who had died. Ranging from the elderly (my mother and father) to middle-aged (my brother, Tom) to my teenaged Lacey, our family had suffered tremendous loss. I caught myself in this sullen thought and wondered, "Am I looking for more pain, and if so, why?"

I told myself I did not *want* to be pain-seeking. I have often communicated with patients in session that any behavior we engage in—whether it's perceived as positive or negative—we wouldn't do if we didn't reap a benefit. I'd say, "Assuming this to be true, what is the benefit you are receiving from behaving this way?"

So, I posed this question to me: "What benefit are you receiving, Nancy, for counting deceased family members in a photo and focusing on the losses?" I answered, "I could have more reasons for feeling the way I do" or "this allowed me to feel sorry for myself." Taking it a step further, I asked, "What benefit do you receive from either of those?" I came up with, "Staying in my grief, which perhaps allowed me to avoid moving on." I could have continued with this self-query but stopped. Attempting to self-therapize wasn't productive, I concluded.

☆☆☆

The date arrived for my two cousins, Annie (from North Carolina) and Mary (from New Jersey) to visit me for five days. They told me they were coming to work and asked me to make a list of projects needed to get my house ready to sell. They would help me dispose of the possessions I no longer needed. While on the phone to Mary before they came, I started crying. "You don't understand," I said. "I can't get it together enough to even make a list." She then wrote me an e-mail that said to do *nothing* except be at the airport to give them a hug.

By the time they arrived, I did have a list—all in my head. Our first order of business was going to the grocery store. This had never been my favorite chore, but after Lacey died, it became excruciating because we often shopped together. She loved Propel Fitness Water, and ten months post Lacey, I still had to turn my head when I passed it on the shelf.

While we shopped, my cousins cheered me up. We bought enough food so that after they left, I would not need to grocery shop for some time. They also helped me sort through a storage area, the garage, and several closets. Their stay with me was bittersweet, however, as it was harrowing whenever I found things of Lacey's I'd forgotten about.

The most remarkable find was another of Lacey's stories. At twelve years old, she wrote about what she hoped to have in the future. Her piece specifically stated what type of college she would attend, what type of man she would marry, and how many children they would have, even down to their personalities.

Plus her writing was so typically *her*—full of humor, nonjudgmental, and deep-thinking. "I don't need my husband to be good-looking," she wrote. "I would just like him to be loving, honest, and kind."

In the last paragraph of this story, she wrote about her death. She wanted to be "encased in a tomb, with beautiful purple and pink flowers around the tomb." She also wrote that she wanted lots of people to be at her funeral, and that she wanted to be cremated.

She even described in detail what her urn would look like. *Amazingly, all these things had actually happened.* We did not place her in a tomb, of course, but the church was certainly a metaphor for this image. More than eight hundred people attended her funeral at the church where purple and pink flowers abounded. And she had been cremated.

I will be forever grateful for the time my cousins took to come and be with me. We laughed and cried a lot. This precious experience gave me deeply needed family support—and hope for less grief in the future.

☆☆☆

Not long after Mary and Annie departed, we held the second meeting of the Lacey Jarrell Foundation, and things were coming together. The board solicited art from several students in the Tucson area, and it looked as though we'd be able to stage the first presentation of young people's artwork in local galleries in May. I felt a lift in my spirit.

The Board of The Lacey Jarrell Foundation, 2007. L-R:
Christina Slater, Mel McBeath, Sylvia Intrieri, Will Jarrell,
Nancy Jarrell, Tana Jay von Isser, Debbie Peck, Cyndy Neighbors

The members of the board—professionals I knew through my long-term relationships or met through other connections—were such loving and generous people. I was amazed at how quickly the nonprofit organization was taking shape and how close I was to achieving my dream for the foundation.

However, it still had its challenges. A small glitch occurred with Cyndy, who unexpectedly lost two of her staff, which meant we might not make our May 10th opening. I struggled with the IRS documentation needed to obtain the nonprofit status. It all seemed overwhelming to me. I will be forever grateful for my accountant, Kelly Metzler, who provided instruction on navigating through this complex process, which required me to do a lot of the work myself. The critical thinking I needed as well as the research and writing it required were roadblocks for me. However, I trusted it would all happen and talked about it with Lacey every day.

At the same time, I continued to work on myself. I knew that, even as I was learning to laugh again, I had become a vastly different woman. I would never be the same, but I also knew not all of that was undesirable. I often found myself speaking of gratitude with tears streaming down my face.

Even though the work was excruciating, I continued in grief therapy. One day, I was asked to draw a relationship graph for Lacey and me. The results forced me to look at the times when things had not gone well between us—incidents I did not want to remember. The exercise brought me closer to the reality that Lacey was not perfect, and neither was I. *I did not want to face that truth. To me, she was perfect.*

I prayed that God would let her be in the best place possible.

One evening, I received a phone message from Michelle St. Rose, who had witnessed the accident. She lived on the mountain side of River Road, and I lived on the river side. Our paths had never crossed until my daughter's death, but we began calling each other a friend. We both had daughters, were divorced, and raised older sons alone. She also lived in a large home by herself. However, I knew she had finally received an offer to sell her home and intended to move.

Her message said a change of timing regarding the sale of her house had occurred. She had to be out of it *in two days*. For months, I said I wanted to come over and stand on her porch in the spot from where she watched the accident. I had not yet found the courage to do so, but it was now or never. I went over the night before she planned to move.

It was early evening, and at the end of April, we still had daylight. Michelle and I talked for a bit and then eventually made our way to the porch on the second level of her home. She had been standing there that sweltering summer day, talking to her sister on her cell phone. The screeching of tires shifted her attention toward the hilly, winding road. Knowing River Road has limited visibility at some points, I was shocked to see what a clear view she must have had of the entire accident. Suddenly, I started to shake. I forced myself to focus on my breathing.

As we stood there, she described exactly what she saw and how she had 911 on the phone before the car had stopped rolling. I disconnected from my emotions to shift into my intellectual self and ask questions. I wanted to retain every piece of information I could!

Michelle continued to describe the accident. That's when I realized what I had understood based on the police reports was not accurate. From this porch, I could see where Lacey first lost control of her car and where she hit the dirt berm. As Michelle described it, I understood how the Subaru had first rolled back and forth across the two lanes and then rolled three more times down the hill. This confirmed the violence of the accident. *How could Ernie have lived through it?*

Then I recalled seeing Lacey's iPod on the seat of the car at the auto salvage shop and marveled at its ability to still play music. *How did this tiny piece of technology keep functioning when my daughter did not?*

As Michelle continued, I learned which direction the car faced when it made its final landing. I had been confused by a newspaper photo of the crushed shell of the car and the paramedics on the scene, not realizing until this moment—almost ten months later—that they had moved the vehicle after they lifted it off my daughter. Consequently, the location of Lacey's memorial was not exactly where she had died.

I was grateful to just be learning this information now as I felt a little more grounded than in months past. Rather than experience a huge emotional response and demand to move the memorial, I chose to be thankful that I knew more of the truth.

After Michelle and I finished going over all the details, we looked at each other and burst into tears. We held each other and cried for several minutes as she whispered, "I am so sorry." I cried the words I have said over and over: "She was just a little girl. She was a good girl."

Once we composed ourselves, I asked Michelle the question that had troubled me for months: Who was the third woman who arrived on the scene and identified herself as a physician? Michelle's eyes grew wide. Just two days before, she had taken her daughter to a dance class. While there, she made eye contact with a woman she thought she knew but could not place. After class, the woman approached Michelle and said, "I know you. We were both there at the accident."

She was the physician, an endocrinologist, and she asked Michelle to give me her love. I was so happy this woman who had also held my daughter's foot and prayed as she died was a mother, a loving and caring person. I never did learn her name.

By asking for answers to my still-unresolved questions, I was getting what I asked for once again. At this time, I also remembered the other woman who stopped that day and held Lacey's foot as she passed had called me a day or so after the accident. She shared with me that within the past year or so, her brother had been killed in a car accident. I don't recall the details, but I do remember she said the car was on fire, and he had not been extricated from the vehicle before the fire made saving him impossible. Her story was tragic and traumatic, and I knew she desperately wanted to prevent Lacey from being another statistic of a vehicular accident.

As more pieces to the puzzle of Lacey's death took shape, I basked momentarily in the gratitude of knowing three loving, caring women were with my child when she transitioned.

Chapter Twenty-Six: A Contract
of Souls

I had my own notion of grief.
I thought it was the sad time
that followed the death of
someone you love.
And you had to push through it
to get to the other side.
But I'm learning there is no other side.
There is no pushing through.
But rather, there is absorption.
Adjustment.
Acceptance.
And grief is not something you complete,
but rather, you endure.
Grief is not a task to finish
and move on,
but an element of yourself.
An alteration of your being.
A new way of seeing.
A new definition of self.

"Grief"
~ Gwen Flowers

May 2007 arrived, and along with it a recognition of how conflicted I remained about the facts surrounding Lacey's death.
Since standing on Michelle's porch, I had experienced an internal
shift, one that distanced me from my emotions and moved me

toward a more intellectual, logical, and analytical thinking approach to my life.

In general, the left hemisphere of the brain is language based and responsible for logical, rational, and concrete thinking. It looks for cause and effect. Perhaps this was self-protection, a way to avoid the pain of imagining Lacey's accident again and again and obsessing over my continuing suspicion that Ernie did something to cause her to lose control of the car that day. The Pima County Sheriff's Department never did prove, to my satisfaction, who was driving, and merely took Ernie's word for it that Lacey was behind the wheel. At times, I could step away from this tortuous internal questioning, but under my emotional radar lurked a chronic gnawing that I still did not have the whole truth of what happened that morning.

May 2nd was the two-year anniversary of my mother's death, but I barely cried that day. I had my usual talk with Lacey, and I even spoke a little to my mother. Those conversations revealed what different relationships I had with each of them. I never communicated with my mother the way Lacey and I did. I had moved across the country in my teens and wasn't close to my mother, yet Lacey always felt like a part of me. We talked so much—every day. I felt increased gratitude for the time I had with my daughter.

Due to the decrease in my tearfulness I experienced feelings of guilt. I worried that only ten months had passed, but I didn't cry as hard every day anymore. Of course, this thinking was irrational. *How should I assess this? Did it mean progress in my healing or that I was forgetting about Lacey?*

I tormented myself with these questions. When I could access my rational thinking, I knew these thoughts were flawed due to changes in my brain from the trauma. And I knew I loved her deeply, tears or no tears. So, after giving myself a reality check, I chose to simply look at it as I did not cry as much one day as the day before. Nothing more. I did not need to analyze it or try to understand it. In fact, doing so only made me feel worse. I reminded myself again to choose my thoughts carefully, pick the ones that helped me move forward and feel hope rather than those that exacerbated my pain. It was seldom easy.

I wanted to be sure Lacey knew how much I loved her. If she could see me from the other side, I wanted her to know she still meant so much to me and that I missed her presence *horribly*. And yet having known Lacey, I realized she would never want to see my daily anguish. Rather, she would want me to be more active, social, and ebullient.

This created a serious conflict within me. During the past month, I had been aware that I felt Lacey's presence less and less. While talking to her at one point, I gave her permission to move on and advance her soul, saying, "Please move ahead if that's best for you. I'll remain on earth to do any suffering and any goodness that God demands of me. I would sacrifice my happiness and my life—anything—for you."

I think she heard me.

☆☆☆

After this brief period of no tears, of course, the tears did resume. They did not last as long or feel as hard as in the early days, but they continued to come. When I experienced a series of decent days, I mistakenly assumed this meant the hard times were behind me. *My days would all get better, and soon I would access peace and achieve happiness.*

This was not true, however. I had some good days, but then the terrible days disabled my previous hope. I reminded myself that waves were a part of the process, and I came to accept them as such.

One day at work, I spoke with a man who always presented as cheerful. I never heard him complain, and he seemed clothed in optimism. (His wife, who also worked with me, was the same way.) I asked him about his consistently positive attitude and how he achieved it. He said, "I wake up every morning and say, 'Today is going to be a great day!'" Although he may have had huge problems I did not know of, he seemed genuine.

Inspired by him, I decided to engage in this practice to help me. Many a morning found me making the statement, "Today is a great day" as tears spattered my blouse. I also knew I wouldn't magically feel better. *There is no cure for the permanent wound of losing a child.*

☆☆☆

My thoughts about Lacey were changing. For a long time, I focused only on her death, why it happened, and how much I missed her. While I often recalled conversations we had in the months before her death, I had not gone back to memories of her infancy or when she attended elementary school. I had not thought about the times she rode horses, or we took trips together, or the sports events I watched her in. So I started allowing these wonderful memories to bring me joy, even as they felt agonizing.

In grief therapy, my therapist asked me to look back at my relationship with Lacey and compile a list of things for which I needed her forgiveness. This process rendered me as raw as a patient cut open in surgery with no sutures to close the wound, but I agreed to do the work. My therapist said again that my relationship with Lacey needed completion—create a clean slate—so I could move on with contentment. I responded with "No, I will not move *on*. I will move *forward*."

The words "move on" ignited a visceral response in me. At times, I struggled to believe she was not ever coming back home. Intellectually I knew she was gone, but emotionally I felt so close to her that my brain refused to assimilate her death—her absence.

Again, I disagreed with my therapist that my relationship with Lacey needed "completion." Grief can be a controversial subject. Some clinicians believe effective grief therapy occurs when the griever overcomes the loss. Others believe grief cannot be treated. In these cases, grief is being generalized and, although I'm focused on losing a child, loss comes in many forms that do not necessarily involve death.

While my personal experience results in my believing the loss of a child is something a mother "never gets over," I do believe an empathetic therapist can provide compassionate support to a griever and be a conduit for processing her journey through to wellness.

In terms of "completion" of my relationship with my daughter, the mere suggestion seemed insensitive. In struggling with the permanence of the loss, to consider my relationship with Lacey had to end was more than I could fathom. Although I knew my therapist had the best of intentions, she'd never had children—nor did she have experience working with a bereaved mother. Consequently, I did not engage in the completion portion of grief therapy. In terms of the possibility of healing from my loss, at best I believed transforming any bit of it into something positive could help and that functioning in life was possible. Still, I did not entertain thoughts that someday I would be healed.

In fact, Lacey's death disoriented me so much that I had lost any accurate perception of time. Events became disorganized in my memory. I became aware through conversations with others that some things I thought happened actually had not. I would later learn from trauma expert Dr. Robert Scaer in a lecture I attended that "trauma is a complication of memory."

For example, when I read her phone bills and saw the calls the day before and the morning of her death, I thought Ernie had phoned her several times before she left the house. After Michelle and I stood out on the porch and revisited the facts of the accident, I was in doubt. *Did I have all the information filed correctly in my head?*

Looking at the phone bills again, I was stunned to see there were no calls from Ernie that morning, at least not before the accident. I had thought Ernie's call came an hour before she left the house to meet him. But as I listened again to the messages and checked the phone's accuracy regarding date and time, I realized that Ernie's message—sweet and gentle, asking Lacey to wake up—came in about ten minutes *after* the accident. I did not know what to think. Whatever the answer to that riddle—a faulty time stamp or a de-layed delivery from Lacey's cell phone carrier—I knew that it would not bring back my daughter.

Still, it plagued me not to know.

Ernie and I did not have contact anymore. I had called him on occasion, but he did not return my calls. Lacey's friends told me he was doing poorly, and I felt incredibly sad about this. I knew he had to have been traumatized by the accident, but I also bounced back and forth in my emotions toward him, feeling compassion one moment and anger the next.

My heart broke every time I lingered on the fact that I would never have Lacey's account of the accident in this lifetime.

☆☆☆

I continued to pray to God adding my new technique of yelling at Him. The yelling was not anger; I simply stated my needs in a very loud voice. But I also had periods of soft conversations with Him in which I *was* truly angry.

One evening, I opened the newspaper and read a story about two local sisters who had just received an award. They worked as volunteers in a nursing home, providing elderly people with companionship and comfort. The girls were only ten and fourteen years old. After the award ceremony, the girls' seventeen-year-old cousin offered to drive them home. Ten minutes later, their car collided with another vehicle at a stoplight. The fourteen-year-old died, the ten-year-old was in critical condition, and the seventeen-year-old was in intensive care. I burst into tears. Another Tucson family faced the loss of one daughter and possibly a second, as well as their niece. *What was the sense in all of this, God? Why, why, why?*

I spent time pondering this question and asked for an answer. Later, I came upon a reading that a friend had sent me. It tried to explain what seems like senseless events.

The article had been excerpted from a series known as the Matthew Books. Matthew was a seventeen-year-old teenager who was tragically killed in a car accident in 1980. Fourteen years later, his mother claimed he came to her through automatic writing. In these daily messages, Matthew shared what it was like to be on the other side. He also talked about politics, the war in Iraq, and global warming. *What did he have to say about soul growth and the afterlife?*

One of his concepts seemed plausible to me: Before taking on this incarnation, while still in a soul state, we all agreed to play the roles that we have assumed on earth. We predetermined all our experiences and relationships. According to Matthew, if we had a certain experience in our lives, it was because we had the *opposite* experience in a former life. I interpreted it to mean that, long ago, Lacey and I (as well as others) agreed she would die in an accident at an early age. We agreed I would be the mother who suffered. All agreements would have been based on the best way to advance our souls to the next stage. These types of experiences, while tragedies in this earthly life, were ultimately opportunities for soul growth.

From this, I understood that in a previous life, I may have been a child who died at an early age and Lacey may have been my long-suffering mother.

The idea of souls contracting together and mapping out their return to earth appealed to me because it stopped me from blaming myself or anyone else for Lacey's accident. Whatever belief struck me at any given moment was permissible if it helped with the pain I felt.

At this point, I gained some awareness of how different my life had become, that I was falling into a form of comfort with it. I was accustomed to the pain and loneliness, which paradoxically gave me relief. That's when I realized I could live in our big house alone, and I have tools to help me with my traumatic grief.

Despite the sadness, I affirmed my faith in believing I would be all right.

Chapter Twenty-Seven: Endings

And now I'm glad I didn't know
The way it all would end, the way it all would go
Our lives are better left to chance
I could have missed the pain
But I'd have had to miss the dance.

Stanza from the song "The Dance"
~ Tony Arata

In that spring of 2007, I became aware of increased anxiety and fear looming around me as I registered an upcoming event: what would have been Lacey's high school graduation. I dreaded facing this and yet knew I could not ignore it. St. Gregory's seemed conflicted in the way the school would honor her. I felt angry about it and thought about writing the headmaster at the end of the year. I thought he needed advice on how to work with parents should this type of tragedy ever occur again.

On top of it, I thought the school was negligent with its frequent e-mails with requests for donations. Then one day a letter arrived that began with the words, "You must be getting very excited that your student is about to graduate from high school."

I dropped to the floor in tears. *How could the school send me such a letter?* I knew it was not intentional, but I needed a moment to access my rational brain, as initially I could only view this as insensitive and careless. I was also baffled that this oversight could occur at such a small school where everyone knew me. The parents who signed the letter had even been friends of mine through the years; our kids grew up together. Clearly, the school did not know how to handle my situation. I hope another parent never goes through what I did.

Not long after Lacey's passing, I offered to donate a shade structure for the soccer field in her name. I had watched many a game in which the girls wholeheartedly exerted themselves, only to rest occasionally on the sidelines with no reprieve from our ceaseless desert sun. By the time I finally received a response to this, the school had a different donation in mind, and it all collapsed in what I interpreted as a lack of interest. No one could explain to me the rationale for this disinterest or even say who was in charge of the decision. *It was abominable.*

As the date of Lacey's class's graduation approached, I felt nervous, yes, but I also knew I had numbed myself to avoid the pain— something we humans do as a survival strategy when difficult and overwhelming emotions flood our nervous systems. This is not healthy in the long term, but it is one of the ways we get through trauma. I know many grieving parents who blame themselves for becoming numb, but the numbness truly protects them when they're traumatized.

☆☆☆

About that time, a friend and her two daughters, both of whom were Lacey's close friends, invited me to a picnic at a local park— just the four of us. They came with gifts for me that included a collage of Lacey and the girls in photographs going back to when Lacey was ten years old. Each girl had drafted a beautiful story, originally conceived as a school project, describing the impact Lacey had on them. We all cried, and then they invited me to their graduations.

The love that surrounded me that day moved me deeply. The older girl, Kelsey Wong, who was Lacey's age, held my hand most of the morning. She reminded me so much of Lacey, because that is what she would do. Her hand even felt like Lacey's, and for a moment, it seemed like Lacey was really there. I guess she was.

☆☆☆

The Lacey Jarrell Foundation had scheduled its first student art presentation for May 10th. Some of the local galleries agreed to let us display student art along their walls and allow five students to sell their work. I had no goal for the foundation to make any money at the event; I simply wanted to help the students. When I saw an ad for the foundation in the Sunday paper, I could not believe it! Things were coming together that both excited and panicked me. I wanted everything to go perfectly for Lacey, but I felt disorganized.

Knowing our board of directors is incredible, I focused on letting go of my worry and trusted that all would go well. The trust extended to Lacey, for she had a strong influence in everything I did, and she guided the many good things in my life. At least that was how I viewed it.

My sense was this had been "other" directed. Everything that came together begged the question, "How did this happen?" Truthfully, I made things happen, but I had an extremely trying time recognizing my accomplishments. Functioning and accomplishing goals were paradoxical experiences that left me conflicted and guilt-ridden at times. I felt conflicted about still functioning and accomplishing things when Lacey was dead. I still felt I should be dead, and that moving on with my life meant leaving her. My crying continued daily but with a lesser intensity, and I could not feel Lacey's presence as much as I previously could. These periods were transient, however.

The pain and acceptance of her death was becoming more real, totally draining me some days. I did not want to think about its permanency. At the same time, I was able to joke again and find pleasure in others' humor. Having gone through so many cycles of grief since her death, my world as I knew it had forever changed. Although some of my loneliness had decreased, this current cycle felt foreign and vexatious. Looking back, I am eternally grateful for the friends who stayed with me—I could not have lived without their support

☆☆☆

During this time, I became aware that our current goal to help students show their art was not singularly what I wanted. Rather, I wanted to help students who were struggling—those who were willing to get direction from us to present their work. I also wanted them to be accountable, which meant showing up and getting their bios in on time. This did not happen. Three of the five students did not do that. *How could I serve them if I did not hold them accountable?* I could not justify helping someone by going out and doing all the work to sell their art if they were not willing to participate.

I also knew I wanted to target youth and families going through grief and loss issues and provide them with counseling support. I was glad to arrive at these ideas and find more clarity in my mission.

The first Lacey Jarrell Foundation event actually went quite well. I had felt apprehensive that day and struggled to pinpoint the source of my anxiety. The event was beneficial to me in that I learned a great deal from the gallery owners. Later, however, I became incensed. I realized my anxiety was related to feeling at the mercy of the gallery owners.

Four exclusive galleries kindly and generously gave us permission to show student art for sale. However, the other gallery owners snubbed us. I felt frustrated thinking I needed their permission to get the foundation going, that I also needed their acceptance of my organization and the student art. What I later came to understand was that I did *not* need them after all. If this were to work, I would try something else. *I have never been a quitter, and I was not about to quit now.*

As it turned out, one of the gallery owners did not like the student art itself, and we agreed to take it out after the initial evening show. One of the board members who helped create this art event agreed to bring back a different piece of art for him to approve. I told her, "Forget about it. Tell him the Lacey Jarrell Foundation does not want its art in his gallery." The old Nancy had come back, at least in part. My rebelliousness and discomfort with not holding my power had returned. Defiantly, I refused to be at this man's mercy; we would be fine without his support. Fortunately, however, my wise friend did not follow my directive, and we did not insult that gallery owner.

The month of May brought the death of a friend who succumbed to liver disease complicated by acute alcoholism. Her daughter was also friends with Lacey and Will. The funeral was held at the same church as Lacey's service, and many of the faces attending were the same—some of the people I had not talked with since Lacey died. It surprised me when several families came over and said they were concerned for me. They wondered if it was an appropriate time for me to attend a funeral. Even when I went through the line to extend my condolences, grieving family members mentioned my loss. I told them, "This is about your pain and loss today, not mine." I cried a lot when they showed videos of my friend. Worried, people came over to comfort me. When they asked if I needed to leave, I explained, "This is just what I do now—I cry a lot, and it's okay."

The evening after my friend's funeral, I found myself alone with my now-familiar companion: grief. I began obsessing once again about how Lacey ended up in her car that morning, barefoot, with none of her possessions, still dressed in the clothes she slept in. I could get away from the thought for longer periods, but the question of what really happened continued to plague me periodically.

☆☆☆

That same evening, I received an e-mail from one of the gallery owners who gave me advice and encouragement on my mission statement. Then she included bullet points with the heading: *The Lacy Pederson Foundation.* I was shocked. Lacy Pederson, who had been in the national news a few years earlier, had gone missing while pregnant. Eventually, the police recovered her body and charged her husband with her murder and that of their unborn child. It was a horrible and painful story. *What was the gallery owner thinking?*

Eventually, I realized this woman just made an oversight, but I struggled accepting that as true. After all, she had been my neighbor for the past seven years. She knew, unquestionably, that my daughter's name was Lacey Jarrell. And many fliers had been left in her store with Lacey's name on it.

However, this mix-up left me with an eerie feeling that Lacey might have been the victim of actions by her passenger. *Could it really be true?* My thoughts felt chaotic at times, and I knew I should not take this as a message from Lacey. Later that night, I was looking up a word in the dictionary and came across another of Lacey's poems—another one of her things, particularly her poems, that showed up unexpectedly in the house. This poem was eerie as well, reading in part:

> *Parked in the warm seasoned cushion*
> *Cold hands placed firmly on the wheel.*
> *But I am not steering the car this time*
> *This life*
> *The unyielding lines that mark my fate.*

Unbelievable! By then, I had found several poems indicating a prediction of her death. I knew my thinking was distraught with traumatic loss, that I was immersed in grief, and yet it became hard to ignore them. This noesis—this sense of knowing—was shared by Lacey and me. I knew her deep intuitiveness. In later years, I would learn about how both the heart and the intestines send chemical messages to the prefrontal cortex area of the brain. From this pathway comes intuition. Related to that, I could not forget Lacey telling me, "Mama, my stomach hurts. I feel like something bad is going to happen."

The compilation of the poems, her words, and my thoughts added to my fear that her passenger was the one steering the car, not her. My anguish and despair grew deeper. *Yet I knew nothing would ever bring my daughter back.*

☆☆☆

I felt overwhelmed anticipating the approaching graduations and Mother's Day. Many of the kids and adults I knew were attentive to me, realizing that Mother's Day would be hard for me, and May was the month both Lacey and Will would have graduated. Due to a course incompletion when he learned his sister had died, Will still needed three credits to graduate college, which would happen in the summer. This May, there would be no Jarrell family graduations as originally planned.

Although several of Lacey's friends from various schools invited me to attend their graduation ceremonies, I knew I could not. I marveled at the networking she had done in her short life and how many people she loved and who loved her back. I knew the St. Gregory School graduation ceremony would be emotionally challenging, but that's the one I would attend without question.

The head of the high school had told me the ceremony would not include anything to honor Lacey at the graduation. I felt hurt about this and told her I was not asking for anything. However, when parents and students complained, it would *not* be okay for the school to use me as an excuse, saying, "We did not want to upset Mrs. Jarrell." They had used this tactic before. I was told Lacey would be in the yearbook and the literary magazine was dedicated to her. I was happy with that.

☆☆☆

That evening, something jogged my memory regarding the pre-view article the newspaper ran to promote the feature on Lacey. I had glossed over it when I first saw the publication and intended to get back to reviewing it. Above her photo was a small article written by the same reporter on the alleged UFO occurrence over Phoenix in March of 1997. The article addressed the belief by former Arizona Governor Fife Symington that the sighting was unexplainable. Lacey, Will, and I happened to be driving to Phoenix the night of these sightings, and we clearly saw three unidentifiable, odd-moving objects in the sky. We watched them from our car and even pulled over, mesmerized and excited by what we were seeing.

We had no doubt this was something extraordinary. Lacey never forgot this and talked about it many times, even in the months before her death. That this article on the sighting showed up years later on the same page that previewed her series signified something greater than coincidence to me. As was the pattern, I chose to believe this to be a message from Lacey, perhaps signifying her presence or telling me she had confirmation that what we viewed that night was indeed extraordinary. I felt relieved and happy that she was communicating with me in this new way.

I am aware how crazy this might sound. Yet I engaged in a lot of magical thinking that first year. My son called it "Lacey phenomena," and although I thought my beliefs were crazy at times, too, I also knew any belief or action that elevated my mood, if only for a moment, was not crazy at all.

Chapter Twenty-Eight: Reversals

In my troubles,
I was someone else to myself, a stranger,
Another woman, someone else altogether.
In the mirror I was like a tree
In the distance
A tree you see and have seen,
A tree you recognize
But whose name is unknown to you.

A stanza from *"Santa Teresa in Nogales"*
~ Alberto Rios

By mid-May, there was no protective shock anymore. This really *was* my life. I missed my daughter more as reality set in. Yet I knew there were many facets to my emotions, aside from the now-permanent ache of losing Lacey Jane.

Some shattering truths were no longer deniable. One was that Jack would leave June 4th, fewer than three weeks away. I knew his plans, and yet I still didn't feel as if he had ever told me the whole story. *How did he feel about me? Why was he moving?*

I didn't know how I could tolerate all my feelings when he left. I was beginning to feel annoyed that I had spent so much time with him, someone who didn't communicate about such life-changing events. *What was going on with him?*

Feeling insignificant, I just wanted his move to happen, so I counted the days on the calendar and marked them off. *Waiting for the hurt, I just wanted to get it over with.* I was finally admitting this relationship was a medication and distraction I used to quell my pain.

I wanted to curb my anger so I could be kind to him when he left—and so I could genuinely wish him a good life.

When I thought about dating someone else, though, I became tearful. *I would never want to date someone who did not know Lacey.* Jack had witnessed my last year with my daughter and also what happened after she died. He was my container—the one person who could give me true feedback on how things were.

I reminded myself that no loss could compare to losing Lacey. So, when Jack did leave as he planned, if all I did was cry and feel lonely and depressed, then that's what I would do. I would not die, for I had not died from what I thought would kill me. Even though I was tired of the pain and trying to find ways out of it, I resolved to live with all my emotions.

There is no way *out* of pain but *through* it, meaning we need to experience all the feelings rather than try to avoid, numb, or medicate them. Pain needs to be processed and felt fully before it can move through us.

☆☆☆

One night on my way to grief therapy, I asked Jack if he thought Lacey knew how much I loved her. "Without a doubt," he told me. He then described how I would light up when she entered the room, and how I would have her sit on my lap as I stroked her long brown hair. He described our relationship in terms of how much she cherished the love I gave her and how much she loved our relationship—and me. *I needed to hear details like that.*

As Graduation Day approached, a new sense of dread arrived. Instead of a celebration, it represented an ending. As Lacey becomes a student of the past, there would no longer be reason for me to have contact with her school. All these things culminated in extreme sadness for me.

Many of Lacey's friends who had been my support would be going off in their own directions and moving on to their next stages in life. I would miss them. One of Lacey's best friends had called and said she was moving to California in five days. This young woman had promised in a letter to Lacey she would take care of me—and she had stayed close to me. I felt another loss, knowing she would soon leave Tucson.

At this same time, I asked at St. Philip's in the Hills where we'd held Lacey's funeral if I could have a memorial service there on the anniversary of her death. I received a genuinely nice reply from the minister who had facilitated her service. She told me the Episcopal Church did not do that. Even though I understood why they would not do a service, this response affected me emotionally. I needed another way to honor the day of her passing, but I also knew I could not keep her memory alive forever for everyone. *Doing this was really for me.*

My hope around Lacey's foundation was fading. Had I formed it too quickly? I was still not clear on my mission and how to implement it. I had relied on kind, wonderful volunteers, but I had to respect that they had busy lives, jobs, and families. They could not do it all for me.

Also, Jack's departure affected his position on the board. And although he said we'd work together through conference calls, I could not imagine doing that. Added to that, the IRS had not yet qualified the foundation for a 501(c)(3) nonprofit status.

I felt so disoriented and perplexed at times. I had no idea how much Jack would be in my life once he moved. *Was maintaining contact with him good for me? Should I sever all ties with him once he left?*

The undulating pattern continued. I now understood that after losing a child, the life of a bereaved parent would not look like a graph plotted with an upward line indicating a clear path to better times. Rather, there are waves within any day—with some unbelievably bad days and nights. I had no control over any of this. That was the bottom line and the lesson—I had no control. I could not stop my pain. I could not stop Jack from moving. I could not make the church do the service I wanted. I could not make the school honor Lacey more fully. *I could not bring Lacey back.*

What *could* I do, though? I could get out of bed. I could write this book. I could be there for my son. I could go to work each day. I could help people at Sierra Tucson. I could make therapy appointments, even when I did not want to go.

But I could not bring myself peace. Nor could I fully alleviate the emotional pain I carried. Sometimes I visualized my body as a cylinder filled with pain in the form of a clear liquid. I waited for the liquid to slowly evaporate, but the line demarcating the level of pain remained static. Just to lose a few drops in the cylinder would have brought exhilarating relief.

God knows I tried. By this time, I had seen and talked to doctors, therapists, life coaches, psychics, and mediums. I had gone to church, read the Bible, concentrated on helping others, focused on gratitude, and asked God and my guardian angels for help. Plus I continued to work out.

At times, I had placed myself in the arms of danger by walking alone to Lacey's memorial site at night. I'd sit there in the dark for hours. I'd visit local psychics in their homes in unsafe parts of town. Sometimes, I behaved carelessly and recklessly. Right after Lacey died, I even received two speeding tickets, and one was on River Road, the same thoroughfare as her accident. As tears rearranged my makeup, I tried to explain the irony of this to the sheriff. He did not understand it.

On May 16th, I felt especially hopeless and exhausted. Even waking up was painful. What could I do to make myself feel better? *I'd have to give it over to God and let go. Again.*

Letting go is an extremely difficult concept for me—to take no action and stop trying to control everything around me. Not easy. I tried to keep faith that "everything happens for a reason," that "when one door shuts, another door opens," and that "this too shall pass." But all the tired clichés failed me. Once more, I turned my pain, my grief, and my troubles over to Him—admitting I clearly had no power over any of this.

I sincerely hoped I could write about how it *did* work rather than how it failed.

☆☆☆

Well, it did work! I was graced with another reprieve. It happened later in the afternoon on that same day, May 16th. Despite feeling challenged to do anything but cry into the pillows on my couch, I forcefully demanded myself to get out the door—to a nail salon. Pampering myself was good, although like so many places, visiting the nail shop left me feeling conflicted, because Lacey and I had gone there together. Her absence from familiar places grated on my soul. On the other hand, the owners of the shop and their staff all knew Lacey, and I preferred to be with people who knew her.

Once I got out of the house, I found it easier to get to the gym, always a big win for me. As I listened to my iPod while working out, I cried at the same time. I wondered which parts of my brain had been activated and if my limbic system—the area of the brain regulating emotion—became over-activated following the trauma of Lacey's death. *What else was changing? Was I running completely on emotion?*

My son called that evening to say he was coming home for about ten days. I was elated. He was flying in the next day. After Will's call, I went grocery shopping. Shopping for him took me through every aisle. As I passed varying products, I thought, "Now this is what Will likes, and this is what Lacey likes." Consequently, Lacey was present in my thoughts as I realized that, for twenty-two years, I had been grocery shopping for my children.

Now, I felt out of place in the store. I had been buying little food for myself. When I did shop, I found myself in the gift/party section looking for items to leave at Lacey's memorial site. In the past month, I had gained an increased ability to navigate the grocery store, though probably in a dissociated state as I focused on selecting the few things I needed quickly and then left.

On this excursion, however, I cried the entire time I walked through the aisles. Some time before, I had given up concerning myself with what people thought if they saw me crying. It just did not bother me anymore. I rarely wondered if—or when—the tears would ever stop. At eleven months post Lacey, still the tears came and spilled onto my blouse. There was little chance of reversion for me in any grocery store, especially since seemingly wicked boxes of cereals and children's beverages stared down at me from their shelves.

I found it harder to keep up my practice of positive thinking and seeking to understand the bigger picture. As I told a friend, "I am either very sad or very angry." This was difficult to admit. I experienced emotional extremes and knew that those of us suffering PTSD tend to either overreact or underreact. However, that evening, I felt thrilled that my son was coming home (despite my appearance while shopping).

As I hauled in the groceries, I checked my phone messages. An art gallery owner had called to let me know a piece of student art had just sold! It had only been a week since the Lacey Jarrell Foundation event, and we had already sold a piece of art! One of the major goals of the foundation—to help students sell their art works—was real. And the gallery owner was almost as excited as I was!

I cried again, but with tears of complete and heartfelt joy. I e-mailed all the board members, and everybody celebrated the sale. Then Jack called, and his emotional response was obvious. I became aware of the extremes. Emotionally, I had gone from hopeless to hopeful in a short span.

These reversals continued to happen, and I thanked God and my daughter. I stated aloud what I felt grateful for as I saw my daughter above me, dancing, cheering, laughing, and celebrating with me. Her presence brought tranquility to my evening.

Later, I sat quietly in my sizable living room and watched the mountains fade in colors of amber, azure, and crimson, guiding the sun to bed for the night. The sky began its transition to navy as the soft blue stars rose to rule the heavens. *How long did I watch this miracle of the universe?*

I felt the open calmness of the earth; I felt the world's despair. And for a moment, I was able to comprehend the wisdom that nothing—absolutely nothing—happened in my world by happenstance and that I and those I loved would be okay.

With renewed hope for the foundation, I was ready to face the demanding work of keeping it going. It *was* such demanding work that I could be performing it as a full-time job, except I needed an income. Besides, I loved my job at Sierra Tucson. I felt fortunate I was paid to do something I truly loved and lucky to work with the compassionate and talented professionals there.

I also loved the location of my work and the opportunity to sit on a porch for lunch and face the backside of the beautiful, inspiring Catalina Mountains. All of us—staff, patients, and guests—were privy to nature's dramatic play. Wise cacti held vertically onto the mountainsides, a ravishing herd of deer roamed the area, and the ever-present Arizona sky changed on a whim, its penetrating light accentuating the mountains. I prayed in gratitude for this daily drama.

During that May, I noticed that when I spoke to people about Lacey, I became "little"—that is, I felt incredibly young, like a four-year old. My voice became tiny, my tears welled up, and I felt fragile and vulnerable in my sorrow. I was sorry people at work saw me this way, but I could do nothing to stop it. Although I'd learned to accept myself with all these feelings, I knew others struggled to understand them.

It might be more accurate to say they struggled to see me so sad. More people than I realized were vigilant in monitoring my facial expressions, my movements, my mood, and my ability to function. The moments I joked or laughed seemed to be particularly important to those who cared for me. At times, I did not notice I was being fun or funny again, but when it happened, people gave me positive feedback. They'd comment that I was moving better or that I did not seem to have as much back pain, for example. I realized then that those close to me were genuinely elated when they saw me feeling better or resuming old behaviors. This helped me immensely.

After a traumatic event, movement is critical in healing the body and the brain. I had developed a slower pace than normal since Lacey's death, and I had a different body posture, too. Eleven months later, I noticed slight improvements in that as I applied some tools and adjusted to my new life.

Athletes have known for years that exercise causes a release of endorphins, which are the feel-good hormones that boost mood. Exercise also stimulates the production of brain-derived neurotropic factor (BDNF), which produces genes in the hippocampus. In 2019, Dr. Ottavio Arancio, a researcher at Columbia University, led a study on a recently discovered hormone called irisin that is released into the metabolism during physical activity.[23] Dr. Arancio was studying a possible link between irisin and Alzheimer's.

The brain's hippocampus is a critical area for sustaining memory and learning. Dr. Arancio and colleagues found irisin present in the human hippocampus and noted that its levels were reduced in Alzheimer patients. Over the years, I learned more about how exercise promotes healthy brain function, improved mood, memory, and cognitive function. I knew little of these benefits in the early times following my loss, but I came to reflect on how fortunate I was for having been able to take those long hikes in Aspen, work out at the gym, and discover yoga.

One afternoon while driving down a main road in Tucson, I suddenly heard a voice in my head say, "Go to yoga." This was not Lacey's voice or even a gender-specific voice but rather a precise, brief, and clear message of direction. As I stopped at the next traffic light and looked to the right, I saw a yoga studio. *I had never attended a yoga class before.*

After doing a bit of research, I attended my first yoga class a few days later at the studio I had seen. When I arrived, I was greeted by a welcoming face. A man I had once worked with at Sierra Tucson was conducting the class. A psychotherapist who specialized in trauma treatment, Tom had left this career to focus on teaching and enhancing his yoga practice. About ten years before, Tom and I with two other clinicians had developed Sierra Tucson's Program for Sexual and Trauma Recovery.

What a relief to see his familiar face! I told him I was struggling and had never done yoga before. With that began my commitment to yoga. In the class, I found myself experiencing a full ten minutes within the hour when I felt present in my body and emotionally balanced. That provided some relief from the ball and chain I dragged around. *This relief was enormous.*

☆☆☆

I was well on my way toward understanding what circumstances, activities, and situations contributed to my feeling better. I always felt happier around my son. With him, I tried to manifest confidence, wisdom, and emotional progress while appearing to have transcended my ferocious grief. This was only minimally possible, however, and along the journey, I learned Will needed to see his mother in all her truth, tugging the pain along and still waking up to another day. I wanted to show him I had the confidence and skill to persevere in the face of adversity despite the loss putting me in unchartered territory.

I did model resilience for Will, although I was not aware of this at the time. In later years, I studied resilience and learned that, as humans, everyone has access to this important survival mechanism, but it is more easily activated if we have witnessed others being resilient.

This caused me to reflect on my childhood when resilience was modeled for me. I realized how much I'd learned from my parents after losing my brother and from my two grandmothers. One had lost her son and the other her husband when their children were young. This led me to being fascinated with multi-generational repetition of trauma history, a phenomenon I'd seen when facilitating genograms with people in family therapy sessions. In the coming years, I ultimately developed a new paradigm of treatment for behavioral health known as The Sabino Model: Neuroscience Based Addiction and Trauma Treatment™. Many things I learned since losing Lacey influenced the creation and development of this model, which was already in process in 2007. The model primarily targeted the treatment of trauma, and I developed a family therapy component of the clinical program that involved communication about multi-generational trauma and trauma repetition in families.

In addition, I had started reading about neuroplasticity, which refers to the capacity that neural networks have to adapt and change as a result of meaningful repetitive experience. In essence, the brain has the ability to change itself when exposed to consistent experiences. *Could I reduce my sadness through daily positive experiences?*

When Will came to visit, I was thrilled to see him and welcome him home. He had plans to return to Boulder and attend the Summer Writing Program at Naropa University. (He is actually the most talented poet and writer in our family.) He also planned to study for the L-Sat exam and begin the admission process for law school. His girlfriend of three years had graduated the previous semester and moved to California for a marketing position. They continued their relationship, but both were unclear how they'd make it work. It was hard to ignore that both my son and I were living parallel experiences, with his girlfriend having moved to California and Jack heading to Colorado. *What is the universe up to with this one?*

During Will's visit, we had many meaningful discussions about Lacey and the pain we both felt. We were also able to talk about a multitude of life challenges in depth and with a splash of humor. I felt grateful to have this kind of relationship with my son. Still, at times, I felt guilty around him, because I was aware that his presence, while a joy and comfort to me, also enlarged the absence of

Lacey. After she was born, there were few times the three of us were not together during their childhood.

As I drove home from work one night, I called Will at the house and asked what he wanted to do for dinner. For years, I had asked Will or Lacey if they wanted me to cook them dinner. As they grew older, they would have already grabbed a burger after school or had plans with friends. This night, when I made the traditional offer, Will responded with such exactness, it surprised me. He requested boneless, skinless chicken breasts with rice—a dish I used to make and one of his and Lacey's favorites.

I felt delighted but anxious about cooking as I had prepared only a handful of meals since Lacey's death. When alone, I either went out with friends or did not eat. So I hurried to the grocery store and bought the few ingredients I needed for Will's request, not allowing myself to focus on the distressing content in many of the aisles. I also went to a store I did not usually frequent, which helped me avoid the sadness I have described. *Maybe I did not need to keep returning to the same grocery store where Lacey and I had shopped together.*

The dinner that evening came off with ease. When Will and I sat down, though, I noticed I had set out three placemats completely unconsciously—one each for Will, Lacey, and me. *I had set the table for three!* When I noticed it, I tried to ignore it and hoped Will did not see it. I hadn't yet put out plates, so my action was subtle—but not to me. These kinds of unconscious actions occurred often. I had to remind myself that everything I did had to be normal, because there is no normal after losing a child. *There is no instruction book on how to live after losing a child.*

☆☆☆

I took extra days off from work to spend time with Will. By this point, I had been looking at houses to buy for seven or eight months. But with ten thousand homes for sale in Tucson, I could not find one I liked. Despite my emotional state, I would not be impractical and make a decision that would compromise me financially. And I'm fussy. While Will was in town, we went with my agent to look at more houses. We found one or two that appealed to Will, but I thought it was because they had a pool or Jacuzzi. Certainly, I didn't want the job of taking care of a pool or Jacuzzi I'd rarely use. Rather,

I desperately wanted mountain views and a yard for a dog or another pet.

When we got home that afternoon, I was surprised to see I had missed four calls from work. Although I frequently received calls on my days off, four was excessive—and on a day I had intentionally left my work cell at home. As I listened to the messages, I learned that my horse, Mo, who lived in the stables where I worked, was near death. *Sierra Tucson, was an incredibly special place—where else could I work and see my horse from my office window?*

As mentioned earlier, Sierra Tucson is an in-patient psychiatric hospital nestled in the valley of the Catalina Mountains, just north of Tucson. It treats adults with a variety of disorders, including addictions, trauma, mood disorders, pain issues, eating disorders, and other mental health issues. The facility looks like a resort but is not. Nor is

My horse, Mo, helped me provide
equine-assisted therapy at Sierra Tucson.

it a lock-down facility. The campus is open, with a barn and outdoor stalls to accommodate about twenty horses. This allows the hospital to offer equine-assisted psychotherapy to patients as a part of their treatment. For several years, I had overseen the equine program and facilitated the equine-assisted psychotherapy.

Some years before, when we struggled to find quality horses for equine therapy, I brought my horse, Mo, to help. Very quickly, Mo became a loved member of the Sierra Tucson community. After a large company purchased the hospital, I gave ownership of Mo to that organization, since she was clearly there to stay. And for reasons of liability, the corporation wanted only horses owned by the company on the grounds. I certainly wanted Mo to live out her life on this property I loved and hoped she would be buried there.

The phone messages said Mo had gone down several times and was unable to get up. She appeared to be swollen and in pain. Mo had been with me for more than twenty years, and I calculated her age as thirty-two—a good old age for a horse. She had lived a full life.

I raced up to work, my mind spinning as I remembered the many things I had deeply shared with this generous horse. I recalled placing my children on her back when they were just babies, and later, Lacey riding her in shows and winning first-place ribbons. I had so many adventures with this mare—through endurance racing, cattle round-ups, team penning, and three-day camping and riding trips. Mo and I had a long and pleasurable history.

When I arrived at Sierra Tucson, I had to decide: *Do I put her down or wait for her to die? I struggled with the moral decision. Did I have any right to dictate the fate of any animal or being? Who was I to order the death of my precious animal?* Didn't God say, "Thou shalt not kill?" I had put many animals down through the years but had not struggled with it this much.

So I spoke with our wrangler, a deeply religious man, and I asked him how he dealt with this dilemma. He told me that God also said, "Be merciful." That was how he justified euthanizing our wonderful animals. He helped me immensely, and after tears and hugs, I agreed to have Mo put down rather than suffer anymore. The wrangler offered to call the vet and take care of other details, staying into the evening to facilitate what needed to happen.

I went to spend thirty special minutes with my horse. I thanked her for all the gifts she brought me in her life and apologized for some of my behaviors, particularly that I had ignored her over the past few months. I had done this intentionally as a way to avoid the pain of her eventual death. Of course, that did not work.

Mo nudged me and stayed remarkably close to me, keeping her head on my chest as I whispered in her ear. I told her Lacey would be meeting her soon, and she seemed calm and comfortable. Then I said goodbye.

As I drove home that night, I cried for Mo, for Lacey, for Will, for the rest of my family, and for all those who are suffering losses. I found comfort, however, in the next few days, as I captured a truly unclouded vision of Lacey and Mo together. I knew their reunion made them both happy, especially Lacey whose joy I could almost feel. I absolutely believed that people and animals went to the same place after death—a place of exquisite beauty and compassion, flawless wisdom and strength, and above all, mountainous Divine Love.

It was vital for me to believe my child and my horse were experiencing divine, supreme love together. They both deserved it.

Although I felt grateful I could say goodbye to my wonderful horse, it still tormented me that I never got to say goodbye to my beautiful daughter.

Chapter Twenty-Nine:

A Play Called Life

I'm going. What is today? Where am I?
What cruel nature wires a brain like this?
To give it pleasure
And then let pleasure make itself a pain?
To say you loved a person
To say that person no longer exists.
A tragic flawed fate going on and on and on.

"No Exit"
~ Mary Jo Bang

One morning driving to work while in conversation with Lacey, I visualized her with ease at the top of our stairs wearing a simple white t-shirt and blue jeans, her long hair down and her long legs kicking out side-to-side as she playfully danced like the scarecrow in *The Wizard of Oz*. She would laugh, and dance, and cheer me on.

I talked out loud to her, then waited a moment to hear what she said in return. I clearly heard words, although not an accompanying voice. Whatever popped into my head, I went with it, and believed that whatever came up was Lacey speaking to me. Her message was always positive.

On this particular morning, I asked Lacey if she would like to take some kind of action (if she could) that would let me know she was with me. I focused extremely hard on paying attention to my environment, so I would not miss any sign or communication she might offer. I wanted to have fun with her and play, and I had a keen sense she was on board with my suggestion.

After about an hour at work, a staff person entered my office and asked to speak with me. As we began talking, Kathy noticed my computer's desktop image, a full-blown photograph of Lacey wearing angel wings. She loved the photo and asked if I would copy it and send it to her. Always ready to share Lacey with people, I said, "Well, let's try to do that now." Kathy pulled her chair close to me, and we went to my computer to search for where the photo was stored. We could not find it! In fact, as we searched, the photograph of Lacey disappeared entirely from my desktop.

We continued to look in "My Pictures," hoping to bring the photograph back to my desktop. We clicked on one photo icon, and a completely different image appeared—a photo of Lacey and me the night before her prom. We were happy and smiling, and most important, together. I had no recollection of sending this photo to my work computer. In fact, I was sure I had not. It then showed up on the desktop, and I must have accidentally clicked something else, because the picture suddenly broke down into sixteen smaller blocks, all across my computer. The number sixteen did not escape me. *Was Lacey still sixteen on the other side—the age she loved?* My co-worker, Kathy, and I tried different options to get the Angel Wings picture back, but we never could find it.

I knew instantly Lacey was playing with me. I loved it! The photo of the two of us signified we were together. I so often believed and felt she was always with me. I chose to believe she had heard me and communicated with me that day. And I found comfort knowing I could still access her. *Everything was okay.*

☆☆☆

The date of Lacey's high school graduation, May 27th, drew closer. Unfortunately, the many phone calls and last-minute requests from the school had me confused and exasperated. Several times, teachers or students called me at work, requesting a DVD of Lacey, photos, or a poem she had written. Although they wanted me to provide the material that day, I could not put together their requests in time. As mentioned earlier, the school had dedicated both the literary magazine and the yearbook to Lacey, but she would not be honored at the commencement ceremony. Still astounded about that, I let the head of the school know I would be attending the ceremony as a guest of Lacey's classmates. When the school director heard my shaky voice, she fumbled with her words and said, "Well, we didn't want to upset you by doing anything." Yet, I had asked her weeks before not to do this, knowing it would become the excuse they would use.

My response to the head of the school again was this: "When the kids complain about it, I want you to be perfectly clear that you may not use me as your excuse. Nothing is being done because you do not want to do anything. That has nothing to do with *not* upsetting me. Do not *ever* tell the kids you did not do anything because Mrs. Jarrell would be upset. Mrs. Jarrell is upset because you are *not* doing anything." She understood.

I did not like that I snapped into anger like this to still defend my child—as I'd always done for both of my children. I could not accept that the school officials wanted to pretend this had never happened. It was as if they conveyed an unspoken message to me and the students, saying, "Let's just get over it. We need to move on."

In agony, I couldn't accept I no longer had a child at the school or that along with my child's death, everything we were involved in had come to an abrupt halt—school classes and activities, soccer practice and games, even speaking to the school counselor about college admissions.

Before graduation night came, I asked a friend to go with me. Will was home, but we both agreed he did not need to go. Having been away at college through her high school years, he wasn't as close to Lacey's friends as I was. And he managed his grief differently than I handled mine. I was proud of Will and his ability to make the best choice for himself. I learned again that Will was highly capable of managing his emotions and did not need me to take care of him.

So, going to graduation felt like the last thing I needed to do to close out my life with St. Gregory School. Between Will and Lacey, I'd had children in that school for twelve years. Graduation was a time to honor Lacey again and be there for her friends. Although I experienced great distress, I am so glad I attended. As

I walked in, parents, children, and teachers approached me and opened themselves to me with hugs, tears, and offers of support. This continued throughout the evening.

As the ceremony began and the kids walked down the aisle to the stage, many of them turned their backs to me so I could see they had placed Lacey's initials, along with two green stars, on the back of their caps. I froze. And then came the tears. *So beautiful and moving.* I was overwhelmed with sadness that my daughter was not there, yet many talked about how they felt her presence in the room.

During the ceremony, the class valedictorian, Amber Rose, stood up and began her speech by noting that a classmate was missing. In her beautiful and passionate speech, she talked about Lacey's life and how she died. Following that, another of Lacey's classmates, Nathan Levy, also focused his speech on Lacey. He talked about her wonderful qualities, and what he most wanted to remember— her laughter and how fun and funny she was. He read a poem she had written titled "Laughter" that I had printed on a two-sided card with two photos and two of her poems—cards I had given to Lacey's classmates about two months after she passed. He held up the card, which was wrinkled, creased, and worn, and said he carried it everywhere with him. *His speech was an extremely dear, loving declaration!*

As the ceremony continued, the head of the school thanked Buddy (who sat alone) and me for attending. Everyone looked at us and clapped, many in tears. I was embarrassed as I had such mixed feelings about being there. I did not want my presence to add sorrow to anyone's celebration.

I also felt sad for my ex-husband, Buddy. I had come with a friend and had many young people nearby wanting to hold my hand. But Buddy did not want to sit with me, explaining he needed to be close to the door if he felt the need to exit early. I understood his feelings but also knew he just did not like to be around me. Lacey's death had moved us even further apart than when we first divorced. The physical separation at the graduation activated another layer of grief I thought I had processed.

After the ceremony, I sought out five of Lacey's closest girlfriends to give them cards. Many kind people surrounded me, wanting to hug me and say kind words. Several kids also wanted to have photos taken with me. I wonder now how those photographs came out, as I remember thinking, *How can I mask my pain and pull off a genuine smile?*

After thirty minutes or so, I was able to weave myself out of the crowd. The love and attention gave me further evidence that my daughter had affected many lives, that the loss of a child truly becomes a *community* loss. I was grateful for the love and the people who kept me going through the worst of times.

☆☆☆

The next day was another graduation party for a friend of Lacey's who attended another school. But I felt frozen all day and cancelled my attendance there. Crippled by the emotion of the previous night, I could not leave the house. Again, here was a pattern I had experienced many times since her death—that is, participating in something emotional and connected to Lacey, then feeling immobilized the following day. Again, I had to remind myself there is no *normal* in grieving a child, and that whatever I did or did not do was okay. Friends told me repeatedly how courageous I was, and yet I felt fragile, weak, and needy. I was incredibly grateful that Will was home. We spent our time watching episodes from a comedy television series he liked.

When Will returned to Colorado for the summer, my loneliness returned and yet I felt fortunate to have many compassionate, kind people in my world who would help me in a heartbeat if asked. I was often surprised when people approached me in parking lots, gas stations, or grocery stores. Remembering my photo in the newspaper series in March, they followed their recognition of me with a big hug. These astounding encounters affirmed that many extraordinary people touched my life.

☆☆☆

In the mail one day was a letter and invitation from a woman I did not know—Anita Smith-Etheridge. She had also read the newspaper article and offered me two complimentary tickets to a musical she had written and directed titled "Why I Sing." When I arrived at the theater, she instructed, I was to find an usher who would take me to reserved seating. She told me to use the code word *Jonathan.*

I wrote Anita an e-mail accepting her invitation. Then I invited my girlfriend, Cyndy, to go with me, as Jack was leaving Tucson two days later. Cyndy and I went to dinner and then to the play with little information about what we were about to see. When we arrived, I asked the usher to direct us to reserved seating and told her the code word Jonathan. She said, "Oh, yes," and, with a smile, led us down to the first row and sat us front and center, as close as one could be to the stage.

We giggled about the great seats we had, especially because no one else was seated in the row. As the musical unfolded, it became obvious that my soon-to-be-friend, Anita, had written, directed, and was acting in a play about the death of her son. He lived in a wheelchair for several years due to being shot outside their home, and then he died of cancer at the age of twenty-six. That had happened five years before. Her story retold the horrible night of the shooting and Anita's time of mourning when she rarely got out of the house, obsessing on photos of him and replaying a video recording of his funeral.

Ultimately, the final act was one of joy, happiness, and humor. It revealed how Anita had eased her intense grief through singing, friendship, God, and changing her behaviors to focus on the positive. She let her son go by not watching the funeral tape all the time, and by celebrating his birthday rather than mourning it. I was in tears throughout, but I also laughed at the humorous parts. What an extremely powerful and moving production. The acting and singing were superb, and Anita's surviving daughter played herself, the anguished sister. Realizing Anita was another bereaved parent, I was in awe of her incredible tribute to her son.

A lot of the play had a gospel flavor to it. All the actors were African American and belonged to the National Association for the Advancement of Colored People (NAACP). I loved being around them, as I had grown up in a racially mixed community in New Jersey. (There is not a large community of African Americans in Tucson.)

As the show ended, the ushers encouraged the audience to stay for a special presentation. The president of the Tucson NAACP came on stage and presented Anita with a bouquet of two dozen red roses. Anita then spoke, and as she did, she looked at me and said, "You are Nancy, correct?" When I said yes, she turned back to the audience. "I would like to honor Nancy this evening. She lost her daughter in a tragic car accident not long ago." She then presented me with the flowers. My tears flowed as I accepted them and kissed her hand. I had no idea this would happen. And I could not believe the kindness.

Afterward, I met all the actors and Anita's family, and we all hugged. Anita apologized for making me cry but I replied, "Anita, you know *you* didn't make me cry. Crying is what I do every day." She smiled and said, "Yes, I do know about that." Later, we had photos taken together for her family and for the media.

As I exited, I ran into Lacey's middle school softball coach, Rebecca. Lacey had loved her, and so did I. She had been at the funeral, but I was surprised to see her at the play. She said, "Nancy, I hope you don't mind that I gave Anita your address. She works with me at the city manager's office, and we had talked of you by chance one day." *Another unexpected occurrence!*

I chose again to believe Lacey had orchestrated this introduction to Anita. Here was another bereaved mother who had used her creative ability to manage her pain and take positive action to carry on, despite her earlier state of debilitating grief. Meeting Anita caused me to reflect on my methods of managing tormenting questions about the human condition of suffering. I contemplated the efficacy again of moments when I asked, "Why me, why my child, why my family?" It was followed by my process of turning this thought around and asking instead, "Why not me?" I am just another dot on this planet journeying through life as millions have over a countless number of years. We've been riding through the storms of suffering and also relishing in the joy and comfort of sunlight, love, and connection.

The night of the play, I received Anita's loving gift of roses as though they came from Lacey, too. I felt so connected to her while experiencing so much love from and for these strangers who had offered me support. I was also grateful for Cyndy's love and support.

That night, I recognized how perspicacious both Anita and I were in our ability to navigate this transmutation day after day.

As I looked back over the eleven months since Lacey's death, I became increasingly aware I had experienced all sorts of circumstances that propelled me into a remarkable new web of people and situations. Many unusual experiences could not be dismissed as coincidental. Again, I was aware that some "other" was directing this play that was my life. Somehow, in all of this, Lacey and I seemed to be at its center.

Although I often felt the trauma and grief were larger than I could bear, I received the gifts of love and new connections. The result? The birth of a belief that I had more to do in this lifetime on earth.

PART THREE: ONE YEAR GONE

Chapter Thirty: Transformations

Love to be real, it must cost—
it must hurt—it must empty us of self.

~ Mother Teresa

In the first week of June, Jack moved to Colorado. The night before he left, I felt pierced, cut open by a sharp knife. I reminded myself how I had felt brutally stabbed and ripped apart when Lacey died, so this loss was more like an incision. Still, I was hurting.

I know that trauma becomes detrimental to one's emotional, physical, and spiritual health. The accumulation of traumatic events over time creates the most psychological damage, and I was living this truth. I struggled to avoid a wounded, victim-like stance, and yet when I perceived myself progressing, it seemed the losses kept piling up, even after I thought I couldn't hold any more.

Although Jack's move represented another loss to me, I knew that ultimately something better would come out of it. Despite my sporadic ability to maintain a faith that I'd experience better times, I also felt I had been hurled into a rapid, gushing river that kept me reaching for something sturdy to hold onto, to save me. But every time I grasped a branch along the shore, it broke, and with it my hope for rescue.

☆☆☆

That night after I said goodbye to Jack, I got in my car and drove around the north side of the city, close to the mountains. I had no direction. I cried and cried, and although God and I had shared many talks in the past months, this time it was different. I did not yell at

God or tell Him that He'd gotten it wrong. I went through a list of everything I could think of that I'd done in my life I considered wrong. And then, while I was driving, I apologized aloud and repeatedly as I begged for forgiveness. I was convinced God was punishing me for something, and because I was not sure why, I came up with everything I could remember.

Sometimes the tears blinded my view of the road. I felt crazy. I *often* felt crazy. So I begged God to show mercy on me and became humble. Then I drove to my daughter's memorial site, stopped my car, walked in the dark to the marker, and wept like a baby. When I arrived home, I got down on my knees in front of my bed. Again, I asked God for mercy. That night, I cried myself to sleep.

☆☆☆

When I awoke, I was surprised to feel okay. I had spoken to God and affirmed my faith that He would pull me through, that He had a plan for me, and that I would get to the other side of all this suffering. Still, I never expected my pain over losing Lacey to go away; I accepted this was my life.

The day continued. Although Jack drove away to start his new life, for the first time since Lacey's death, I felt content for an entire twenty-four hours. *This was enormous!* When I shared this with friends, they asked me, "What happened that made it a good day for you? Did you do something fun? Did something really neat happen?" Well, nothing happened at all, except that I had experienced a mind shift that left me settled in believing my life would get better. *My prayers had been heard.*

Yet, something actually *had* happened. Jack had left. What I had been dreading was done, so ironically, this finality relieved me. The *anticipation* of perceived pain had exacerbated my sense of doom. *I was okay.*

I acted as if I were having the most wonderful day of my life. I shouted aloud in my car, saying things like "I am loving life today!" and "Today is a *fantastic* day!" Although I didn't actually feel this, I was trying the fake-it-until-you-make-it routine. And for that day, it worked.

When I got home from work, I focused on getting ready for my gym workout, determined not to sit at home feeling miserable. I had told both Lacey and God that I felt ebullient—all was going well for me. And I was starting to feel these things, even though Jack was gone. Just another day, but yet *not* another day.

★★★

As I approached my walk-in closet to retrieve my gym shoes, suddenly one of my many shoes flew off the shelf, spun in the air, and landed on the closet floor in perfect alignment for me to place on my foot. The shoe was not something I'd wear to the gym, but one of a crazy pair of casual dress shoes. It was a blue-and-black slip-on shoe with a leopard-like printed pattern. Lacey made fun of me for buying them. I made fun of myself for buying these shoes, too. I rarely wore them and frequently wondered, "*What was I thinking?*"

Three thoughts prevailed at that moment: 1) I could not believe what I was seeing; 2) someone was in my closet; and 3) Lacey had done this. I had been standing about six feet away, but then I slowly approached my closet. Finding no one there, I knew Lacey had caused this. Had a different shoe come off the shelf, it would not have been as clear a message. Lacey knew my favorite color was the blue in this shoe, and that we had laughed about these crazy shoes so often.

I had never seen anything like it, but I knew things like this happened. I had heard of people seeing objects move and believing their loved one was responsible, but this had not happened to me. This shoe lived on the third shelf of my closet. It could not have just flown off by itself.

As I accepted that Lacey did it, I began to laugh. *She was cheering me on for having my first full day of ease and learning to celebrate my life.* Her personality was fun and goofy, and she always said her passion was cheering people up. No small task, but she accomplished it for me then.

Once I registered it all, I thanked Lacey and continued through the evening amazed! I told her she had an incredible amount of energy to make that shoe fly off the shelf. People often commented they felt her energy around them. I would hear it from parents of Lacey's friends, her teachers, and adult family members—not only the kids.

I went to the gym and felt peaceful there. When I went to bed that night, I still had a heightened mood. *I had enjoyed an entire day. It wasn't full of the old, familiar, deep, searing pain!* Coincidentally, this occurred on the day Jack moved out of state.

Before I settled between the covers that night, I received three different phone calls from people who knew Lacey. Each call began with them saying in overly excited voices they had to tell me what had happened. Each caller described an incident that had occurred that day. And each incident involved something out of the ordinary the caller believed related to Lacey's presence.

For example, one story involved a young woman who was driving with her four-year-old son. He said to her, seemingly out of the blue, "Lacey is in Heaven." The mother was surprised, and she asked why he had thought of Lacey at that moment. When she looked ahead, she saw a car with the license plate that read "Lace." She shivered and wept. The boy could not read yet.

As I became aware of Lacey's presence that day, I wondered what it was about June 5th that brought her close to me and others. I looked at last year's calendar, trying to remember what we had done that day the year before. I had not written down anything special, so I thought about numerology. This was new to me, and since Lacey had died, I paid a lot more attention to numbers, interpreting them for their significance. According to numerology, Lacey's number was eleven, which is a master number and indicates high spiritual qualities. Lacey knew she was an eleven. She included the number in her e-mail address and identified it as her lucky number. June 5th represented a total of eleven—June is the sixth month, and I added five to six for a total of eleven.

It suddenly made sense that Lacey was all around that day. I know many would think I am deranged, but for me, these kinds of beliefs helped me think the separation was not as profound as I often believed. It felt as if we still had a devoted attachment that death could not sever.

For anyone who has lost a child, my advice is to just do and believe whatever works for you. Whatever brings you even an ounce of joy or one minute away from the ever-present pain is fine, no matter what others think. Your critics have not lived in your world, and unless they have experienced it, no one can understand what it is like to lose a child and walk around feeling both alive and dead. It is a foreign and lonely existence from what we have known. Your relationship with your child is unique, as are all our relationships. They cannot be compared.

☆☆☆

I became accustomed to living alone. I did not love it, but I was doing it, even embracing the experience. I would later come to see it as a blessing—like crying. I did not mind it—I expected it and accepted it. I was recognizing, too, that the suffering and pain I experienced was a prerequisite for something better. I held on to that belief tightly.

When I felt able, I continued reaching out to other bereaved parents when asked, but only then. People frequently thanked me for my acts of kindness. They did not know they had helped me, for receiving gratitude from other mothers was a gift. *There is so much amazing love all around me in the world.*

I felt sad that it takes a tragedy for people—including me—to offer more love to others. Never again would I tolerate that isolation in my life. I want to live with compassion for others, reach out and take a minute to write a "thinking of you" card, buy flowers, or just give a hug. I hope to emanate grace and tenderness to others who are suffering.

☆☆☆

During the week that Jack left, I made plans with friends and scheduled activities so I was not stuck in my house feeling frozen. By chance or not, I discovered another organization in Tucson, The Drawing Studio, that is devoted to bringing art to the community. I had one connection to this group, Tana Jay von Isser, the daughter of one of the directors. Lacey had been close friends with Tana. I received an invitation to a board meeting and a party. Although I felt uncomfortable about attending, I went anyway. Knowing only one person there left me feeling skittish and exposed. I was afraid of my emotions.

As I entered the party, Tana's mother, Janice Angevine, greeted me warmly. She and her husband Kent von Isser had been at Lacey's funeral, but I could not remember their faces. She became tearful as she talked and went on to say how honored she was that I had come. I told her I felt honored to be invited. She said she had loved Lacey, that whenever my daughter entered their home, the room lit up. She shared cute stories of Lacey and then told me that I, too, lit up the room. I appreciated her kind comment, but I could not imagine someone who's carrying such grief as I was could light up a room.

She brought me into the board meeting, and I told the group about our nonprofit organization—the Lacey Jarrell Foundation. They gave me ideas on how to get things moving and suggested I become a part of their organization. By the end of the night, I had met so many warm and kind people that I felt inspired. I was also surprised at how many of them knew of, or knew my daughter, and I wept as they spoke to me. *Amazing.*

At the end of the night, I met a man who had lost a son in a car accident four years earlier. He was very sullen, but we instantly had a connection. We knew each other's heaviness and recognized how, due to our shared experience, we felt separate from the rest of society. He and I agreed we always have one foot in life and another foot in the afterlife. It often felt like a tug of war, but where was the destination?

He understood why I had thought of dying and admitted he still struggled with that feeling. He said he no longer had a purpose in life, but he stayed on earth because he had two daughters. I had said the exact words in terms of having no purpose other than to be here for my son. He related to my PTSD symptoms of depersonalization, impaired memory, dissociation, and the distortion of time— never knowing what day it is, or how time either passes quickly or so slowly. We both said we would live out our days until we meet our child again. The conversation was sad, and we both wept. At this point, I left the party. How ironic to be one of the last to leave after initially feeling nervous about going alone.

Once again, I reminded myself that despite all this suffering and loss, I would experience happy times again. I was determined. *My daughter would not want to see me suffering so deeply.*

☆☆☆

With all of the sadness, there have been many days when I've felt connected to a higher existence, a divine nature, a universal healing love. When these moments occur, I can access peace and even have fun. By the eleven-month mark, I think my sense of humor and ability to laugh had, for the most part, returned. Perhaps I did not laugh at things I once did. But I could laugh; I could be funny; I could make jokes again. Before my loss, I seldom watched funny movies and rarely watched television, except for the news. Yet now I had a whole collection of comedy shows, funny movies, and CDs of comedians. When I was particularly low, I would play one of these, even just as background noise while I was alone in my house. It helped some.

I could no longer watch movies with trauma, death, and violence. One night I went to a movie with two friends, and none of us knew anything about the film. It soon became evident this was a scary, traumatic movie. When a scene appeared of a car rolling and crashing, I shook, jumped, and had to look away. My PTSD could still be activated by reminders.

The duality of my new life—what my loss had taken and brought to me—weighed on my mind. The phrase "The painful arithmetic of the human condition—gain and loss" kept playing in my head. Still, I did receive an increased amount of love around me. Although I felt lonely at times, I knew that, because of my story, numerous people were available to comfort me—but only if I reached out to them.

Yet, I was not particularly good at reaching out. I was beginning to feel comfortable with my isolation, though I knew that would not bring me what I wanted. Everything still took enormous effort.

The anniversary of Lacey's death was three weeks away.

I was still keeping up the Myspace site, although spending less time with it. Activity on the site had died down, as many of Lacey's friends had gone away on summer vacations and were busy preparing for college.

By June 26th, the summer heat was registering up to 105 degrees each day. My drives past her accident site decreased to a few times a week, and generally, I did not stop. I sometimes pulled over across from it at night and just stared, saying prayers and talking to her. I would suddenly remember this was not where she had *lived*—rather, it was where she *died*. I recalled that Alan had told me that months ago when I was still consumed with the happenings there. I continued to leave flowers and wind chimes, or other knick-knacks, but not as frequently.

Once more, I rallied and went out with my real estate agent to look at homes to buy. Another morning lost, having arrived home without liking anything. At times when we entered a neighborhood or a certain area, I would literally feel sick to my stomach. Something was not right about any of this. *I was not supposed to be moving. I was not supposed to be running from a home that had once been full of love and connection but was now filled with sorrow and pain. Would I ever feel that I belonged anywhere?*

Often, I just felt that nothing short of having Lacey with me would suffice.

By this time, I had looked at more than 200 homes, and on the last outing, I experienced increased depression. I had gone out determined to find a house that day and failed. *I give up,* I thought. *Perhaps I'm not meant to move after all.*

My realtor, Cathy Erchull, was an angel to keep going out with me day after day, patiently taking me to see multiple houses. She later told me she knew all along I was not ready to move, but she believed I had to discover this for myself. Cathy was a mother, too, and her kindness and indulgence of me was admirable.

I did not know what my final giving up meant. Part of me still believed it best that I move. Another part of me saw this desire as an act of avoidance—another false hope that moving would lessen the loss. *Maybe God had something else in mind.* Maybe I had been trying to do too many things at once—find a house, draft a book, get Lacey's foundation going, work, find fun, exercise, be social, write the IRS application, and on and on. Recognizing this, I decided to let it go and turn it all over again to God. *Please take care of it for me, God. I'm not getting far on my own.*

I stepped back from the pressure I placed on myself to keep doing, doing, doing. Instead, I focused on the foundation and eventually completed the IRS application. I continued to isolate. Truthfully, I had no interest in socializing. I came to find comfort in living alone. Although I knew too much time alone was not healthy for me, I was stuck in that conflicted state of knowing what to do to improve mood and yet not being able to follow through with action—one of the profound symptoms of traumatic grief and major depression. Like a lost puppy, I had to fend for myself in the harsh desert.

I frequently felt sorry for myself, but I did not want that to be my life. I did not want to be a victim. I tried everything I'd learned on how to develop a positive attitude. I recalled the philosophy that every thought we put out to the universe is like a ripple in a pool, and that these thoughts come back to us. This meant that if I were resenting somebody, then that negative energy would come back to me. But if I were sending love to someone, then love is what I would get back. I added this practice to my growing list of ways to help myself feel better. My mood went up and down from day to day. As the calendar drew closer to the one-year anniversary of Lacey's death, *I was not doing very well.*

I had not seen my therapist in over a month. She had to travel east unexpectedly when her mother took ill and was dying. I was not sure if, on her return, she would be able to continue the grief work with me while she dealt with her own loss. I felt concerned and sad for her as well.

Repeatedly, I asked God for help, but it did not feel like I was getting much. I needed someone to make me a schedule on my days off and push me out the door or accompany me to something that involved activity, movement, and people. But I didn't let anyone know I needed this. I was so tired. I was treading water in a vast ocean, bobbing up and down, trying to keep my head above water. *My constant battle to feel better.*

Chapter Thirty-One: It Doesn't Get Better; It Just Gets Different

You don't get over it
You don't get past it
You don't get around it
You don't outlast it
You don't fight it
You don't lose it
You don't believe it
But you don't undo it
You don't get over it
You just get through it.

"Get Through It"
~ Jon Randall, Mairtin O'Connor,
and Alison Brown

At this point, what more could I do to change my life into one I wanted to live? My daughter would never be back with me, and I needed to combat my solitary lifestyle. Seeing all the psychics and mediums, starting the foundation, working and overworking, helping others, hiding my feelings, not hiding my feelings, looking for houses, not looking for houses—all gave me only temporary reprieves from the pain. So, I decided to do nothing. I often tell people in therapy that "when you don't know what decision to make, don't make one. That in itself is a decision." I stopped asking God for help and pretending I was having a good day. I also stopped being grateful for things that had not even happened yet.

Truthfully, I was angry with God again. I felt deserted, abandoned. I hated feeling this loss. I did not want to become bitter like
some of the bereaved parents I had met. Instead, I wanted to be the
way Lacey would want me to be—happy, joyful, living life to its
fullest. Yet, I could not get unstuck. *Perhaps my anger would give
me energy.*

☆☆☆

One day at work, I asked one of the young staff members to have
lunch with me. I wanted to discuss one of our programs and a specific group she facilitated. After talking business for a bit, she looked
at me and said, "How are you doing? You look tired and really sad."
I was surprised at the question and even more so by my response—
bursting into tears and falling into my little girl voice. I told her I
was struggling and asked for her feedback on how she saw me. She
said I had little energy, looked bereft, and seemed exhausted. She
was right—I was feeling all those things, plus I was not eating well.
I struggled to keep on weight.

Her feedback was useful for me. I had not known this young
woman in such a kind and compassionate way. She was tearful with
me, which was frequently the case any time I talked to someone
about missing Lacey. *The loss of a child is universal.*

People feel their own level of pain over this, but of course, no
one felt the depth of *my* pain. I knew I needed to stop overworking, that I needed a vacation. So I asked for time off the week before
Lacey's anniversary and a few days the following week. Doing so
scared me, knowing I struggled when I was home alone, and I had
not made plans to leave town.

However, I knew I needed a break. *Somehow, I would survive
without going to work for ten days.*

☆☆☆

That night, June 15th, I came home to find a packet in the mail from
my accountant. All the IRS paperwork for nonprofit status of Lacey's
foundation was complete. I had been waiting for this! As soon as
the IRS acknowledged receipt of the paperwork, I could legally
accept donations.

Looking up to the sky, I threw my arms into the air and shouted, "Lacey, we did it! We have the beginning of a foundation! It is almost the real deal now." I was elated.

Still, I needed to hear from the IRS one more time, granting us the final approval to fully operate. That night, I reminded myself that good moments exist, that I was extremely fortunate the Lacey Jarrell Foundation had come together so quickly. Thinking about it, I had no idea how all of this happened, and yet, of course, I had a great deal to do with it. Writing the eighty-plus pages of documentation for IRS acceptance seemed "other directed." I just did it, and I felt optimistic I'd receive final approval from the IRS.

Lacey would not want me sitting home alone, yet I had made no plans. So, I went to a movie by myself, something I could do easily even though I had never gone to a movie alone when she was alive.

☆☆☆

Sunday, June 17th did not start out well. When I woke up, I had no internet access. Usually, I'd spend hours on my computer, writing to people, researching assorted topics, working on foundation material, and checking e-mails. That morning regimen had become as natural as brushing my teeth.

Naturally, that put me on edge that morning, and I called my local internet company. Fortunately, a tech worker came out first thing that day, but I feared I'd have to miss an appointment with a dear friend of mine, Joe King, who had co-facilitated Lacey's funeral service. He wanted to take me to a new spiritual church where he was a deacon. As it turned out, the tech resolved my computer issue quickly, so I went off to meet Joe at the church. Yet despite his directions, I never found it.

I returned home feeling frustrated. Having lived in Tucson for thirty-plus years, I thought I knew the town inside and out. Lately, though, I often got lost—likely the resulting dissociation from my traumatic grief.

When I returned home, I absolutely had no idea what to do with myself, but I knew I needed to get out of the house. Once again, I found it difficult to look at Lacey's photos, read her poetry, or play the DVDs of her. For so many months, I'd wanted to see these every day, but on this day, it just felt too painful. *I was consistently being inconsistent.* Over time, though, I learned that my capricious thoughts and behaviors were normal responses to traumatic grief.

As I sat at my computer, I felt frozen again, not knowing how to get out of the chair and into another room. The "spells" I often experienced were truly debilitating. Sometimes, I could not physically move and stayed stuck in the freeze—a familiar state that often occurs following a traumatic event. When I slumped over in hard and heavy tears at my desk, I found enough motivation to move over to the couch. I grabbed what had been Lacey's little blue blanket, curled up into a compressed position to disappear into the fabric, and cried. Feeling sleepy, I closed my eyes and said aloud, "Please, my guides, my guardian angels, my Lacey, my God— please tell me what to do to help myself. Just get me through this day."

Although I was becoming drowsier, I continued to ask for help. And then I got a noticeably clear message: "Go get a massage." I could almost hear Lacey saying it, for it was not something I would have thought to do for myself. I immediately got up and called a place, but it had no openings. The second place I called had an opening in thirty minutes, so I got ready and headed for the door.

The massage was beneficial and soothing, but the experience was unlike any massage I had experienced. I could not feel the massage therapist touching my body. She kept asking me if this or that hurt, but it did not—I could hardly feel a thing. *Was I that disconnected from my body?* Then I decided I would somehow get to the gym in the evening, which helped me feel better. When I returned home, two things happened.

The first was receiving a message from a young girl writing to me on Myspace. She was a grade below Lacey, and they had connected from their love of soccer. She had written on Lacey's site a while back and stated, "I am going to die, because I can't play soccer." I wrote to her and told her she would not die if she could not play soccer. Then I asked her what was wrong and learned about an injury that prevented her from playing for a long time. She would die, she said, because soccer was her life.

I told her she needed to focus on the positive, that if she got well, she could play. "If you want to play, then you will play," I told her. I also said if I did not die from losing my daughter, she certainly was not going to die from not playing soccer. Later, she told me I had helped her.

A few weeks earlier, this girl had read something on Myspace, in which I had written a depressing message to Lacey that alluded to a wish to die. On this Sunday evening, she told me, "You helped me, and now I'll help you. *Two* people don't have to die because of that accident." It was an immensely powerful statement.

Not long after I read the Myspace post, my son called in a good mood—the second thing. He knew I was sad, and I told him I could not make up my mind about flying back to New Jersey for a family wedding. "Mom," he said, "the last three times you saw all of these people was at your dad's funeral, your mom's funeral, and Lacey's funeral. This may be the last time you see Aunt Alice. She is old. They all came for us. Now it's time to go to them and celebrate something. No more funerals, Mom. It's time to start living your life again."

He made my day. I was so proud of him.

The messages from Will and the young girl were right. I did need to start living life instead of staying so connected to death. I immediately made reservations to go to the wedding and, by the end of the day, I had found peace and felt hope again.

☆☆☆

As I came into work after the weekend, one of the doctors I work with greeted me. She had a middle-school-aged child who went to the same school as Lacey. She thoughtfully brought me the middle-school yearbook, dedicated to Lacey. In fact, it devoted a whole page to her. The yearbook also had a DVD attached.

Although I wasn't watching Lacey's DVDs anymore, I took this one home and played it that night. I saw multiple photos of her as well as one of her accident site and another of the star the school had hung in her memory in the garden. Many of the young children had written poems to say goodbye, or they authored stories about what she meant to them.

Once again, Lacey's positive effect on these young students floored me. I did not know them, but they clearly knew her. The network of people Lacey created, both before and after her death, continued to grow.

✩✩✩

As July approached, my ten days of time off from work began and included Lacey's death anniversary of July 6th. To stop isolating, I had to reach out again and connect to a few friends. I was incredibly grateful to have them. *How would I handle ten days off from work? Would I go into my frozen mode and not be able to leave my house?*

As if by telepathy, one of my friends sensed this. She called and asked me what I wanted to do on the anniversary. People were waiting to hear from me, so they could help. I told her, "All I know is that I don't want to be alone." With that said, she and I discussed things we could do, and I began to feel less fearful.

I was acutely aware that, although I would survive that day, the next day would be July 7th, and my world would not have changed—I would still carry my pain. This pain resides in me, runs through me, and escorts me everywhere I go. I did not try to attach to it and set myself up for more sorrow. It just was.

Having completed a year since her death would not mean I would magically feel better. In talking to other bereaved parents, I knew that the pain never leaves. We might get used to having our loved one gone, but the heartache remains part of our lives. *The pain doesn't get better; it just gets different.*

✩✩✩

The next morning, I awoke with a clear memory of having dreamed about Lacey. I felt soothed whenever she presented to me in dream state. Seeing her again in the netherworld of sleep, however, brought me head on with the reality of what I had tried to numb and avoid: *the permanence.* In the dream, I crawled into bed with her, hugged her, and held her the way I used to when she was young. It felt so real, and I had just been thinking how much I missed hugging her. *I could have Lacey in my dreams but never again alive on earth with me.*

That afternoon, two of Lacey's precious male friends, Corey and Andy, stopped over to visit. They also came to help me fix the damaged lighting around my house and my mailbox, the result of a rogue car in the neighborhood. I mentioned I had dreamed of Lacey the night before, and they both looked surprised. They had dreamed

- 282 -

of her as well! And this hadn't happened for any of us in a long time. *How ironic!*

We also determined we all dreamed about her at approximately the same time—early in the morning, around sunrise. All of us had awakened, then gone back to sleep and dreamed of her. We decided she knew we were planning to be together, so she came to us.

What an emotional day, one of aching and tenderness. The boys and I talked about Lacey for hours.

I knew I could not keep speaking about her with everyone. It was hard on the people who cared about me, and I needed to scale it back for myself. I credit other people, including my son, for giving me this knowledge.

I was absorbed with death and preoccupied with the day of and days immediately after Lacey's death. Again, I remembered Alan's wise statement when, early on, I told him I was driving up and down River Road trying to recreate what happened that morning: "You need to remember, Nancy, that River Road is where she died. It was not where she lived."

Still, I yearned for some satisfactory explanation of what happened and subconsciously believed remaining close to those days would provide me the answer. My reaction to the words "move on" remained visceral. Every time I heard or saw that phrase, I felt an uncomfortable tingling sensation that zapped my body like lightening. Moving on would mean betraying and abandoning my daughter.

Yet, I also knew at some level that re-engaging in life was vital for me to find purpose and to one day access the joy of a life worth living. I had not come very far with it, but at least I was aware that this was my next step. At times, my heartache made it impossible for me to stand up.

☆☆☆

I was surprised to have another dream of Lacey—two dreams in three days. I had asked her to help me with my resignation to *not* move out of our house. In the dream, a younger Lacey, her brother, her father, and I were all living together as a family. *I missed having a family.*

In the dream, we had just moved into a new house. I was not sure if I liked it, then Lacey led me into what would be my bedroom and showed me the view out the window. It was a spectacular scene of the moon hanging over the ocean, looking out over a beach where we lived. The moon seemed alive, radiant, and mercurial as its amber light flushed against the azure and cyan sea. From my bedroom, I could see how close our house was to the water. This astounding view sold me on being content with our new home.

When I awoke, I wondered about a message in this dream such as leaving the desert to be close to water. Lacey always loved the water when we took vacation trips to the beach, saying she wanted to live by the ocean someday. Perhaps this was a message of hope telling me there's still beauty to be found in this world. I thanked her for coming to me again.

☆☆☆

My short trip to New Jersey for my cousin's wedding was imminent. All my cousins wanted me to attend, since many had not seen me since Lacey died. It was at the wedding I learned how much grief several had experienced around Lacey's death.

For example, Ali, the daughter of my cousin Mary, came up to me, held my hand, and burst into tears, explaining, "I never even wrote you an e-mail about this, Aunt Nancy, and I love you and Lacey and Will so much." Her confession warmed and saddened my heart.

"Oh, Ali, please forgive yourself for this," I told her. "I love you and know you care. Besides, I received such an outpouring of love in e-mails, cards, phone calls, and visits that I would not have known you did not write. We all handle our grief differently, and if your way was to stay quiet, that is acceptable to me. I would never judge you about how you need to process your grief."

This was entirely true. I came to understand that how each of us managed our sorrow was just how we did it, and that way was okay.

☆☆☆

I had many precious conversations that weekend in New Jersey. My Aunt Alice, who was well into her eighties and the only surviving sister of my mother's generation, held me close and looked me in the eye. She told me she needed to do this and had for a long time. Then she told me how much she loved me, and that she prayed for me daily. I teared up, and she did as well. I had rarely seen this incredibly strong woman cry.

The entire weekend was highly emotional for me. I found it difficult to hold on to any exhilaration I accessed at the wedding and reception. Instead, I struggled to connect to the fun, and my efforts to hold back tears were futile. I did not want to ruin anyone's enjoyable time by seeming needy or appearing fragile.

And yet periodically, I joined in with my cousins and laughed about when we were kids. We got a chuckle from the fact that, only two years earlier, after my parents died, I had made the grand statement, "I will never return to the state of New Jersey." And here I was.

We faced an additional source of sadness. My sister, who lived only fifty miles away, did not attend the wedding. No one explicitly stated why, but it was apparent she did not come because both my brother and I would be there. However, I was emotionally prepared to see her. I had been through so much that having my sister distance herself from me and an agreement to sever our relationship over nonexistent estate issues was just another scrape. It hurt, but like everything, this hurt paled compared to the tragedy of losing Lacey.

☆☆☆

The next day, I went out to eat with my cousins. Almost at once, I became aware I could not stay focused on anything. I felt uncomfortable in my body as though I wanted to run from the table, run from the town, run from my life. I could not engage in conversation as I faked my way through the meal and felt I did not belong anywhere. *Not even here with the family I loved and who loved me.*

Losing my child continued to set me apart from the rest of the world—or at least that's how it felt. I still had one foot in life and one foot in the afterlife, a common malady of bereaved parents.

When I got on the plane to return to Tucson, I was sincerely glad to be going home. On the other hand, I dreaded the "nothing and no one waiting to greet me at my door" part. This was the first time in my life I had flown home with no one to call about picking me up or asking if I got home safely. After hiring a driver, I arrived at my silent home very late that night.

Missing Lacey goes without saying. That is a constant. I also missed my son and, added to the list, I was missing Jack. It had been three whole weeks since he moved to Colorado.

I was mad at myself for missing him. He left me.

I told myself I should never speak to him again, though I did talk with him occasionally. Sometimes it helped; other times, it ignited a greater flame of desolation within me. *He knew what life was like for me some days.* Yet, because I did not share my feelings with him anymore, he really did not know what I was going through.

☆☆☆

My goal: to keep moving forward and do things that would help me feel more engaged in life. I had no expectation of great times and joy, but I hoped for positive change. I wanted something new—new activities, new goals, anything that might decrease my despair. I was in a constant battle with my grief. *Oh, God, please give me just five minutes without this puncturing pain.*

On some days, I marveled that I did not return to drinking alcohol. However, I knew that relapsing would only bring more sorrow and shame, and that I could not tolerate myself for even a second if that happened. I also believed that to drink again would dishonor the memory of my daughter. She never knew me when I was actively engaged in my alcoholism. So I stayed sober and kept the faith that someday I would feel better.

My grief resided in me everywhere I turned. I was resigned to having no option but to keep feeling my open wound, tending to it, and allowing the suffering to walk me through each day.

Although at times I had regressed into an almost infantile state, the profound awareness of my loss made me realize I had finally become an adult. The adult experience of being "grown up" was apparent in my knowledge of true suffering. I also had greater insight into the priorities of life, as well as an instinctive ability to pull from every single resource in my personal and physical repertoire. Perhaps all my experiences that felt so meaningless at times were actually intentional events, designed to deliver the coping skills I needed to tolerate what seemed intolerable and unbearable.

Our reactions are colored by our life experiences, including grief from past losses left unattended, whether it be job loss, a divorce, a health issue, or a sense of how to manage subsequent losses. Consciously or not, we all develop coping mechanisms that we use to defend ourselves from the overwhelm of undesirable feelings. Every time we navigate through unwelcome distress, we gain knowledge on how to survive in trying times, and we strengthen the neural pathways in the brain that maintain the coping skills used. What happens in our lives and how we manage it shapes how we'll likely respond in the future.

Despite previous losses and working through denial, my new life as a bereaved parent continued to shock me at times. Nothing, absolutely nothing, was like anything I had imagined for my life. Yet, somehow, I was passing the days. *How am I still alive after almost a year?*

☆☆☆

I knew without question that my greatest joy and comfort was in being a mother. I loved being a mother—from the moment I learned I was pregnant and then gave birth. I was dedicated to my children unconditionally. Although I remained a parent to both my children for life, the active parenting for Lacey had ended. And with Will living in Colorado, life changes kept me from the hands-on, day-to-day parenting I had so enjoyed. My son was doing exactly what a twenty-two-year-old young man should be doing—exploring options, furthering his education, and gaining independence from his father and me. I missed him, though, and wanted to see him more than every few months.

As I continued making my daily gratitude statements, I always started with the words, "I am happy and grateful that Will is my son and that Lacey is my daughter." I never used the past tense. No, Lacey is still my daughter, who exists in another form. But I could not deny it any longer. She's gone from this earth forever. *This is permanent.*

My heart was broken, splintered across the desert where Lacey lost her life. I desperately needed a new role for myself, a new place to fit. Thankfully, my work environment was a place of familiarity and comfort, and I did fit there. However, I did not want my life defined solely by my career. I wanted other identities, like a philanthropist, to fill the void. And implementing the Lacey Jarrell Foundation was moving me toward the new.

☆☆☆

Then in the depths of the living darkness, once again, something happened. I shifted my behavior. I stopped considering drastic, unhealthy options to end my suffering. Instead, I became more diligent about my own personal safety so I could affirm with a vengeance that my life would be lived with fullness during my time on earth.

I reflected on the miracles of the year since Lacey's passing. Retrieving the silver pendant I had found in St. Mary's church in Aspen. Receiving the old book of poems with the green paper bookmarking a poem on Heaven and Hell. Recalling the episodes in which the lights had flicked on and off seemingly at will, and the time the alarm had set itself off. Laughing about the blue–and–black shoe jumping off my closet shelf. The astounding number of people—angels, really—who entered my life to bring guidance and comfort.

Was there a way I could gather and embrace all these miracles? Could I blend every detail of each phenomenon into a personal intuitive manual to guide me in living a life with more purpose and devotion to the values I found paramount to be the best woman I could be? Integrity, honesty, grace, kindness, forgiveness, and empathy—could I practice these and incorporate them into all my actions going forward? Could I demonstrate that despite my pain like no other, I could find inspiration from my suffering? And if even my words helped one individual, could I embrace gratitude whole heartedly and absorb myself in a life worth continuing? *I must remain teachable. There is so much I have yet to learn.*

Chapter Thirty-Two:

I Have Learned . . .

And this I learned from you, dear Loss
That the soul is deepened from the pain and the despair
And that life returns, even though the mountain burned.

"From You I Learned"
~ Nancy Jarrell

Just a week before the one-year anniversary of Lacey's death, I prayed to the Virgin to please remove my loneliness, my bitterness, and any resentment I held.

Within short order, I felt a lessening of my pain.

Then Jack reached out to me in a very genuine way. He let me know how he felt about me and said he missed me. I was able to accept him as he was, where he was, and feel settled, knowing that we loved each other. It felt okay. To a degree, I understood that Jack had his own journey to travel. His twenty-five-year marriage that ended in divorce was still very raw and recent. I remembered those early years after my own divorce during which I often felt rudderless. It took time for my new identity to emerge after so many years of being Buddy's wife and having someone else to share responsibility for major life decisions. Jack needed his own time and space to manifest his new identity and to reflect on the emergence of his new role in life. I had done the same.

Suddenly, I no longer felt angry with God. I began to realize that He had carried me through the past year. Somehow in those soporific months, I had managed to stay alive. Before Lacey's death, I remember saying many times, "I would die if I ever lost one of my children." But I had not imploded as I often thought I would. *I was still here on earth.*

Of course, I was dreading July 6th, which was fast approaching. I rose above my anxiety and in the midst of my fear, I said, "I will not have another funeral, but I will have a party." A party would be a wonderful way to celebrate Lacey's life and thank the many people who had been there for me—loving me and helping me through the year. I also wanted to thank all those who had been there for my son.

I took this idea to the board of directors of Lacey's foundation. Those incredible women rallied around me, and though the date was only seven days away, they quickly helped me organize a party at one of the local resorts. I selected a menu, rented a room, and hired musicians. The board organized a silent auction, which would benefit the foundation and give us the opportunity to advertise what we were doing.

Suddenly, my fear turned to excitement. Cyndy put together a beautiful professional-quality invitation that we e-mailed to people and posted at my work. We later realized we had put the wrong phone number on the flier, but I was able to laugh about it. Initially, I had counted about seventy-five people who had sent an RSVP. *Before long, I had no idea how many would come. I let it be. If hundreds showed up, then we would manage it.*

☆☆☆

I had a good feeling about all of it, for there were plenty of reasons to *not* feel so alone. The women of the board were incredibly supportive and helpful, of course, but something else mattered, too. For some time, I had a winged messenger—a red-tailed hawk—that flew over me every morning on my way to Sierra Tucson. The hawk would come to me on command. If I did not see him at our usual place, I would "ask" him to show up, and he would appear and soar with me the last half mile to the hospital. This faithful, familiar hawk brightened the entrance to the place where my entire world stopped turning, where I had first learned the terrible news about my daughter. In some way, I felt he was Lacey, appearing to lift my life of chronic distress and give me hope.

A few days before the celebration, I went to a store to buy decorations for the party. Of course, I was purchasing a lot of stars, particularly green ones. The woman at the check-out counter happily asked, "What are you going to do with the stars?" After I told her, she rang up my purchases and then abruptly turned away. As I gathered my bags, I thought I must have upset her. Just as I turned to leave, she said, "Please wait. I want to blow up this green star balloon for you. Why don't you take it home? When the time feels right, make a wish to your daughter and let it go off into the sky."

She tied the balloon around my wrist with green ribbon, and I felt exceedingly small, like a little child. Though the clerk was significantly younger than I, she appeared like the older woman taking care of me. It touched my heart, and I became tearful. Thanking her, I let her know how much this meant to me, and that she had brought comfort into my day. Again, I realized the kindness from strangers. My experience in the last year had been one of giving and receiving love from more people than I had ever before experienced.

Although I longed for my Lacey Jane and her bountiful hugs and kisses, I had to remember how much love came from all around me.

☆☆☆

Preparing for the celebration, I had several days when I felt okay in the world, and I was grateful to experience more of these. On my better days, I began to truly live life again. I reminded myself my daughter would want me to participate *in* life, not just pass through it, as I had been doing. Still, I had continued to mark off days on the calendar like a convict in prison. Waiting for what? Keeping track of what? I did not know.

I tried to be realistic about the day after Lacey's one-year anniversary. I told myself it would not mean the entire world had changed and everything would get better. One of the many myths about grief is that it decreases once you get through all the holidays that first year. This did not happen with the deaths of my parents. *How could I expect it to happen with the most significant loss of my life?*

I was not totally surprised, then, when I took a backward turn on July 4th, as I remembered the previous July 4th all too well. Lacey was out and called me several times, which was not unusual because she often checked in. That night, she was concerned that I would be watching the fireworks alone. Although I felt a bit down at the time, I was all right being by myself. I had intended to work the next morning and planned on being in bed at nine.

Instead, I decided to sleep on the couch and wait for Lacey to get home. I drifted off, not knowing how long I had been asleep when a late-night storm rolled through. The loud thunder and torrential rains awakened me. Then the phone rang. Lacey. She was driving in the storm.

"I'm scared, Mama," she said.

I was scared, too. I wanted to meet her and have her leave her car until tomorrow. She said she was close to home. I directed her to take the safest route to our house and told her how to pump her brakes after going through water. Then I got up and paced until I heard her car come up the road. When she walked in, we hugged and talked about how scary it can be to drive in a monsoon. I thanked God she had made it home safe and sound.

In less than forty-eight hours, however, she would not make it home safely. Driving before noon on a sunny cloudless day, she would perish for no reason at all.

The last day I saw my daughter alive was July 5th, 2006. A year later, I was compiling everything I have learned in the twelve months that followed.

☆☆☆

Today, I know it is vital to tell our loved ones *every day* how we feel about them. It is just as important to clear up any unfinished conflict by day's end for we are never promised a tomorrow. I remain forever grateful that my last words to Lacey were, "Goodnight, Lacey. I love you."

☆☆☆

I had cried for almost three hundred and sixty-five consecutive days, but so often, my tears were not only of sadness but also of reverence for humanity. It's a quality I acquired through the privilege of receiving compassion and kindness from others. I felt a connectedness to nature and many of life's intricacies that I had never noticed before. I recalled when I yelled at God: "You got it wrong this time, God. You selected the wrong woman for this despair. I really can't do this." I saw how a power greater than I weaved our lives like mathematical equations and took me through the brink of darkness back into light—and through a pain like no other I have known.

It was not over yet, however, and I intuitively knew it did not have an ending.

☆☆☆

Common experiences occur due to the loss of a child. Feeling numb or dazed; struggling with staying present; being unable to think or remember clearly; experiencing varying waves of pain, sorrow, hurt, anger, and guilt. For me, the most difficult part was dealing with the rawest emotions I have ever known.

It was also the most disorienting experience of my life. I felt depersonalized, disconnected from myself and my body. Time was distorted. I seemed bewildered. My world was disarranged. Life seemed surreal. Losing Lacey altered every cell in my body, and I felt as if a vital organ had been yanked out of me the moment I learned that Lacey was dead. Disemboweled forever.

There are no adequate words that can fully explain the depths of terror and trepidation of losing a child. For me, all previous losses were merely pinpricks on my skin. Losing my daughter peeled me down to my last layer of protection. *Raw. Exposed. Unconcealed. Excoriated.*

☆☆☆

How did I get through each day after losing my child? By keeping myself open to receive the love available to me. *This was so, so important.* It would have been a vastly dissimilar experience had I not allowed the love to come in from all who crossed my path—strangers, friends, family, even short-term acquaintances. Looking back, I grabbed hold of anything I could to help walk me through the agony. I now know how important it is to receive the emotional nourishment available. It saved my life many times.

During that first year, I saw psychics, mediums, channelers, therapists, and medical doctors. I read books, began authoring this book, formed a nonprofit foundation, completed a grueling IRS application, went to grief counseling, and attended a five-day psychodrama retreat. I also attended another funeral and celebrated a wedding. In my everyday life, I went out to dinner, felt grateful, prayed, and listened to music—all with the hope of feeling better. When I did not, I declined invitations, overworked, stayed frozen in my house, and felt sorry for myself. I yelled in my car and screamed even more while alone in my house. For a time, I even refused to pray or listen to music.

What have I learned from all this?

I have learned that *everything I did was okay*. These are just things I did, behaviors, nothing more or less. They brought me to where I am today. What I learned, too, is that I did not need a clairvoyant or a medium to connect me to my daughter—I already had the ability to do so. I simply call on her, and she is with me. Always. She is in my thoughts—her image, voice, personality, laugh, movements, and gestures are hardwired into my brain. She runs through my blood, my heart, my cells, and my veins. Lacey is everywhere.

I have learned that Hell is on earth. I believe I lived there, and yet for as much pain as I felt, there will be comparable joy. I do not know if I will experience this joy while on earth, but I know it is out there—somewhere.

I have learned that love is the answer to all sorrows, and that the opposite of fear is faith.

I believe in an afterlife and that we go through life fulfilling our previous contracts with each other. We are all souls dwelling on earth for the moment, trying to support the growth of each other's souls. I believe Lacey died to advance my soul and her own. I also believe I will see her again, and that perhaps earth is the hardest place to live.

I believe in a power greater than myself, whom I choose to call God.

I have learned that focusing on gratitude and positive thinking can make an enormous difference in a day.

I have learned that we all have a place somewhere inside where we can hold intolerable and unbearable pain. Yet, while in the depths of despair, we can transcend this plane of existence and become privy to another perception of our world in which color and detail are profoundly clear.

I have learned about resilience. We all have access to this and, as humans, can survive what might seem insurmountable.

I have learned that love is the most powerful primal emotion. It both elevates and devastates. And nature is a natural healer, which is why we all need to participate in taking care of this earth and all of God's creatures.

I have learned that sunlight is very healing. I frequently felt more grounded and present when I placed myself in the grandeur of the sun. The sun emits a certain light known as blue light that releases melatonin into our systems, relaxing us, and preparing us for sleep.

I have learned that mostly there is good in the world and that the loss of a child affects a whole community, whether we knew the child or not.

I have learned that my suffering has given me more wisdom and growth, and that profound learning can come from suffering. I also know that suffering is a natural life process that comes from having loved. Suffering is part of the human condition. There is no zip code, village, city, or country in which people are immune from suffering.

I have learned I have the capacity for enormous love, that I have loved with an intensity and passion and commitment, and that I know my daughter felt loved on earth and on the other side. She, too, has this ability for love. And for the privilege of being her mother, I will forever be grateful.

I have learned that I can tolerate loneliness, that I can live alone, and that compassion and forgiveness are vital for our survival.

I have learned there are no set stages of grief. We each grieve individually in our own way and in our own time. Also, there is no right or wrong way to process our emotions and feelings. We find on our own what works to make it through another day, or another hour, or another minute. Eventually, it was acceptable to me to commiserate with myself. I did not get there quickly or with ease.

☆☆☆

Looking back on July 6th, 2007, exactly one year since Lacey's death, I couldn't believe a year has gone by. *What have I done? This numb, conflicted state has become familiar.* Yet, I know what I have done.

Although my life took this horrible turn, I could say I was growing used to it. That morning, I flipped through the newspaper as though it were any other day, but I could not remember a thing I read. I looked at the "in memoriam" piece I had published there, and I felt good about the poem I wrote to Lacey.

Afterward, I went downstairs to her room and laid on her bed. This was scary, as I had not wanted to disturb anything on her bed or risk losing her scent. This day was different. Only her bed was left in the room. Although I gave away her other furniture, I kept all the blue and green stars on her wall. *They will come down when I move. If I move.* My heart and mind constantly changed about this, even though it once seemed a necessity. Running was not the answer. I could never run from my consciousness, anyway. That was impossible.

☆☆☆

The air inside my house felt still while my son still slept. Lying on her bed, I softly spoke to Lacey and thanked her for coming into my life. I talked to her about my faith, and my belief that I will see her again. I heard her tell me she is happy. She likes it where she is. She can fly, change the colors of things on a whim, and create her own landscapes at will.

I asked if she needed to tell me anything. I could hear her in my head saying, "No, Mama. You have everything you need inside of yourself. You already know what you need to do." I told her I would take part in life again and find my way. I wanted her to know I would survive.

Just then, I saw a sharp vision of Lacey wearing the little plaid boxer shorts she slept in and the blue T-shirt she died in, with the words "Passion" and "Intelligence" on the back. Then I sensed her cuddle up next to me, and it felt real and peaceful. I felt my hand touch her leg and rub the side of her thigh, just as I used to when she was little, and I would tell her she had beautiful legs.

It remained noticeably quiet in the room. I kept my eyes closed the entire time and lay very still. Tears came, and after a few minutes, I opened my eyes. The room was exceptionally bright and white. It looked different—bright, white, and comforting. I knew she had been there with me. As I got up to leave, I felt drawn to look under her bed. There, I spotted a white feather—a small, white, silky feather like so many I had found since she passed. I picked it up and smiled. I felt at peace.

Later, I went to the roadside where she died. I wanted to be there at 11:30 and stay there until noon. I wanted to see the conditions and just be silent at her place of death at the time of her death. I planned to buy fresh flowers and lay them there. Then I had to get ready for the celebration party in her honor. We were expecting between one hundred and one hundred fifty people. I felt nervous, but only for a breath. *What is there to be anxious about? It will be as it will be. I have no control over what happens. It's the irony of life.*

☆☆☆

On that day, July 6th, 2007, I shuffled through the mail and found an envelope from the IRS. I bolted inside to retrieve a knife to open it carefully. And there it was—the final approval letter from the IRS designating the Lacey Jarrell Foundation as a 501(c)(3) non-profit organization. Done!

I tilted my eyes toward the sky and yelled to Lacey. "We did it! We developed a nonprofit in your name!" Then I did a little dance around my kitchen, holding the paperwork as my dance partner. *You're behaving like Lacey,* I thought. And I was.

☆☆☆

As I come to the end of this book, I have fulfilled the commitment I made to write it. I am again reminded of the last words I ever spoke to my daughter: "Goodnight Lacey. I love you." I will continue to feel grateful they were the last words I said before her time on earth ended. I part today with these words to her: "Good morning, precious angel. My love for you is constant and forever. I know I will see you again where the stars kiss the heavens, my precious, shining star forever."

Epilogue

My life did not suddenly change just because the calendar turned to July 7th—one year and one day post Lacey. Everything—the constant grief, the daily tears, and even the feeling of having lost a vital body part—carried over into the second year. Synchronistic events continued to happen, experiences I could not just write off as coincidental. Lacey was still clearly near me that second year.

I am often asked by other newly bereaved parents, "How long does this pain last?" I cannot answer that using a measure of time; I can only say it can be different for all of us. It depends on our life experiences, our relationship with the child, how the child died, our coping skills, and the support from people in our lives. I only know that my personal experience involved little change for *four* years after Lacey died. By the fifth year, my condition improved little by little, year after year, as the setbacks subsided.

Today, many years later, I can look back at those first four years and see the gifts in my living alone, grieving alone, and having the private space to do so. Had I not been alone—a time I cherished—I would not have allowed myself to emote so freely. All the yelling, screaming, crying, and dropping to the floor or couch would not have occurred. Instead, I would have protected myself and others from allowing my vulnerability to become a burden.

Mostly, had I not been alone, I believe my ability to keep moving forward may have been compromised. This does not mean I believe someone needs to be alone for years to manage traumatic grief—not at all. But this was the experience given to me, and I feel immense gratitude for that.

☆☆☆

In February 2008, I checked the mail one evening and became anxious when I saw a handwritten envelope addressed to me. It was from someone I did not know, living in Logan, Utah. I took several deep breaths, then opened the envelope to find a handwritten letter from Gregg, a twenty-one-year-old man and student athlete at Utah State University. He was very polite and sensitive to my reaction to his words.

In short, Gregg stated that a year before, he began to question his faith in God. He told me the name "Lacey" came to him in "a dream." He awoke with the name on his mind, went to his computer, and searched the name on YouTube. He found a video someone had posted honoring Lacey Jarrell. That's when he learned about Lacey's death. He had never met or heard of her before.

Gregg forgot about this occurrence for eight or nine months, he wrote. And then for some reason he could not explain, he searched the name "Lacey" again on YouTube and asked, "What is the connection? Is this a message about wearing my seatbelt? I never wear my seatbelt." He also googled her name and found my name and address. He said he took this "as a sign to write you." He asked me to contact him if "you have it in your heart" to do so. I intuitively knew the letter was genuine, and he had more to share. So I called Gregg the following day, and we spoke for more than an hour.

Gregg was a dear, kind, and compassionate young man. As we talked, we learned that our families had remarkably similar dynamics. His mother had divorced his father due to his alcoholism, and he had one sister. He was the same age as Will, and his sister was the same age as Lacey when the divorce happened. He was majoring in psychology and wanted to become a paramedic. An African American man from California, he had received a football scholarship to Utah State University. Sadly, he struggled there as the only African American on the team and an outcast in a closed Mormon community. As a result, he was miserable and severely depressed.

The night that Lacey's name came into his head, Gregg had taken multiple over-the-counter medications in an attempt to commit suicide. It did not work, and with the name "Lacey" running through his head, he was distracted from continuing with the attempt. As I spoke to him on the phone, he told me my call had interrupted his plan for a second suicide attempt. Upon learning this, I spoke to him at length about how his mother and sister would suffer. I also shared my life experience of hope and the knowledge I'd gained that life would get better. He thanked me profusely.

After that, we became friends on Facebook and kept in touch over the years. I am happy to know that, today, Gregg is living a rewarding life in California. He finished college, found his way to the other side of depression, and started his own successful fitness business. We both believe our connection happened through divine intervention. We call it a miracle—a Laceysend!

☆☆☆

In 2009, Paul Smith, the paramedic, got married after being introduced by Michelle St. Rose to one of her best friends, Elaine. When I arrived at their wedding, I was stunned when Alan, Paul's paramedic colleague, escorted me into the church and sat me in the front row. The church was decorated with beautiful green and white flowers. The wedding colors, from the bridesmaid dresses to the decorations, featured a medley of green, including emerald, sage, forest, viridian, and more. The bride and groom requested no gifts but rather donations to the Lacey Jarrell Foundation. They both told me they believed Lacey had brought them together, and they wanted to honor her. I was overcome with emotion.

☆☆☆

About this book, it was not until the fourth year that I could go back and edit what I had written in the first year. At that point, I only ran a spellcheck—that was all—because it was too painful to revisit many of the episodes I'd described. At the same time, I had to admit I had been trying everything I could to keep Lacey alive. It was deeply wounding to realize I had to let her go entirely. Still, I spoke to her in depth about this, and following our communication, it became clear she was no longer around as much as before. And when she was, the intensity was diffused. I continued to cry daily.

In the fifth year, I took this manuscript to an editor. After it was returned to me, again, I did not read it for another four years. Then I put in two more years of sporadic writing and rewriting before stashing it away once more. In 2015, I was introduced to another editor, and I tackled the manuscript again. This pattern of working with the manuscript and then not being able to read it continued until early 2019. Finally, I had the stamina and emotional stability to rework it consistently over several months.

Years later, I have insight into why and how it was best that I took so many years to finally polish this manuscript—to make it into something other than a daily recording of my anguish. Writing in that first year gave me another reason to keep getting up in the morning; I convinced myself I had something important to do.

The fact that I can return to this writing and add to it my experience since Lacey's death gives me increased confidence to put this book into the world. Over the years, I have been hard on myself for not completing it. Today, however, I see this differently. Once again, someone was taking care of me, knowing better than I when I could share my story and have the greatest chance of helping others.

☆☆☆

In June 2010, after a surprising turn of events, Jack proposed to me, and we married that November. Will served as best man, and Jack's daughter, Laura, was maid of honor. We all talked about Lacey afterward and honored her spirit. I had incorporated hues of green into the décor as a way to include her.

Jack and I on our honey-
moon in Peru, 2010

In 2011, I resigned from Sierra Tucson as the clinical director. For a year, I grieved over this, which in some ways seemed like another loss. But for many reasons, it felt like the right time for me to move on. Four months later, I opened my own psychotherapy practice, which grew quicker than I could have imagined.

While reviewing parts of my manuscript in 2012, I reread the piece on the young man I met at the warehouse art district in Tucson who had suggested I read *Intra Muros*. Six years later, I searched for the book online and learned it was written by Rebecca Ruter Springer and first published in 1898. The book was difficult to find, but ironically it had just been republished by Forgotten Books, which uses current technology to digitally remaster historical writings. I found it at www.forgottenbooks.org.

The story, written in the first person, eloquently describes the author's near-death experience and paints an image of an afterlife that is welcoming, warm, and comforting. Its archaic language made it difficult to read, but I found the contents affirming and hopeful about what happens after death.

I never did sell my house. In fact, I still live in it today with Jack and our two mixed-breed rescue dogs. We did some remodeling and feel happy and content here. At times, Lacey fills the air, and we believe we hear her when unexpected noises startle us. Things still turn on and off by themselves, too. Her energy lives on.

☆☆☆

In my private practice, I've noted that, no matter what my clients presented with—addictions, depression, anxiety, relationship concerns, and mental health issues—addressing the traumatic events in their lives tended to resolve them. They all had experienced something traumatic, even though some did not recognize a pivotal incident as traumatic at first.

I enhanced my skills working with trauma and developed a new model of treatment based on the philosophy that *unprocessed trauma* is the root cause of most behavioral health problems. Today, I employ interventions specifically intended to effectuate neuroplasticity—healthy brain change.

I also began to see bereaved parents in my practice and started a group for bereaved mothers. It was intended to last only six weeks, but I ended it two and a half years later. It was taking its toll on me. Somehow, though, these mothers and I held onto each other week after week. We shared our unwanted bond and supported one another as our lives continued with both joys and sorrows.

☆☆☆

For several years, I researched religions including Hinduism, Buddhism, Islam, and the Baha'i Faith. In 2013, I was privileged to travel to India with a group of female colleagues to study the culture, meet with psychologists, tour hospitals, and volunteer in an orphanage.

This enhanced my beliefs about the existence of an afterlife and my faith that I would see my daughter again.

I also went back to riding horses. Although I had a nasty horse accident that broke my ribs in 2013, I returned to them yet again. Despite being injured, horses have been healing creatures to me since I was a little girl. I sought them out at the neighboring farms and stables where I grew up. Once I finally persuaded my parents to allow me to receive riding instructions at a local barn, the horses became my safety, my comfort, particularly on those childhood days riddled with family conflicts. I also knew my horse accident was just that—a horse accident.

We horse lovers don't just stop riding because we get injured. My horse had no intention of harming me. I knew that intuitively.

Will went on to law school at California Western. He graduated in 2012, despite being hospitalized in 2010 after a bad accident playing basketball that delayed him one semester. He passed the California Bar Exam and become a criminal defense attorney in San Diego. After accepting a job with a law firm in the La Jolla area, he took and passed another bar exam. This provided him with the opportunity to be licensed to practice law in twenty-three states besides California. I am so proud of him.

Will and I at his wedding in 2016

He also met a lovely woman, and Will and Katherine Grace Jarrell married in June 2016. I love her and am grateful she and Will found each other. Sadly, she too had lost a sibling. Then in April 2017, Jack's daughter, Laura, married Eddie Bielecki. I love them both as well. All of them are precious in my life. Ironically, Eddie had also lost a sibling.

In 2019, Will and Katie had a baby boy. I am now blessed with a precious grandson. This gift is helping me move along the spectrum from grief to more joy.

Katie, Will, and Liam, 2020

☆☆☆

Jack and I were able to realize our dream of working together. We had been seeking properties on which we could develop a start-up residential behavioral health facility using the treatment model I had been developing over the years. While considering one property in Tucson in 2013 that had Sabino Creek running through it, I decided to name my treatment program The Sabino Model: Neuroscience Based Addiction and Trauma Treatment™. The name was also influenced by the Spanish meaning of the word "sabino," which means "painted" and refers to paint horses. Jack and I both own and ride paint horses, thus the name seemed perfect. Unfortunately, we could not negotiate a workable lease on that property. But in 2014, we secured a lease on another property at the base of Sabino Canyon. Although it required a considerable amount of remodeling, it provided a perfect location for implementing The Sabino Model. We intended to spend the rest of our careers growing and improving this treatment center based on kindness, compassion, and empathy.

In October 2015, I obtained licensure to open a fifty-bed residential behavioral health facility called Sabino Recovery on this property in Tucson. We combined Jack's business acumen with my clinical expertise. We were privileged to actualize my dream and develop every aspect of the facility as we put The Sabino Model into practice. This neuroscience-based treatment model came together as a result of my work in mental and behavioral health, my study of neuroscience (specifically neuroplasticity), and my suffering and learning as the result of losing my child.

We designed this to use neuroplasticity as the driver of every patient's treatment plan and effectuate brain change. I introduced my model as a new paradigm to treat behavioral health issues in the United States. Every paint color I chose, every piece of furniture, and the time of day we scheduled activities and therapy sessions were all based on my research. The goal? To develop a holistic model of care that combined allopathic and naturopathic medicine. Despite significant challenges, I was able to implement every piece of my vision by mid-2016.

I thought Sabino Recovery and the testing program I co-created would be my legacy. Implementing outcome studies and providing data on the efficacy of my model would be my work for years to come. More important, though, I wanted it to be a tribute to my daughter. And I wanted Sabino to become a place of respite for bereaved parents. What happened to Jack and me at our facility, though, was nothing short of tragic. Again, I found myself in shock when my dream was taken away due to legal issues beyond our control. *How could this even be possible?*

Despite this setback, I am grateful we met our goals by helping many individuals with my model that emphasized kindness, compassion, and empathy. Jack and I still own a small amount of equity in Sabino Recovery, although we are not involved in day-to-day operations. What we accomplished there is gone, but we've extracted these valuable life lessons: We are not promised another day; change is what's to be expected; the best laid plans are not guaranteed to happen. Most important we learned that, despite the shock, hurt, fear, anger, shame, and emotional wounds, we all have the ability to access resilience. Without it, there would be no human survival.

Even though this business was another loss, it was nothing compared to losing Lacey. I hold on tight to the memories of the loving people who entered my life in those early years. I refuse to lose faith in the goodness of others, and I do not want to become jaded.

☆☆☆

Since 2016, the deep, searing pain from losing Lacey has subsided enough to allow me to enjoy life again. But I still miss her beyond description. Not a day passes that she is not my first thought when I awake and my last thought when I lie down at night. The tears still come, but very seldom.

While tackling this book again, only then did I fully realize my consistent seeking of God and prayer, and my continual return to the religion I was raised in. I thought I had successfully fled from Catholicism years ago, but it played a paramount role in my choice of coping tools. Clearly, if I ever thought I was not religious, my behaviors over the past fourteen years left me no rational ability to deny it.

Yes, I still consider myself to be spiritual. However, my journey of loss has brought me face to face with my Creator, my beliefs, and my faith in something so powerful, so clearly present to me, that I could not ignore the salvation I experienced time after time following my pleas and prayers for help. These conversations with God were not always gentle. I directed every primal emotion I had with congruency toward my God. I am grateful I was heard—even when sometimes the answer I received was a "No, Nancy, this is not my plan for you today."

☆☆☆

In 2017, a chance meeting with another clinician led me to providing consulting services for a women's residential and out-patient treatment program, The Haven. The women are mostly young, indigent adults, and some are homeless—a population I had not worked with before. This work once again humbled me while also bringing me face to face with my pain. Many of these women have lost children, not to death but to the Department of Child Services as a result of their addictions. It does not escape me that some are the same age Lacey would be.

I acknowledge that their grief is different from mine as I place mine aside to support them in processing the pain, guilt, shame, and responsibility they have for their losses. I experience gratitude every time I work with these women.

☆☆☆

In 2019, I received an unexpected phone call from one of Lacey's former classmates, Tim Milner. Tim informed me he was a teacher at what had been St. Gregory School, now called The Gregory School. *Where had the time gone? How could Tim be a teacher now?*

He shared with me his sadness being on campus and seeing the deteriorating memorial his class had created for Lacey in an obscure area of the grounds. He also shared his intent to receive my blessing in re-creating the memorial. He wanted to commission an artist to create a new star and move her memorial to a prominent site on the campus near the senior student area.

When I heard this, I teared up with gratitude—not only for Tim's kind and generous gesture but for the knowledge that others still missed Lacey and loved her. To finance this endeavor, Tim created a GoFundMe page on Facebook for his and Lacey's classmates and successfully raised the funds. Lacey's former teacher and coach, Jeff Clashman, was also involved in promoting this renewal of Lacey's memorial. When they met me at the school one morning, I hugged them both hard. With their generous and genuine welcome, I was able to let go of my past resentments toward the school and its former administration. They both reminded me that "this place is your home and community, too, and we welcome you here."

During this visit, I was struck with how many years had passed and how I had remained frozen in 2006, still feeling the incident and my loss in a raw way. This visit was cathartic. It let me gain true distance from the tragic day she passed and allowed me to stop expecting her to trot up the stairs in our home.

☆☆☆

After the Lacey Jarrell Foundation took off, it remained active for the first eight years after its inception. I did not keep up the annual fundraising events, however, and I'm recommitted to growing the foundation again. Lacey remains in my world every day. The memory of her physical life is as fresh and close to me as the day she passed, and I would never want this to be different.

As for my own healing, I continue to focus on gratitude for all that I have experienced—the suffering, the wisdom, and the joy—and for the sixteen years I shared with my precious child on earth. I continue to tend to her roadside memorial and still wonder exactly what happened the day she died.

I am not whole. The loss still lives in me, but I have learned to manage and accept this while keeping my faith that I will see my Lacey Jane again.

Today, I continue to work with indigent women at The Haven as well as mothers who have lost children and people suffering from trauma, grief, addiction, and other behavioral health concerns in a specialty private practice. I am expanding on my treatment model and teaching others how to implement it. I supervise associate-level clinicians to assist them in acquiring licensure with the State of Arizona for practicing psychotherapy. I facilitate equine-assisted psychotherapy, provide consulting services to people developing behavioral health facilities, and assist them in acquiring licensure. I provide four- to ten-day psychotherapy intensives for both individuals and couples in the United States and Europe. I also author articles for publication in magazines on the treatment of addictions and mental health issues.

Mostly, I strive to embrace life to the fullest.

☆☆☆

One more thing. For years, I met with Ernie at least once a year, and we cried together and would go over that day in detail. The first two years, he struggled with depression and then sought professional help for it. I assisted him and his family in acquiring that help.

Today, Ernie has his college degree and has become a kind, sensitive, motivated young man. For a while, we communicated via phone, e-mail, and social media. He never hesitated to answer a call or an e-mail from me, and I knew he would be there for me whenever I needed him.

I have come to accept that Lacey's death was an accident with no one to blame. Although, I still question the circumstances causing the accident, I am at peace with knowing there was no malicious intent that tragic day. Looking back, I can understand how my obsession with trying to figure out what happened was a subconscious attempt to maintain denial—and thus to cope. I needed a distraction from having to acknowledge the permanence and to find my way after this sudden separation.

At times, Ernie would ask me, "Do you think if Lacey had lived, she and I would have gotten back together?" I'd answer him with what I know to be true. First, anything is possible and, second, we will never know.

I haven't communicated with Ernie for several years now, but last I did, I could see he had evolved into the person Lacey envisioned. She saw his intelligence and sweetness, which was not always visible to the rest of us as he used aggression to cover the traumas of his childhood. When I told him I recognized he had become the man Lacey had wanted him to be, he responded, "That is the least I could do for her." And he repeated, "I wish it had been me, not her."

A shooting star expelled from the heavens
Came down that day, cached in the midday sun.
And disturbed by the expulsion,
Snatched my shining star on earth.
Taking her in one quick stroke,
To help the other stars continue
Sprinkling the love and joy down to us.
Left on earth hoping to catch one small spark
That will connect us back to you.
Yet it is not at noon when I feel you most,
Not the time of your death, but rather
When the sky turns navy,
Just before the transition from day to evening.
That navy, silent sky,
Calling me to you, the blessed time of your birth.
My love and your love is constant.

And so, my precious darling,
My green star,
I have ached with sorrow
And felt joy for the sweetness,
Knowing I will see you again,
Where the stars kiss the heavens.

~ Nancy Jarrell
July 6, 2007

Endnotes

1 Selby Jacobs, *Traumatic Grief: Diagnosis, Treatment, and Prevention,* (Philadelphia: Brunner/Mazel, 1999).

2 Stephen W. Porges, "The polyvagal theory: phylogenetic substrates of a social nervous system," *International Journal of Psychophysiology,* (International Organization of Psychophysiology, October 2001).

3 John W. James and Russell Friedman, *The Grief Recovery Handbook: The Action Program for Moving Beyond Death, Divorce, and Other Losses,* (New York: HarperCollins Publishers, Inc., 1998).

4 Arnold van Gennep, *Les Rites de Passage,* (France, 1909).

5 Arnold van Gennep, *The Rites of Passage,* Second Edition. Introduction by David L. Kertzer, (Chicago: University of Chicago Press, 2019), vii–xxxv.

6 Victor Turner, *The Forest of Symbols: Aspects of Ndembu Ritual,* (Ithaca: Cornell University Press, 1967).

7 Gregory N. Bratman, J. Paul Hamilton, Kevin S. Hahn, Gretchen C. Daily, and James J. Gross, "Nature experience reduces rumination and subgenual prefrontal cortex activation," (USA: *Proceedings of the National Academy of Sciences,* July 14, 2015).

8 Sarah E. Dowd, Martina L. Mustroph, Elena V. Romanova, Bruce R. Southey, Heinrich Pinardo, Justin S. Rhodes, and Jonathan V. Swedler, "How exercise could help fight drug addiction," (Neurosciencenews.com, November 14, 2018).

9 Irvin D. Yalom, *When Nietzsche Wept: A Novel of Obsession,* (New York: Basic Books, 1992).

10 Leo Buscaglia, *Born for Love: Reflections on Loving,* (Slack, Inc., 1992), 102.

[11] Robert C. Scaer, *The Body Bears the Burden: Trauma, Dissociation, and Disease,* Second Edition, (New York: Routledge Taylor & Francis Group, 2007), 20-21.

[12] Julianne Holt-Lindstad, Wendy A. Birmingham, and Kathleen C. Light, "Influence of a 'Warm Touch' support enhancement intervention among married couples on ambulatory blood pressure, oxytocin, alpha amylase, and cortisol," *The American Psychosomatic Society,* (Provo, Utah: Brigham Young University, 2008).

[13] J. Bowlby, *Attachment and Loss,* Volume 1, (New York: Basic Books, 1968).

[14] Mary D. Salter Ainsworth, Mary C. Blehar, Everett Waters, and Sally Wall, *Patterns of Attachment, A Psychological Study of the Strange Situation,* (New York: Psychology Press, 2014 reprint).

[15] Kenneth Doka, Terry Martin, *Grieving Beyond Gender: Understanding the Ways Men and Women Mourn,* Revised Edition, (New York: Taylor and Francis, 2010), 37-110.

[16] Noam Schneck, Tao Tu, Stefan Haufe, George A. Bonanno, Hanga Galfalvy, Kevin N. Ochsner, J. John Mann, Paul Sajda, "Ongoing monitoring of mind wandering in avoidant grief through cortico-basal-ganglia interactions," *Social Cognitive and Affective Neuroscience* (Oxfordshire, England: Oxford University Press, December 6, 2018).

[17] Ibid.

[18] American Society of Addiction Medicine, *The ASAM Criteria: Treatment Criteria for Addictive, Substance-Related, and Co-Occurring Conditions,* Third Edition, (Nevada: The Change Companies, 2013), 10.

[19] Jon-Kar Zubieta, David J. Scott, Mary Heitzeg, Robert Koeppe, and Christian Stohler, *Pleasure and Pain: Study shows brain's "pleasure chemical" is involved in response to pain, too,* (Michigan: Vice President for Communication Michigan News, University of Michigan, October 25, 2006).

[20] Robert C. Scaer, *The Body Bears The Burden: Trauma, Dissociation, and Disease,* Second Edition, (New York: Taylor & Francis, 2007), 20-21.

[21] Ibid, 23.

[22] Wikipedia: "'Last Kiss' is a song released by Wayne Cochran in 1961 on the Gala label. It failed to do well on the charts. Cochran subsequently re-recorded his song for the King label in 1963. J. Frank Wilson and the Cavaliers, Pearl Jam, and several international artists, including the Canadian group Wednesday, revived the song with varying degrees of success. The song was one of several teen tragedy songs from this period."

[23] Ottavio Arancio, Mychael V. Lourenco, Rudimar L. Frozza, Guilherme B. de Freitas, Hong Zhang, Grasielle C. Kincheski, Felipe C. Ribeiro, Rafaella A. Gonclaves, Julia R. Clarke, Danielle Beckman, Agnieszka Staniszewski, Hanna Berman, Lorena A. Guerra, Leticia Forny-Germano, Shelby Meier, Donna M. Wilcock, Jorge M. de Souza, Soniza Alves-Leon, Vania F. Prado, Marco A.M. Prado, Jose F. Abisambra, Fernanda Tovar-Moll, Paulo Mattos, Sergio T. Ferreira & Fernanda G. De Felice, "Exercise-linked FNDC5/Irisin rescues synaptic plasticity and memory defects in Alzheimer's models," *(Nature Medicine*, January 7, 2019).